a year of
AFGHANS

LEISURE ARTS, INC.
and
OXMOOR HOUSE, INC.

EDITORIAL STAFF

Vice President and Editor-in-Chief: Anne Van Wagner Childs
Executive Director: Sandra Graham Case
Editorial Director: Susan Frantz Wiles
Publications Director: Susan White Sullivan
Creative Art Director: Gloria Bearden

PRODUCTION
Senior Technical Editor: Cathy Hardy
Instructional Editor: Tammy Kreimeyer

EDITORIAL
Managing Editor: Linda L. Trimble
Associate Editor: Janice Teipen Wojcik
Assistant Editors: Terri Leming Davidson and
**   Stacey Robertson Marshall**

ART
Graphics Art Director: Rhonda Hodge Shelby
Senior Graphics Illustrators: Sonya McFatrich and Lora Puls
Graphics Illustrators: Roberta Aulwes and Karen L. Wilson
Color Technician: Mark Hawkins

BUSINESS STAFF

Publisher: Rick Barton
Vice President and General Manager:
**   Thomas L. Carlisle**
Vice President, Finance: Tom Siebenmorgen
Vice President, Retail Marketing: Bob Humphrey
Vice President, National Accounts: Pam Stebbins
Retail Marketing Director: Margaret Sweetin
General Merchandise Manager: Cathy Laird
Vice President, Operations: Brian U. Davis
Distribution Director: Rob Theime
Retail Customer Service Manager: Wanda Price
Print Production Manager: Fred F. Pruss

A Year of Afghans
Published by Leisure Arts, Inc., and Oxmoor House, Inc.

ISSN 1096-5505
Hardcover ISBN 1-57486-126-3
Softcover ISBN 1-57486-127-1

10 9 8 7 6 5 4 3 2 1

*L*ike the ever-changing seasons, this outstanding treasury of afghans offers striking beauty, abundant variation, and heartwarming reminders of times past. Our impressive collection of 52 wonderful wraps — in many different styles, colors, and textures — lets you add the excitement of the vibrant seasons to your decor.

Warm cover-ups featuring pristine snowflakes and patchwork pines are perfect for frosty days. Then bring springtime freshness indoors with throws inspired by lilac bouquets, vivacious violets, and tulips in bloom. Breezy summertime wraps showcase romantic seashells and the charm of wildflower meadows. And finally, welcome cool weather with cozy warmers splashed with fall color and the elegance of harvest mist.

The afghans are equally appealing for your home or as presents. Honor your mother with an heirloom throw that features cascading shells, celebrate the arrival of a precious baby with a sweet blanket, or send messages from Cupid featuring lacy Victorian styling or soft pink "petals." You can even salute the Stars and Stripes with coverlets in all-American colors and sing praises to the Yuletide season with angels and holly.

With step-by-step stitch guides and handy diagrams, it's easy for both beginning and advanced crocheters to stitch a variety of easy-to-follow patterns. After looking at the radiant full-color photographs, you'll want to start stitching right away. So don't delay — begin today to create many months' worth of cozy comfort with A Year of Afghans *as your guide!*

SCRAP-BASKET KALEIDOSCOPE

Like a many-splendored kaleidoscope, this throw dazzles with bright, eye-catching colors. Your scrap basket is a great source of brilliant hues for these granny squares.

Finished Size: 47" x 65"

MATERIALS
Worsted Weight Yarn:
 Black - 28 ounces,
  (800 grams, 1,920 yards)
 Scraps - 28 ounces,
  (800 grams, 1,920 yards) **total**
   Note: We used 10 different
    colors. Each Square requires
    13¾ yards.
Crochet hook, size H (5.00 mm) **or** size
 needed for gauge
Yarn needle

GAUGE SWATCH: 4½"
Work same as Square.

STITCH GUIDE

FRONT POST TREBLE CROCHET *(abbreviated FPtr)*
YO twice, insert hook from **front** to **back** around post of st indicated, YO and pull up a loop *(Fig. 12, page 141)*, (YO and draw through 2 loops on hook) 3 times.
PICOT
Ch 3, dc in top of dc just made *(Fig. 23, page 142)*.

SQUARE (Make 140)
With Scrap color desired, ch 4; join with slip st to form a ring.
Rnd 1 (Right side)**:** Ch 3 **(counts as first dc)**, 15 dc in ring; join with slip st to first dc, finish off: 16 dc.
Note: Loop a short piece of yarn around any stitch to mark Rnd 1 as **right** side.
Rnd 2: With **right** side facing and working in Back Loops Only *(Fig. 21, page 142)*, join next Scrap color desired with slip st in any dc; slip st in next dc, (ch 3, slip st in next 2 dc) around, ch 1, hdc in first slip st to form last ch-3 sp; do **not** finish off: 8 ch-3 sps.
Rnd 3: Ch 4 **(counts as first dc plus ch 1)**, dc in joining hdc, ch 2, ★ (dc, ch 1, dc) in center ch of next ch-3, ch 2; repeat from ★ around; join with slip st to first dc: 16 dc and 16 sps.
Rnd 4: Ch 3 **(counts as first dc)**, dc in next ch-1 sp, working in both loops, dc in next dc, 2 dc in next ch-2 sp, dc in next dc, dc in next ch-1 sp and in next dc, (tr, ch 3, tr) in next ch-2 sp, ★ dc in next dc, dc in next ch-1 sp and in next dc, 2 dc in next ch-2 sp, dc in next dc, dc in next ch-1 sp and in next dc, (tr, ch 3, tr) in next ch-2 sp; repeat from ★ 2 times **more**; join with slip st to first dc, finish off: 40 sts and 4 ch-3 sps.
Rnd 5: With **right** side facing, join Black with sc in any corner ch-3 sp *(see Joining With Sc, page 142)*; 4 sc in same sp, ★ ♥ sc in next tr, † skip next dc on Rnd 3, work FPtr around next dc, skip next dc on Rnd 4 from last sc made, sc in next dc, working in **front** of last FPtr made, work FPtr around skipped dc on Rnd 3, skip next dc on Rnd 4 from last sc made †, sc in next 2 dc, repeat from † to † once, sc in next tr ♥, 5 sc in next corner ch-3 sp; repeat from ★ 2 times **more**, then repeat from ♥ to ♥ once; join with slip st to first sc, finish off: 60 sts.

Continued on page 15.

January

SNOWY DAY

Inspired by a wintry surprise, this cozy throw brings to mind masses of lacy snowflakes floating silently to earth. The quickly worked wrap is stitched with a jumbo hook while holding two strands of soft brushed acrylic yarn together.

Finished Size: 53" x 72"

MATERIALS
Worsted Weight Brushed Acrylic Yarn,
48 ounces, (1,360 grams, 3,705 yards)
Crochet hook, size Q (15.00 mm)

Entire Afghan is worked holding two strands of yarn together.

GAUGE: Each Motif = 6½" (straight edge to straight edge)

STITCH GUIDE

> **FRONT POST DOUBLE CROCHET**
> ***(abbreviated FPdc)***
> YO, insert hook from **front** to **back** around post of dc indicated, YO and pull up a loop ***(Fig. 11, page 140)***, (YO and draw through 2 loops on hook) twice.

MOTIF (Make 95)
Rnd 1 (Right side): Ch 4, 11 dc in fourth ch from hook; join with slip st to top of beginning ch-4: 12 sts.
Note: Loop a short piece of yarn around any stitch to mark Rnd 1 as **right** side.
Rnd 2: Ch 1, sc in same st, work (FPdc, ch 1, FPdc) around next dc, skip dc **behind** FPdc, ★ sc in next dc, work (FPdc, ch 1, FPdc) around next dc, skip dc **behind** FPdc; repeat from ★ around; join with slip st to first sc: 6 ch-1 sps and 12 FPdc.
Rnd 3: Ch 1, sc in same st and in next FPdc, 3 sc in next ch-1 sp, ★ sc in next 3 sts, 3 sc in next ch-1 sp; repeat from ★ around to last FPdc, sc in last FPdc; join with slip st to first sc, finish off: 36 sc.

ASSEMBLY
Join 2 Motifs as follows:
With **right** side of **first** Motif facing and working in Back Loops Only ***(Fig. 21, page 142)***, join yarn with slip st in center sc of any 3-sc group; holding **second Motif** with **right** side facing, slip st in center sc of corresponding 3-sc group ***(Fig. 26, page 143)***, ★ slip st in next sc on **first Motif**, slip st in next sc on **second Motif**; repeat from ★ across to center sc of 3-sc group on **both Motifs**, slip st in center sc on **first Motif**, slip st in center sc on **second Motif**; finish off.

Using Placement Diagram as a guide, join remaining Motifs together in same manner, forming 5 vertical strips of 11 Motifs each and 4 vertical strips of 10 Motifs each.

Join strips in same manner.

EDGING
With **right** side facing and working in Back Loops Only, join yarn with slip st in any sc; ch 1, (slip st in next sc, ch 1) around; join with slip st to first slip st, finish off.

PLACEMENT DIAGRAM

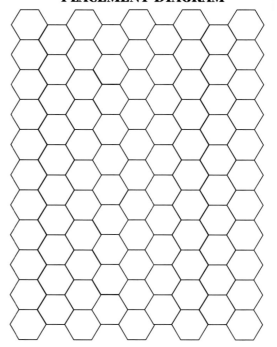

COUNTRY PINES

Stately evergreens are silhouetted against a snowy landscape on this woodsy wrap. The simple-to-stitch granny squares are easily whipstitched together.

Finished Size: 46" x 67"

MATERIALS
Worsted Weight Yarn:
Green - 34¹/₂ ounces, (980 grams, 2,170 yards)
Off-White - 12 ounces, (340 grams, 755 yards)
Red - 2 ounces, (60 grams, 125 yards)
Crochet hook, size I (5.50 mm) **or** size needed
for gauge
Yarn needle

GAUGE SWATCH: 3"
Work same as Square A.

Referring to the Key, page 15, make the number of Squares specified in the colors indicated.

SQUARE A
With color indicated, ch 4; join with slip st to form a ring.
Rnd 1 (Right side): Ch 3 (**counts as first dc, now and throughout**), 2 dc in ring, ch 2, (3 dc in ring, ch 2) 3 times; join with slip st to first dc: 12 dc and 4 ch-2 sps.
Note: Loop a short piece of yarn around any stitch to mark Rnd 1 as **right** side.
Rnd 2: Slip st in next 2 dc and in next ch-2 sp, ch 3, (2 dc, ch 2, 3 dc) in same sp, ch 1, ★ (3 dc, ch 2, 3 dc) in next ch-2 sp, ch 1; repeat from ★ 2 times **more**; join with slip st to first dc, finish off: 24 dc and 8 sps.

SQUARE B
With Off-White, ch 4; join with slip st to form a ring.
Rnd 1 (Right side): Ch 5 (**counts as first dc plus ch 2**), 3 dc in ring, cut Off-White, with Green, YO and draw through, ch 1, 3 dc in ring, ch 2, 3 dc in ring, cut Green, with Off-White, YO and draw through, ch 1, 2 dc in ring; join with slip st to first dc: 12 dc and 4 ch-2 sps.
Note: Mark Rnd 1 as **right** side.

Rnd 2: Slip st in first ch-2 sp, ch 3, (2 dc, ch 2, 3 dc) in same sp, ch 1, 3 dc in next ch-2 sp, cut Off-White, with Green, YO and draw through, ch 1, 3 dc in same sp, ch 1, (3 dc, ch 2, 3 dc) in next ch-2 sp, ch 1, 3 dc in next ch-2 sp, cut Green, with Off-White, YO and draw through, ch 1, 3 dc in same sp, ch 1; join with slip st to first dc, finish off: 24 dc and 8 sps.

ASSEMBLY
With matching color as desired, using Placement Diagram, page 15, as a guide, and working through inside loops only, whipstitch Squares together *(Fig. 27a, page 143)*, forming 15 vertical strips of 22 Squares each, beginning in second ch of first corner ch-2 and ending in first ch of next corner ch-2; whipstitch strips together in same manner.

EDGING
Rnd 1: With **right** side facing, join Green with sc in any corner ch-2 sp *(see Joining With Sc, page 142)*; sc in same sp, ★ † (sc in next 3 dc and in next sp) twice, hdc in joining, (sc in next sp and in next 3 dc) twice, [sc in next sp, hdc in joining, (sc in next sp and in next 3 dc) twice] across to next corner ch-2 sp †, 3 sc in corner ch-2 sp; repeat from ★ 2 times **more**, then repeat from † to † once, sc in same sp as first sc; join with slip st to first sc: 740 sts.
Rnds 2 and 3: Ch 1, 2 sc in same st, sc in each st across to center sc of next corner 3-sc group, ★ 3 sc in center sc, sc in each st across to center sc of next corner 3-sc group; repeat from ★ 2 times **more**, sc in same st as first sc; join with slip st to first sc.
Finish off.

NOSTALGIC GRANNY

This snuggly wrap in faded shades of rose and green brings back memories of grandmother's garden. Large and small squares make up the nostalgic design.

Finished Size: 50" x 73"

MATERIALS

Worsted Weight Yarn:
Black - 25 ounces, (710 grams, 1,715 yards)
Lt Green - 10 ounces, (280 grams, 685 yards)
Dk Rose - 7 ounces, (200 grams, 480 yards)
Green - 7 ounces, (200 grams, 480 yards)
Lt Rose - 6 ounces, (170 grams, 410 yards)
Crochet hook, size I (5.50 mm) **or** size needed for gauge
Yarn needle

GAUGE: Square A or B = 3³/₄"
Square C = 7¹/₂"

Gauge Swatch: 3³/₄"
Work same as Square A or B.

	Square A Make 116	Square B Make 35
Rnd 1	Green	Lt Rose
Rnd 2	Lt Green	Dk Rose
Rnd 3	Black	Black

SQUARES A & B

Referring to table above, make the number of Squares specified in the colors indicated.

Rnd 1 (Right side): With color indicated, ch 4, 2 dc in fourth ch from hook, ch 3, (3 dc in same ch, ch 3) 3 times; join with slip st to top of beginning ch-4, finish off: 12 sts and 4 ch-3 sps.
Note: Loop a short piece of yarn around any stitch to mark Rnd 1 as **right** side.

Rnd 2: With **right** side facing, join next color with slip st in any ch-3 sp; ch 3 **(counts as first dc, now and throughout)**, (2 dc, ch 3, 3 dc) in same sp, ch 1, ★ (3 dc, ch 3, 3 dc) in next ch-3 sp, ch 1; repeat from ★ 2 times **more**; join with slip st to first dc, finish off: 24 dc and 8 sps.

Rnd 3: With **right** side facing, join Black with slip st in any corner ch-3 sp; ch 3, (2 dc, ch 3, 3 dc) in same sp, ch 1, 3 dc in next ch-1 sp, ch 1, ★ (3 dc, ch 3, 3 dc) in next corner ch-3 sp, ch 1, 3 dc in next ch-1 sp, ch 1; repeat from ★ 2 times **more**; join with slip st to first dc, finish off: 36 dc and 12 sps.

SQUARE C (Make 24)

Rnd 1 (Right side): With Lt Rose, ch 4, 2 dc in fourth ch from hook, ch 3, (3 dc in same ch, ch 3) 3 times; join with slip st to top of beginning ch-4, finish off: 12 sts and 4 ch-3 sps.
Note: Mark Rnd 1 as **right** side.

Rnd 2: With **right** side facing, join Lt Green with slip st in any ch-3 sp; ch 3, (2 dc, ch 3, 3 dc) in same sp, ch 1, ★ (3 dc, ch 3, 3 dc) in next ch-3 sp, ch 1; repeat from ★ 2 times **more**; join with slip st to first dc, finish off: 24 dc and 8 sps.

Rnd 3: With **right** side facing, join Green with slip st in any corner ch-3 sp; ch 3, (2 dc, ch 3, 3 dc) in same sp, ch 1, 3 dc in next ch-1 sp, ch 1, ★ (3 dc, ch 3, 3 dc) in next corner ch-3 sp, ch 1, 3 dc in next ch-1 sp, ch 1; repeat from ★ 2 times **more**; join with slip st to first dc, finish off: 36 dc and 12 sps.

Rnd 4: With **right** side facing, join Black with slip st in any corner ch-3 sp; ch 3, (2 dc, ch 3, 3 dc) in same sp, ch 1, (3 dc in next ch-1 sp, ch 1) twice, ★ (3 dc, ch 3, 3 dc) in next corner ch-3 sp, ch 1, (3 dc in next ch-1 sp, ch 1) twice; repeat from ★ 2 times **more**; join with slip st to first dc, finish off: 48 dc and 16 sps.

Rnd 5: With **right** side facing, join Lt Rose with slip st in any corner ch-3 sp; ch 3, (2 dc, ch 3, 3 dc) in same sp, ch 1, (3 dc in next ch-1 sp, ch 1) 3 times, ★ (3 dc, ch 3, 3 dc) in next corner ch-3 sp, ch 1, (3 dc in next ch-1 sp, ch 1) 3 times; repeat from ★ 2 times **more**; join with slip st to first dc, finish off: 60 dc and 20 sps.

Continued on page 14.

Rnd 6: With **right** side facing, join Dk Rose with slip st in any corner ch-3 sp; ch 3, (2 dc, ch 3, 3 dc) in same sp, ch 1, (3 dc in next ch-1 sp, ch 1) 4 times, ★ (3 dc, ch 3, 3 dc) in next corner ch-3 sp, ch 1, (3 dc in next ch-1 sp, ch 1) 4 times; repeat from ★ 2 times **more**; join with slip st to first dc, finish off: 72 dc and 24 sps.

Rnd 7: With **right** side facing, join Black with slip st in any corner ch-3 sp; ch 3, (2 dc, ch 3, 3 dc) in same sp, ch 1, (3 dc in next ch-1 sp, ch 1) 5 times, ★ (3 dc, ch 3, 3 dc) in next corner ch-3 sp, ch 1, (3 dc in next ch-1 sp, ch 1) 5 times; repeat from ★ 2 times **more**; join with slip st to first dc, finish off: 84 dc and 28 sps.

ASSEMBLY

With Black, using Placement Diagram as a guide, and working through both loops, whipstitch Squares together *(Fig. 27b, page 143)*, forming 9 vertical strips, beginning in center ch of first corner ch-3 and ending in center ch of next corner ch-3; whipstitch strips together in same manner.

PLACEMENT DIAGRAM

B	A	A	B	A	A	B	A	A	B	A	A	B
A		C		A		C		A		C		A
A				A				A				A
B	A	A	B	A	A	B	A	A	B	A	A	B
A		C		A		C		A		C		A
A				A				A				A
B	A	A	B	A	A	B	A	A	B	A	A	B
A		C		A		C		A		C		A
A				A				A				A
B	A	A	B	A	A	B	A	A	B	A	A	B
A		C		A		C		A		C		A
A				A				A				A
B	A	A	B	A	A	B	A	A	B	A	A	B
A		C		A		C		A		C		A
A				A				A				A
B	A	A	B	A	A	B	A	A	B	A	A	B

EDGING

Rnd 1: With **right** side facing, join Black with sc in any corner ch-3 sp *(see Joining With Sc, page 142)*; ch 2, sc in same sp, ★ † ch 1, skip next dc, sc in next dc, ch 1, (sc in next ch-1 sp, ch 1, skip next dc, sc in next dc, ch 1) twice, [(sc in next sp, ch 1) twice, skip next dc, sc in next dc, ch 1, (sc in next ch-1 sp, ch 1, skip next dc, sc in next dc, ch 1) twice] across to next corner ch-3 sp †, (sc, ch 2, sc) in corner ch-3 sp; repeat from ★ 2 times **more**, then repeat from † to † once; join with slip st to first sc: 448 sps.

Rnd 2: Slip st in first corner ch-2 sp, ch 1, (sc, ch 2, sc) in same sp, ch 1, (sc in next ch-1 sp, ch 1) across to next corner ch-2 sp, ★ (sc, ch 2, sc) in corner ch-2 sp, ch 1, (sc in next ch-1 sp, ch 1) across to next corner ch-2 sp; repeat from ★ 2 times **more**; join with slip st to first sc.

Rnd 3: (Slip st, ch 2, slip st) in first corner ch-2 sp, ch 1, (slip st in next ch-1 sp, ch 1) across to next corner ch-2 sp, ★ (slip st, ch 2, slip st) in corner ch-2 sp, ch 1, (slip st in next ch-1 sp, ch 1) across to next corner ch-2 sp; repeat from ★ 2 times **more**; join with slip st to first slip st, finish off.

SCRAP-BASKET KALEIDOSCOPE Continued from page 6.

ASSEMBLY

With Black and working through inside loops only, whipstitch Squares together *(Fig. 27, page 143)*, forming 10 vertical strips of 14 Squares each, beginning in center sc of first corner 5-sc group and ending in center sc of next corner 5-sc group; whipstitch strips together in same manner.

EDGING

Rnd 1: With **right** side facing, join Black with sc in center sc of any corner 5-sc group; sc in same st, ★ sc in each st and in each joining across to center sc of next corner 5-sc group, 3 sc in center sc; repeat from ★ 2 times **more**, sc in each st and in each joining across, sc in same st as first sc; join with slip st to first sc: 728 sc.

Rnd 2: Ch 6, dc in third ch from hook, (dc, work Picot, dc) in same st, skip next 3 sc, [(dc, work Picot, dc) in next sc, skip next 3 sc] across to center sc of next corner 3-sc group, ★ [dc, (work Picot, dc) twice] in center sc, skip next 3 sc, [(dc, work Picot, dc) in next sc, skip next 3 sc] across to center sc of next corner 3-sc group; repeat from ★ 2 times **more**; join with slip st to third ch of beginning ch-6, finish off.

COUNTRY PINES Continued from page 10.

PLACEMENT DIAGRAM

KEY

Square A

■ - Green (Make 186)

☐ - Off-White (Make 60)

■ - Red (Make 12)

Square B

◪ - Off-White & Green (Make 72)

ROSE PETAL RIPPLE

Soft pinks cascade in romantic waves down this pretty coverlet, which is perfect for a Valentine sweetheart. Simple clusters produce the rippling effect.

Finished Size: 46" x 61"

MATERIALS
  Worsted Weight Yarn:
    Lt Pink - 17 ounces,
       (480 grams, 1,115 yards)
    Dk Pink - 9 ounces,
       (260 grams, 590 yards)
    Pink - 7 ounces,
       (200 grams, 460 yards)
  Crochet hook, size I (5.50 mm) **or** size
    needed for gauge

GAUGE: Each repeat from point to point =
       3¼"; 4 rows = 3"

Gauge Swatch: 6½"w x 3"h
Ch 28 **loosely**.
Work same as Afghan for 4 rows.
Finish off.

STITCH GUIDE

CLUSTER (uses next 5 sts or sps)
★ YO, insert hook in **next** st or sp, YO and pull up a loop, YO and draw through 2 loops on hook; repeat from
★ 4 times **more**, YO and draw through all 6 loops on hook *(Figs. 17a & b, page 141)*.
ENDING CLUSTER (uses last 4 sts)
YO, insert hook in **next** dc, YO and pull up a loop, YO and draw through 2 loops on hook, YO, skip next ch **and** next dc, insert hook in **last** st, YO and pull up a loop, YO and draw through 2 loops on hook, YO and draw through all 3 loops on hook.

COLOR SEQUENCE
One row **each**: Dk Pink *(Fig. 24, page 143)*, ★ Pink, Lt Pink, Pink, Dk Pink; repeat from ★ throughout.

With Dk Pink, ch 184 **loosely**.
Row 1 (Right side): Dc in fourth ch from hook, ch 1, skip next ch, dc in next ch, ch 1, skip next ch, 3 dc in next ch, ch 3, 3 dc in next ch, ch 1, skip next ch, dc in next ch, ch 1, ★ skip next ch, work Cluster, ch 1, skip next ch, dc in next ch, ch 1, skip next ch, 3 dc in next ch, ch 3, 3 dc in next ch, ch 1, skip next ch, dc in next ch, ch 1; repeat from ★ across to last 4 chs, (YO, skip **next** ch, insert hook in **next** ch, YO and pull up a loop, YO and draw through 2 loops on hook) twice, YO and draw through all 3 loops on hook: 128 sts and 70 sps.
Row 2: Ch 3, turn; (skip next ch, dc in next dc, ch 1) twice, (3 dc, ch 3, 3 dc) in next ch-3 sp, ch 1, skip next 2 dc, dc in next dc, ch 1, ★ skip next ch, work Cluster, ch 1, skip next ch, dc in next dc, ch 1, (3 dc, ch 3, 3 dc) in next ch-3 sp, ch 1, skip next 2 dc, dc in next dc, ch 1; repeat from ★ across to last 2 ch-1 sps, skip next ch, work Ending Cluster.
Repeat Row 2 until Afghan measures approximately 61" from beginning ch, ending by working one row Dk Pink; finish off.

SENTIMENTAL SWIRLS

This feminine throw has a lacy loveliness reminiscent of swirling skirts on pirouetting dancers. An elegant border with ruffly scallops and picots completes the luxurious look.

Finished Size: 49" x 66"

MATERIALS
  Worsted Weight Yarn:
    38 ounces, (1,080 grams, 2,605 yards)
  Crochet hook, size H (5.00 mm) **or** size needed
    for gauge
  Yarn needle

GAUGE: Each Motif = 6¼" (straight edge to straight edge)

Gauge Swatch: 3" diameter
Work same as Motif through Rnd 2.

STITCH GUIDE

DECREASE (uses next 2 ch-3 sps)
★ YO, insert hook in **next** ch-3 sp, YO and pull up a loop, YO and draw through 2 loops on hook; repeat from ★ once **more**, YO and draw through all 3 loops on hook (**counts as one dc**).
PICOT
Ch 3, dc in third ch from hook.

MOTIF (Make 72)
Ch 6; join with slip st to form a ring.
Rnd 1 (Right side)**:** Ch 3 (**counts as first dc, now and throughout**), dc in ring, ch 2, (2 dc in ring, ch 2) 5 times; join with slip st to first dc: 12 dc and 6 ch-2 sps.
Note: Loop a short piece of yarn around any stitch to mark Rnd 1 as **right** side.
Rnd 2: Slip st in next dc, ch 3, 3 dc in next ch-2 sp, ch 2, skip next dc, dc in next dc, (dc, ch 1, dc) in next ch-2 sp, ch 2, skip next dc, ★ dc in next dc, 3 dc in next ch-2 sp, ch 2, skip next dc, dc in next dc, (dc, ch 1, dc) in next ch-2 sp, ch 2, skip next st; repeat from ★ once **more**; join with slip st to first dc: 21 dc and 9 sps.

Rnd 3: Slip st in next 2 dc, ch 3, dc in next dc, 3 dc in next ch-2 sp, ch 3, dc in next ch-1 sp, ch 1, (dc, ch 1, dc) in next ch-2 sp, ch 3, skip next 2 dc, ★ dc in next 2 dc, 3 dc in next ch-2 sp, ch 3, dc in next ch-1 sp, ch 1, (dc, ch 1, dc) in next ch-2 sp, ch 3, skip next 2 sts; repeat from ★ once **more**; join with slip st to first dc: 24 dc and 12 sps.
Rnds 4 and 5: Slip st in next 2 dc, ch 3, ★ dc in next dc and in each dc across to next ch-3 sp, 4 dc in ch-3 sp, ch 3, skip next dc, (dc in next dc, ch 1) across to next ch-3 sp, (dc, ch 1, dc) in ch-3 sp, ch 3, skip next 2 sts; repeat from ★ 2 times **more**; join with slip st to first dc: 42 dc and 18 sps.
Finish off.

HALF MOTIF (Make 10)
Ch 5, place marker in second ch from hook for st placement; join with slip st to form a ring.
Row 1 (Right side)**:** Ch 5 (**counts as first dc plus ch 2**), (2 dc in ring, ch 2) twice, dc in marked ch, remove marker: 6 dc and 3 ch-2 sps.
Note: Mark Row 1 as **right** side.
Row 2: Ch 3, turn; (dc, ch 1, dc) in next ch-2 sp, dc in next dc, ch 2, 3 dc in next ch-2 sp, dc in next dc, ch 2, (dc, ch 1, dc) in next ch-2 sp, 2 dc in last dc: 12 dc and 4 sps.
Row 3: Ch 3, turn; dc in same st, ch 3, dc in next ch-1 sp, (ch 1, dc) twice in next ch-2 sp, ch 3, skip next 2 dc, dc in next 2 dc, 3 dc in next ch-2 sp, ch 3, dc in next ch-1 sp, ch 1, dc in last 2 dc: 13 dc and 6 sps.
Row 4: Ch 3, turn; dc in next dc, ch 3, skip next ch-1 sp, 4 dc in next ch-3 sp, dc in next 3 dc, ch 3, (dc, ch 1, dc) in next ch-3 sp, (ch 1, dc in next dc) twice, ch 3, skip next ch-1 sp, 4 dc in next ch-3 sp, dc in last 2 dc: 19 dc and 6 sps.
Row 5: Ch 4 (**counts as first dc plus ch 1, now and throughout**), turn; dc in next 5 dc, 4 dc in next ch-3 sp, ch 3, skip next dc, (dc in next dc, ch 1) 3 times, (dc, ch 1, dc) in next ch-3 sp, ch 3, skip next 2 dc, dc in next 5 dc, 4 dc in next ch-3 sp, ch 1, skip next dc, dc in last dc; finish off: 25 dc and 8 sps.

Continued on page 25.

VICTORIAN ELEGANCE

Created with brushed acrylic yarn, this Victorian wrap reflects the beauty of rosebuds and blushing young misses. The gorgeous edging gets its grandeur from sumptuous shells and puff stitches.

Finished Size: 49" x 67"

MATERIALS
Brushed Acrylic Worsted Weight Yarn:
    41 ounces, (1,160 grams, 2,075 yards)
Crochet hook, size I (5.50 mm) **or** size needed
    for gauge

GAUGE: In pattern, (V-St, ch 1, sc, ch 1) 3 times = 5";
        8 rows = 4$^1/4$"

Gauge Swatch: 5$^1/4$"w x 4$^1/4$"h
Ch 24 **loosely**.
Work same as Afghan Body for 8 rows.
Finish off.

STITCH GUIDE

> **V-STITCH (abbreviated V-St)**
> (Dc, ch 1, dc) in sc indicated.
> **SHELL**
> (2 Dc, ch 2, 2 dc) in st or sp indicated.
> **BEGINNING PUFF STITCH**
>   **(abbreviated Beginning Puff St)**
> (YO, insert hook in **same** st, YO and pull up a loop even with loop on hook) twice, YO and draw through all 5 loops on hook **(Fig. 19, page 142)**.
> **PUFF STITCH (abbreviated Puff St)**
> (YO, insert hook in st indicated, YO and pull up a loop even with loop on hook) 3 times, YO and draw through all 7 loops on hook.

AFGHAN BODY

Ch 114 **loosely**, place marker in fifth ch from hook for st placement.

Row 1 (Right side)**:** Dc in sixth ch from hook, ★ ch 1, skip next ch, sc in next ch, (ch 1, skip next ch, dc in next ch) twice; repeat from ★ across: 18 sc and 55 sps.

Row 2: Ch 1, turn; sc in first ch-1 sp, ★ ch 1, skip next dc, work V-St in next sc, ch 1, skip next ch-1 sp, sc in next sp; repeat from ★ across: 19 sc and 54 ch-1 sps.

Row 3: Ch 4 **(counts as first dc plus ch 1)**, turn; dc in same st, ★ ch 1, skip next ch-1 sp, sc in next ch-1 sp, ch 1, skip next dc, work V-St in next sc; repeat from ★ across: 18 sc and 55 ch-1 sps.

Rows 4-91: Repeat Rows 2 and 3, 44 times; do **not** finish off.

EDGING

Rnd 1: Ch 1, do **not** turn; 2 sc in top of last dc on Row 91; working in end of rows, 2 sc in first row, (sc in next row, 2 sc in next row) across; working in sps and in free loops of beginning ch **(Fig. 22, page 142)**, 3 sc in first ch, skip next sp, sc in next ch and in each sp and each ch across to marked ch, skip marked ch, 3 sc in next ch; working in end of rows, 2 sc in first row, (sc in next row, 2 sc in next row) across; working in sts and in sps on Row 91, 3 sc in first dc, skip next ch-1 sp, sc in next st and in each ch-1 sp and each st across to last ch-1 sp, skip last ch-1 sp, sc in same st as first sc; join with slip st to first sc: 500 sc.

Rnds 2-4: Ch 1, turn; 2 sc in same st, ★ sc in each sc across to center sc of next corner 3-sc group, 3 sc in center sc; repeat from ★ 2 times **more**, sc in each sc across and in same st as first sc; join with slip st to first sc: 524 sc.

Rnd 5: Ch 5 **(counts as first dc plus ch 2, now and throughout)**, turn; ★ skip next 2 sc, work Shell in next sc, ch 2, [skip next 4 sc, (dc, ch 5, dc) in next sc, ch 2, skip next 4 sc, work Shell in next sc, ch 2] across to within one sc of next corner 3-sc group, skip next 2 sc, (dc, ch 5, dc) in center sc, ch 2; repeat from ★ 2 times **more**, skip next 2 sc, work Shell in next sc, ch 2, [skip next 4 sc, (dc, ch 5, dc) in next sc, ch 2, skip next 4 sc, work Shell in next sc, ch 2] across to last 2 sc, skip last 2 sc, dc in same st as first dc, ch 2, dc in first dc to form last corner ch-5 sp: 54 Shells and 54 ch-5 sps.

Rnd 6: Ch 1, turn; 3 sc in same sp, sc in next ch-2 sp, ch 1, work Shell in next Shell (ch-2 sp), ch 1, sc in next ch-2 sp, ★ 5 sc in next ch-5 sp, sc in next ch-2 sp, ch 1, work Shell in next Shell, ch 1, sc in next ch-2 sp; repeat from ★ around, 2 sc in same sp as first sc; join with slip st to first sc, do **not** finish off: 54 Shells and 378 sc.

Continued on page 26.

SWEETHEART SQUARES

A pretty palette of heart-embellished squares creates a lovely effect on this Cupid-pleasing wrap. Puffy clusters form textured hearts on the squares, which are bordered in coordinating shades and whipstitched together.

Finished Size: 53" x 68"

MATERIALS

Worsted Weight Yarn:
- Ecru - 17 ounces, (480 grams, 1,165 yards)
- Mauve - 11 ounces, (310 grams, 755 yards)
- Green - 11 ounces, (310 grams, 755 yards)
- Blue - 11 ounces, (310 grams, 755 yards)
- Rose - 11 ounces, (310 grams, 755 yards)

Crochet hook, size I (5.50 mm) **or** size needed for gauge

Yarn needle

GAUGE: Each Square = 7¹/₄"

Gauge Swatch: 4¹/₂"
Work same as Square Center.

STITCH GUIDE

CLUSTER (uses one ch)
YO, insert hook in Back Loop Only of next ch *(Fig. 21, page 142)*, YO and pull up a loop, YO and draw through 2 loops on hook, ★ YO, insert hook in **same** ch, YO and pull up a loop, YO and draw through 2 loops on hook; repeat from ★ once **more**, YO and draw through all 4 loops on hook *(Figs. 16a & b, page 141)*. Push Cluster to **right** side.

	Square A Make 16	Square B Make 16	Square C Make 16	Square D Make 15
Rows 1-18	Mauve	Blue	Green	Rose
Rnd 1	Mauve	Blue	Green	Rose
Rnd 2	Ecru	Ecru	Ecru	Ecru
Rnds 3 & 4	Green	Rose	Mauve	Blue
Rnd 5	Ecru	Ecru	Ecru	Ecru

SQUARE

Referring to table, make the number of Squares specified in the colors indicated.

CENTER

With color indicated, ch 20 **loosely**.

Row 1 (Right side): Sc in second ch from hook, (ch 1, skip next ch, sc in next ch) across: 10 sc and 9 ch-1 sps.

Note: Loop a short piece of yarn around any stitch to mark Row 1 as **right** side and bottom edge.

Rows 2 and 3: Ch 1, turn; sc in first sc, (ch 1, sc in next sc) across.

Note: Work in both loops of each st across unless otherwise instructed.

Row 4: Ch 1, turn; sc in first sc, (ch 1, sc in next sc) 4 times, work Cluster, sc in next sc, (ch 1, sc in next sc) 4 times: 10 sc and one Cluster.

Row 5: Ch 1, turn; sc in first sc, (ch 1, sc in next sc) across: 10 sc and 9 ch-1 sps.

Row 6: Ch 1, turn; sc in first sc, (ch 1, sc in next sc) 3 times, (work Cluster, sc in next sc) 3 times, (ch 1, sc in next sc) 3 times: 10 sc and 3 Clusters.

Row 7: Ch 1, turn; sc in first sc, (ch 1, sc in next sc) across: 10 sc and 9 ch-1 sps.

Row 8: Ch 1, turn; sc in first sc, (ch 1, sc in next sc) twice, (work Cluster, sc in next sc) 5 times, (ch 1, sc in next sc) twice: 10 sc and 5 Clusters.

Row 9: Ch 1, turn; sc in first sc, (ch 1, sc in next sc) across: 10 sc and 9 ch-1 sps.

Row 10: Ch 1, turn; sc in first sc, ch 1, sc in next sc, (work Cluster, sc in next sc) 7 times, ch 1, sc in last sc: 10 sc and 7 Clusters.

Row 11: Ch 1, turn; sc in first sc, (ch 1, sc in next sc) across: 10 sc and 9 ch-1 sps.

Rows 12 and 13: Repeat Rows 10 and 11.

Row 14: Ch 1, turn; sc in first sc, (ch 1, sc in next sc) twice, (work Cluster, sc in next sc) twice, ch 1, sc in next sc, (work Cluster, sc in next sc) twice, (ch 1, sc in next sc) twice: 10 sc and 4 Clusters.

Rows 15-18: Ch 1, turn; sc in first sc, (ch 1, sc in next sc) across; do **not** finish off: 10 sc and 9 ch-1 sps.

Continued on page 24.

BORDER

Rnd 1: Ch 1, **turn**; sc in first sc, ch 1, (sc in next sc, ch 1) 8 times, (sc, ch 2, sc) in last sc; † ch 1, working in end of rows, skip first 2 rows, (sc in next row, ch 1, skip next row) 8 times †; working in free loops of beginning ch *(Fig. 22b, page 142*, (sc, ch 2, sc) in first ch, ch 1, skip next ch, (sc in next ch, ch 1, skip next ch) 8 times, (sc, ch 2, sc) in next ch, repeat from † to † once, sc in same st as first sc, ch 2; join with slip st to first sc, finish off: 40 sc and 4 ch-2 sps.

Rnd 2: With **wrong** side facing, join Ecru with sc in any corner ch-2 sp *(see Joining With Sc, page 142)*; ch 2, sc in same sp and in next sc, ★ (ch 1, sc in next sc) across to next corner ch-2 sp, (sc, ch 2, sc) in corner ch-2 sp, sc in next sc; repeat from ★ 2 times **more**, (ch 1, sc in next sc) across; join with slip st to first sc, finish off: 48 sc and 4 ch-2 sps.

Rnd 3: With **right** side facing, join next color with sc in any corner ch-2 sp; ch 2, sc in same sp, ★ † ch 1, skip next sc, (sc in next sc, ch 1) across to within one sc of next corner ch-2 sp, skip next sc †, (sc, ch 2, sc) in corner ch-2 sp; repeat from ★ 2 times **more**, then repeat from † to † once; join with slip st to first sc, do **not** finish off.

Rnd 4: Ch 1, **turn**; sc in same st, ★ † (ch 1, sc in next sc) across to next corner ch-2 sp, ch 3, skip corner ch-2 sp †, sc in next sc; repeat from ★ 2 times **more**, then repeat from † to † once; join with slip st to first sc, finish off.

Rnd 5: With **right** side facing, join Ecru with sc in first sc; working **behind** next corner ch-3, (dc, ch 3, dc) in ch-2 sp one rnd **below**, ★ sc in next sc, (ch 1, sc in next sc) across to next corner ch-3, working **behind** corner ch-3, (dc, ch 3, dc) in ch-2 sp one rnd **below**; repeat from ★ 2 times **more**, (sc in next sc, ch 1) across; join with slip st to first sc, finish off: 56 sts and 48 sps.

ASSEMBLY

With Ecru, using Placement Diagram as a guide, and matching sts of bottom edge of one Square to top edge of next Square, whipstitch Squares together *(Fig. 27b, page 143)*, forming 7 vertical strips of 9 Squares each, beginning in center ch of first corner ch-3 and ending in center ch of next corner ch-3; whipstitch strips together in same manner, keeping bottom edges at same end.

PLACEMENT DIAGRAM

A	B	C	D	A	B	C
D	A	B	C	D	A	B
C	D	A	B	C	D	A
B	C	D	A	B	C	D
A	B	C	D	A	B	C
D	A	B	C	D	A	B
C	D	A	B	C	D	A
B	C	D	A	B	C	D
A	B	C	D	A	B	C

EDGING

Rnd 1: With **right** side facing, join Ecru with sc in any corner ch-3 sp; ch 2, sc in same sp, ★ † ch 1, skip next dc, (sc in next sc, ch 1, skip next st) 12 times, [(sc in next sp, ch 1) twice, skip next dc, (sc in next sc, ch 1, skip next st) 12 times] across to next corner ch-3 sp †, (sc, ch 2, sc) in corner ch-3 sp; repeat from ★ 2 times **more**, then repeat from † to † once; join with slip st to first sc: 448 sc and 4 ch-2 sps.

Rnd 2: Ch 1, **turn**; sc in same st, ch 1, ★ (sc in next sc, ch 1) across to next corner ch-2 sp, sc in corner ch-2 sp, ch 1; repeat from ★ around; join with slip st to first sc: 452 sc.

Rnd 3: Ch 1, turn; sc in same st and next ch-1 sp, ch 1, dc in next corner sc, ch 1, sc in next ch-1 sp and next sc, ★ (ch 1, sc in next sc) across to within one ch-1 sp of next corner sc, sc in next ch-1 sp, ch 1, dc in corner sc, ch 1, sc in next ch-1 sp and in next sc; repeat from ★ 2 times **more**, ch 1, (sc in next sc, ch 1) across; join with slip st to first sc: 460 sts.

Rnd 4: Slip st in next sc, do **not** turn; ★ † ch 1, (slip st, ch 1) twice in next corner dc, slip st in next sc, ch 1, (slip st in next ch-1 sp, ch 1) across to within 2 sc of next corner dc, skip next sc †, slip st in next sc; repeat from ★ 2 times **more**, then repeat from † to † once, skip joining slip st; join with slip st to next slip st, finish off.

SENTIMENTAL SWIRLS Continued from page 18.

ASSEMBLY

Using Placement Diagram as a guide and working through both loops, whipstitch Motifs together *(Fig. 27b, page 143)*, forming 6 horizontal strips of 7 Motifs each and 5 horizontal strips of 6 Motifs and 2 Half Motifs each, beginning in first dc to left of ch-3 on one edge and ending in last dc to right of next ch-3, leave corner ch-3 sps unworked; whipstitch strips together in same manner.

PLACEMENT DIAGRAM

Point A

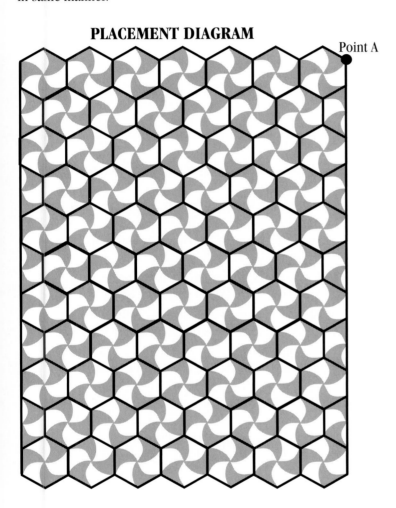

EDGING

Rnd 1: With **right** side facing, join yarn with slip st in ch-3 sp at Point A on Placement Diagram; ch 4, dc in same sp, ch 1, dc in next dc, ch 1, (skip next dc, dc in next dc, ch 1) 4 times, (dc, ch 1) twice in next ch-3 sp, (dc in next dc, ch 1) 5 times, [decrease, ch 1, (dc in next dc, ch 1) 5 times, (dc, ch 1) twice in next ch-3 sp, dc in next dc, ch 1, (skip next dc, dc in next dc, ch 1) 4 times, decrease, ch 1, dc in next dc, ch 1, (skip next dc, dc in next dc, ch 1) 4 times, (dc, ch 1) twice in next ch-3 sp, (dc in next dc, ch 1) 5 times] 3 times, (dc, ch 1) twice in next ch-3 sp, dc in next dc, ch 1, (skip next dc, dc in next dc, ch 1) 4 times, ★ dc in next ch-3 sp, ch 1, skip next joining; working in end of rows on Half Motif, hdc in next row, ch 1, (sc in next row, ch 1) 4 times, sc in ring, ch 1, (sc in next row, ch 1) 4 times, hdc in next row, ch 1, skip next joining, dc in next ch-3 sp, ch 1, dc in next dc, ch 1, (skip next dc, dc in next dc, ch 1) 4 times; repeat from ★ 4 times **more**, (dc, ch 1, dc) in next ch-3 sp, place marker around last ch-1 made for st placement, ch 1, (dc in next dc, ch 1) 5 times, (dc, ch 1) twice in next ch-3 sp, dc in next dc, ch 1, (skip next dc, dc in next dc, ch 1) 4 times, [decrease, ch 1, dc in next dc, ch 1, (skip next dc, dc in next dc, ch 1) 4 times, (dc, ch 1) twice in next ch-3 sp, (dc in next dc, ch 1) 5 times, decrease, ch 1, (dc in next dc, ch 1) 5 times, (dc, ch 1) twice in next ch-3 sp, dc in next dc, ch 1, (skip next dc, dc in next dc, ch 1) 4 times] 3 times, (dc, ch 1) twice in next ch-3 sp, (dc in next dc, ch 1) 5 times, ✝ dc in next ch-3 sp, ch 1, skip next joining; working in end of rows on Half Motif, hdc in next row, ch 1, (sc in next row, ch 1) 4 times, sc in ring, ch 1, (sc in next row, ch 1) 4 times, hdc in next row, ch 1, skip next joining, dc in next ch-3 sp, ch 1, (dc in next dc, ch 1) 5 times ✝, repeat from ✝ to ✝ across; join with slip st to first dc: 378 sts and 378 ch-1 sps.

Continued on page 26.

SENTIMENTAL SWIRLS Continued from page 25.

Rnd 2: Ch 4, dc in next ch-1 sp, † ch 1, (dc in next dc, ch 1) 7 times, dc in next ch-1 sp, ch 1, ★ (dc in next dc, ch 1) 5 times, dc in next 3 dc, ch 1, (dc in next dc, ch 1) 5 times, dc in next ch-1 sp, ch 1; repeat from ★ 5 times **more**, (dc in next dc, ch 1) 7 times, dc in next ch-1 sp, ch 1 †, dc in next dc, ch 1, (skip next ch, dc in next st, ch 1) across to marked ch-1 sp, dc in marked ch-1 sp, remove marker and place marker around dc just made for st placement, repeat from † to † once, (dc in next st, ch 1, skip next ch) across; join with slip st to first dc: 396 dc.

Rnd 3: Ch 6, dc in third ch from hook, (dc, work Picot) twice in next dc, † (dc in next dc, work Picot) 7 times, (dc, work Picot) twice in next dc, ★ (dc in next dc, work Picot) 6 times, skip next dc, (dc in next dc, work Picot) 6 times, (dc, work Picot) twice in next dc; repeat from ★ 5 times **more**, (dc in next dc, work Picot) 7 times, (dc, work Picot) twice in next dc †, (dc in next dc, work Picot) across to marked dc, (dc, work Picot) twice in marked dc, repeat from † to † once, (dc in next dc, work Picot) across; join with slip st to third ch of beginning ch-6: 402 dc.

Rnd 4: Ch 6, dc in third ch from hook, (dc in next dc, work Picot) around; join with slip st to third ch of beginning ch-6, finish off.

VICTORIAN ELEGANCE Continued from page 20.

Rnd 7: Ch 3, turn; work Beginning Puff St, (ch 3, work Puff St in next sc) twice, † ch 1, skip next ch-1 sp, work Shell in next Shell, ch 1, [skip next ch-1 sp and next 2 sc, work Puff St in next sc, (ch 3, work Puff St in next sc) twice, ch 1, skip next ch-1 sp, work Shell in next Shell, ch 1] 14 times, skip next ch-1 sp and next sc, work Puff St in next sc, (ch 3, work Puff St in next sc) 4 times, ch 1, skip next ch-1 sp, work Shell in next Shell, ch 1, [skip next ch-1 sp and next 2 sc, work Puff St in next sc, (ch 3, work Puff St in next sc) twice, ch 1, skip next ch-1 sp, work Shell in next Shell, ch 1] 11 times, skip next ch-1 sp and next sc †, work Puff St in next sc, (ch 3, work Puff St in next sc) 4 times, repeat from † to † once, (work Puff St in next sc, ch 3) twice; join with slip st to top of Beginning Puff St: 54 Shells and 170 Puff Sts.

Rnd 8: Turn; slip st in first ch-3 sp, ch 1, (sc, ch 3) twice in same sp, sc in next ch-3 sp, ch 3, sc in next ch-1 sp, ch 1, work Shell in next Shell, ch 1, sc in next ch-1 sp, ★ [(ch 3, sc in next sp) 3 times, ch 1, work Shell in next Shell, ch 1, sc in next ch-1 sp] across to next corner 5-Puff St group, ch 3, sc in next ch-3 sp, ch 3, (sc, ch 3) twice in next 2 ch-3 sps, sc in next ch-3 sp, ch 3, sc in next ch-1 sp, ch 1, work Shell in next Shell, ch 1, sc in next ch-1 sp; repeat from ★ 2 times **more**, [(ch 3, sc in next sp) 3 times, ch 1, work Shell in next Shell, ch 1, sc in next ch-1 sp] across to last 2 ch-3 sps, ch 3, sc in next ch-3 sp, ch 3, (sc, ch 3) twice in last ch-3 sp; join with slip st to first sc.

Rnd 9: Turn; slip st in first ch-3 sp, ch 3 **(counts as first dc, now and throughout)**, dc in same sp, † ch 2, skip next ch-3 sp, (dc, ch 5, dc) in next ch-3 sp, ch 2, [skip next 2 sps, work Shell in next Shell, ch 2, skip next 2 sps, (dc, ch 5, dc) in next ch-3 sp, ch 2] 15 times, skip next ch-3 sp, work Shell in next ch-3 sp, ch 2, skip next ch-3 sp, (dc, ch 5, dc) in next ch-3 sp, ch 2, [skip next 2 sps, work Shell in next Shell, ch 2, skip next 2 sps, (dc, ch 5, dc) in next ch-3 sp, ch 2] 12 times, skip next ch-3 sp †, work Shell in next ch-3 sp, repeat from † to † once, 2 dc in same sp as first dc, ch 1, sc in first dc to form last ch-2 sp.

Rnd 10: Ch 3, turn; (dc, ch 2, 2 dc) in same sp, ★ ch 1, sc in next ch-2 sp, 5 sc in next ch-5 sp, sc in next ch-2 sp, ch 1, [work Shell in next Shell, ch 1, sc in next ch-2 sp, 5 sc in next ch-5 sp, sc in next ch-2 sp, ch 1] across to next corner Shell, [2 dc, (ch 2, 2 dc) twice] in corner Shell; repeat from ★ 2 times **more**, ch 1, sc in next ch-2 sp, 5 sc in next ch-5 sp, sc in next ch-2 sp, ch 1, [work Shell in next Shell, ch 1, sc in next ch-2 sp, 5 sc in next ch-5 sp, sc in next ch-2 sp, ch 1] across, 2 dc in same sp as first dc, ch 2; join with slip st to first dc.

Rnd 11: Turn; slip st in first ch-2 sp, ch 3, (dc, ch 2, 2 dc) in same sp, ★ [ch 1, skip next ch-1 sp and next 2 sc, work Puff St in next sc, (ch 3, work Puff St in next sc) twice, ch 1, skip next ch-1 sp, work Shell in next ch-2 sp] across to next corner, ch 2, work Shell in next ch-2 sp; repeat from ★ 2 times **more**, [ch 1, skip next ch-1 sp and next 2 sc, work Puff St in next sc, (ch 3, work Puff St in next sc) twice, ch 1, skip next ch-1 sp, work Shell in next ch-2 sp] across, ch 2; join with slip st to first dc.

Rnd 12: Turn; slip st in first ch-2 sp, ch 1, (sc, ch 3, sc) in same sp, ch 1, work Shell in next Shell, ch 1, ★ [sc in next ch-1 sp, (ch 3, sc in next sp) 3 times, ch 1, work Shell in next Shell, ch 1] across to next corner ch-2 sp, (sc, ch 3, sc) in corner ch-2 sp, ch 1, work Shell in next Shell, ch 1; repeat from ★ 2 times **more**, [sc in next ch-1 sp, (ch 3, sc in next sp) 3 times, ch 1, work Shell in next Shell, ch 1] across; join with slip st to first sc.

Rnd 13: Slip st in first ch-3 sp, ch 5, turn; skip next ch-1 sp, work Shell in next Shell, ch 2, ★ [skip next 2 sps, (dc, ch 5, dc) in next ch-3 sp, ch 2, skip next 2 sps, work Shell in next Shell, ch 2] across to within one ch-1 sp of next corner ch-3 sp, skip next ch-1 sp, (dc, ch 5, dc) in corner ch-3 sp, ch 2, skip next ch-1 sp, work Shell in next Shell, ch 2; repeat from ★ 2 times **more**, [skip next 2 sps, (dc, ch 5, dc) in next ch-3 sp, ch 2, skip next 2 sps, work Shell in next Shell, ch 2] across to last ch-1 sp, skip last ch-1 sp, dc in same sp as first dc, ch 2, dc in first dc to form last corner ch-5 sp.

Rnd 14: Ch 1, turn; 3 sc in same sp, sc in next ch-2 sp, ch 1, work Shell in next Shell, ch 1, sc in next ch-2 sp, ★ 5 sc in next ch-5 sp, sc in next ch-2 sp, ch 1, work Shell in next Shell, ch 1, sc in next ch-2 sp; repeat from ★ around, 2 sc in same sp as first sc; join with slip st to first sc.

Rnd 15: Ch 3, turn; work Beginning Puff St, (ch 3, work Puff St in next sc) twice, † ch 1, skip next ch-1 sp, work Shell in next Shell, ch 1, [skip next ch-1 sp and next 2 sc, work Puff St in next sc, (ch 3, work Puff St in next sc) twice, ch 1, skip next ch-1 sp, work Shell in next Shell, ch 1] 16 times, skip next ch-1 sp and next sc, work Puff St in next sc, (ch 3, work Puff St in next sc) 4 times, ch 1, skip next ch-1 sp, work Shell in next Shell, ch 1, [skip next ch-1 sp and next 2 sc, work Puff St in next sc, (ch 3, work Puff St in next sc) twice, ch 1, skip next ch-1 sp, work Shell in next Shell, ch 1] 13 times, skip next ch-1 sp and next sc †, work Puff St in next sc, (ch 3, work Puff St in next sc) 4 times, repeat from † to † once, (work Puff St in next sc, ch 3) twice; join with slip st to top of Beginning Puff St.

Rnd 16: Do **not** turn; slip st in first ch-3 sp, ch 1, (sc, ch 5, sc) in same sp and in next ch-3 sp, sc in next ch-1 sp, (sc, ch 5, sc) in next Shell, sc in next ch-1 sp, ★ [(sc, ch 5, sc) in next 2 ch-3 sps, sc in next ch-1 sp, (sc, ch 5, sc) in next Shell, sc in next ch-1 sp] across to next corner 5-Puff St group, (sc, ch 5, sc) in next 4 ch-3 sps, sc in next ch-1 sp, (sc, ch 5, sc) in next Shell, sc in next ch-1 sp; repeat from ★ 2 times **more**, (sc, ch 5, sc) in next 2 ch-3 sps, [sc in next ch-1 sp, (sc, ch 5, sc) in next Shell, sc in next ch-1 sp, (sc, ch 5, sc) in next 2 ch-3 sps] across; join with slip st to first sc, finish off.

GRANNY'S POSY PATCH

Inspired by grandmother's posy patch, this soothing wrap transforms scraps into a sprinkling of gracious flowers. We used nine shades of pink and purple to highlight the squares, which are joined as you stitch.

Finished Size: 48" x 63"

MATERIALS
Worsted Weight Yarn:
Dk Green - 26¹/₂ ounces,
(750 grams, 1,815 yards)
Green - 12 ounces,
(340 grams, 825 yards)
Scraps - 9 ounces,
(260 grams, 615 yards) **total**
Note: We used 9 different colors in shades of pink and purple.
Crochet hook, size H (5.00 mm) **or** size needed for gauge

GAUGE SWATCH: 3³/₄" square
Work same as First Motif.

FIRST MOTIF

With Scrap color desired, ch 4; join with slip st to form a ring.
Rnd 1 (Right side): Ch 3 **(counts as first dc, now and throughout)**, 19 dc in ring; join with slip st to first dc, finish off: 20 dc.
Note: Loop a short piece of yarn around any stitch to mark Rnd 1 as **right** side.
Rnd 2: With **right** side facing, join Green with slip st in any dc; ch 4 **(counts as first dc plus ch 1)**, (dc in next dc, ch 1) around; join with slip st to first dc, finish off: 20 dc and 20 ch-1 sps.
Rnd 3: With **right** side facing, join Dk Green with slip st in any ch-1 sp; ch 3, 2 dc in same sp, 3 dc in each of next 3 ch-1 sps, ch 7, skip next ch-1 sp, ★ 3 dc in each of next 4 ch-1 sps, ch 7, skip next ch-1 sp; repeat from ★ 2 times **more**; join with slip st to first dc, finish off: 48 dc and 4 ch-7 sps.

ADDITIONAL MOTIFS

Work same as First Motif through Rnd 2: 20 dc and 20 ch-1 sps.
Rnd 3 (Joining rnd): Work One or Two Side Joining, arranging Motifs into 12 vertical rows of 16 Motifs each.

ONE SIDE JOINING

Rnd 3 (Joining rnd): With **right** side facing, join Dk Green with slip st in any ch-1 sp; ch 3, 2 dc in same sp, 3 dc in each of next 3 ch-1 sps, ★ ch 7, skip next ch-1 sp, 3 dc in each of next 4 ch-1 sps; repeat from ★ once **more**, ch 3, holding Motifs with **wrong** sides together, sc in center ch of corresponding corner ch-7 on **adjacent Motif** *(Fig. 26, page 143)*, ch 3, skip next ch-1 sp on **new Motif**, 3 dc in next ch-1 sp, † skip next 3 dc on **adjacent Motif**, sc in sp **before** next dc *(Fig. 25, page 143)*, 3 dc in next ch-1 sp on **new Motif** †, repeat from † to † 2 times **more**, ch 3, sc in center ch of next corner ch-7 on **adjacent Motif**, ch 3; join with slip st to first dc on **new Motif**, finish off.

TWO SIDE JOINING

Rnd 3 (Joining rnd): With **right** side facing, join Dk Green with slip st in any ch-1 sp; ch 3, 2 dc in same sp, 3 dc in each of next 3 ch-1 sps, ch 7, skip next ch-1 sp, 3 dc in each of next 4 ch-1 sps, ch 3, holding Motifs with **wrong** sides together, sc in center ch of corresponding corner ch-7 on **adjacent Motif**, ch 3, skip next ch-1 sp on **new Motif**, ★ 3 dc in next ch-1 sp, † skip next 3 dc on **adjacent Motif**, sc in sp **before** next dc, 3 dc in next ch-1 sp on **new Motif** †, repeat from † to † 2 times **more**, ch 3, sc in center ch of next corner ch-7 on **adjacent Motif**, ch 3, skip next ch-1 sp on **new Motif**; repeat from ★ once **more**; join with slip st to first dc, finish off.

EDGING

With **right** side facing, join Dk Green with slip st in any corner ch-7 sp; ch 3, 6 dc in same sp, ★ † skip next 3 dc, 3 dc in sp **before** next dc, skip next 3 dc, 3 hdc in sp **before** next dc, skip next 3 dc, 3 dc in sp **before** next dc, [3 dc in each of next 2 sps, skip next 3 dc, 3 dc in sp **before** next dc, skip next 3 dc, 3 hdc in sp **before** next dc, skip next 3 dc, 3 dc in sp **before** next dc] across to next corner ch-7 sp †, 7 dc in corner ch-7 sp; repeat from ★ 2 times **more**, then repeat from † to † once; join with slip st to first dc, finish off.

EMERALD TRELLIS

The refreshing color and pleasing pattern on this verdant wrap remind us of lush foliage climbing a garden trellis. Each row is worked across the length of the afghan, with long fringe trimming the ends.

Finished Size: 56" x 75"

MATERIALS
Worsted Weight Yarn:
Green - 51 ounces, (1,450 grams, 3,495 yards)
Lt Green - 23 ounces, (650 grams, 1,575 yards)
Crochet hook, size J (6.00 mm) **or** size needed for gauge

GAUGE: 16 tr and 7 rows = 5"

Gauge Swatch: 5" square
With Green, ch 19 **loosely**.
Row 1: Tr in fifth ch from hook **(4 skipped chs count as first tr)** and in each ch across: 16 tr.
Rows 2-7: Ch 4 **(counts as first tr)**, turn; tr in next tr and in each tr across.
Finish off.

STITCH GUIDE

JOINING WITH DC
Begin with slip knot on hook, YO, holding loop on hook, insert hook in st indicated, YO and pull up a loop (3 loops on hook), (YO and draw through 2 loops on hook) twice.

JOINING WITH TR
Begin with slip knot on hook, YO twice, holding loops on hook, insert hook in st indicated, YO and pull up a loop (4 loops on hook), (YO and draw through 2 loops on hook) 3 times.

Each row is worked across length of Afghan. When joining yarn and finishing off, always leave a 6" end to be worked into fringe.

AFGHAN BODY
With Lt Green, ch 242 **loosely**.
Row 1 (Wrong side)**:** Sc in second ch from hook, ★ ch 7, skip next 3 chs, sc in next ch; repeat from ★ across; finish off: 61 sc and 60 ch-7 sps.
Note: Loop a short piece of yarn around **back** of any stitch to mark **right** side.

Row 2: With **right** side facing, join Green with dc in first sc; ★ working **behind** next ch-7, tr in 3 skipped chs on beginning ch, dc in next sc on Row 1; repeat from ★ across; finish off: 241 sts.
Row 3: With Lt Green, ch 3, with **wrong** side facing, skip first 2 sts, holding first ch-7 **behind** next tr, sc in next tr working through ch-7 sp, ★ ch 7, skip next 3 sts, holding next ch-7 **behind** next tr, sc in next tr working through ch-7 sp; repeat from ★ across to last 2 sts, ch 3, leave remaining sts unworked; finish off.
Row 4: With **right** side facing and keeping ch-3 to **front**, join Green with tr in first unworked dc one row **below** ch-3; tr in next tr, dc in next sc on previous row, ★ working **behind** next ch-7, tr in next 3 sts one row **below** ch-7, dc in next sc on previous row; repeat from ★ across, keeping ch-3 to **front**, tr in last 2 unworked sts one row **below** ch-3; finish off.
Row 5: With **wrong** side facing and holding first ch-3 **behind** first tr, join Lt Green with sc in first tr working through first ch of ch-3 *(see Joining with Sc, page 142)*; ch 7, ★ skip next 3 sts, holding next ch-7 **behind** next tr, sc in next tr working through ch-7 sp, ch 7; repeat from ★ across to last 4 sts, skip next 3 sts, holding last ch-3 **behind** last tr, sc in last tr working through last ch of ch-3; finish off.
Row 6: With **right** side facing, join Green with dc in first sc; ★ working **behind** next ch-7, tr in next 3 sts one row **below** ch-7, dc in next sc on previous row; repeat from ★ across; finish off.
Repeat Rows 3-6 until Afghan measures approximately 56" from beginning ch, ending by working Row 4.
Last Row: With **wrong** side facing and holding first ch-3 **behind** first tr, join Lt Green with sc in first tr working through first ch of ch-3; sc in next 3 sts, ★ holding next ch-7 **behind** next tr, sc in next tr working through ch-7 sp, sc in next 3 sts; repeat from ★ across to last st, holding last ch-3 **behind** last tr, sc in last tr working through last ch of ch-3; do **not** finish off.

EDGING
TOP
Ch 1, turn; slip st in each st across; finish off.

BOTTOM

With **right** side facing and working in free loops of beginning ch *(Fig. 22b, page 142)*, join Lt Green with slip st in ch at base of first sc; slip st in each ch across; finish off.

Holding 3 strands of each color together, add additional fringe evenly spaced across end of rows *(Figs. 28b & d, page 143)*.

ROMANTIC RIBBONS

As light and breezy as a breath of spring, this tan and cream coverlet features intriguing ribbon-like panels. A romantic border enhances the gorgeous mile-a-minute afghan.

Finished Size: 52" x 69"

MATERIALS
Worsted Weight Yarn:
Cream - 34 ounces, (970 grams, 2,090 yards)
Tan - 14 ounces, (400 grams, 860 yards)
Crochet hook, size J (6.00 mm) **or** size needed for gauge

GAUGE: Each Strip = 4³/₄" wide

Gauge Swatch: 4³/₄"w x 7"h
Ch 61 **loosely**.
Work same as Foundation Row and Border of First Strip.

FIRST STRIP
CENTER
With Tan, ch 897 **loosely**.
Foundation Row: Working in back ridges of beginning ch *(Fig. 2b, page 139)*, sc in second ch from hook and in next 4 chs, ch 2, place marker around third sc made to mark **right** side and place second marker around ch-2 just made to mark joining placement, sc in same ch and in next 4 chs, skip next 2 chs, sc in next 5 chs, ★ ch 2, sc in same ch and in next 4 chs, skip next 2 chs, sc in next 5 chs; repeat from ★ across, finish off: 81 ch-2 sps on **each** side.

BORDER
Rnd 1 (Right side): With **right** side facing, join Cream with sc in marked ch-2 sp *(see Joining With Sc, page 142)*; remove marker, (ch 2, sc in next ch-2 sp) across to last 10 sc, ch 2, sc in end of last sc, ch 6; working across second side of Foundation Row, (sc in next ch-2 sp, ch 2) across to last 9 chs, sc in end of first sc, ch 6; join with slip st to first sc: 164 sps.
Rnd 2: Ch 4, (dc, ch 1, dc) in same st, (ch 1, dc in next ch-2 sp, ch 1, dc in next sc) across to next ch-6 sp, (ch 1, dc in same st) twice, (ch 1, dc) 3 times in next ch-6 sp, (ch 1, dc) 3 times in next sc, (ch 1, dc in next ch-2 sp, ch 1, dc in next sc) across to last ch-6 sp, (ch 1, dc in same st) twice, ch 1, (dc, ch 1) 3 times in last ch-6 sp; join with slip st to third ch of beginning ch-4: 340 ch-1 sps.

Rnd 3: Ch 1, sc in same st, † ch 3, (sc, ch 3) twice in next corner dc, sc in next dc, (ch 3, skip next dc, sc in next dc) across to next corner dc, (ch 3, sc) twice in corner dc, ch 3, (sc in next dc, ch 3, skip next dc) twice †, sc in next dc, repeat from † to † once; join with slip st to first sc: 178 ch-3 sps.
Rnd 4: Slip st in first ch-3 sp, ch 1, (sc, ch 3, sc) in same sp and in each ch-3 sp around; join with slip st to first sc, finish off.

REMAINING 9 STRIPS
Work same as First Strip through Rnd 3 of Border: 178 ch-3 sps.
Rnd 4 (Joining rnd): Slip st in first ch-3 sp, ch 1, (sc, ch 3, sc) in same sp and in next 90 ch-3 sps, sc in next ch-3 sp, ch 1, holding Strips with **wrong** sides together, matching sts and sps, and markers at opposite ends, sc in corresponding ch-3 sp on **previous Strip** *(Fig. 26, page 143)*, ch 1, sc in same sp on **new Strip**, ★ sc in next ch-3 sp, ch 1, sc in next ch-3 sp on **previous Strip**, ch 1, sc in same sp on **new Strip**; repeat from ★ across to last 4 ch-3 sps, (sc, ch 3, sc) in last 4 ch-3 sps; join with slip st to first sc, finish off.

EDGING
Rnd 1: With **right** side of short edge facing, join Cream with sc in right corner ch-3 sp; ch 3, sc in same sp, † (ch 3, sc in next ch-3 sp) 5 times, ★ ch 1, skip next joining, sc in next ch-3 sp, (ch 3, sc in next ch-3 sp) 5 times; repeat from ★ 8 times **more**, ch 3, sc in same sp, (ch 3, sc in next ch-3 sp) across to next corner ch-3 sp †, (ch 3, sc) twice in corner ch-3 sp, repeat from † to † once, ch 3; join with slip st to first sc: 272 ch-3 sps.
Rnd 2: Slip st in first ch-3 sp, ch 1, (sc, ch 3, sc) in same sp and in each ch-3 sp around; join with slip st to first sc.
Rnd 3: Slip st in first ch-3 sp, ch 1, (sc, ch 7, sc) in same sp, ★ ch 3, (sc in next ch-3 sp, ch 7, sc in next ch-3 sp, ch 3) across to next corner ch-3 sp, (sc, ch 7, sc) in corner ch-3 sp; repeat from ★ 2 times **more**, ch 3, (sc in next ch-3 sp, ch 7, sc in next ch-3 sp, ch 3) across; join with slip st to first sc: 276 sps.

Rnd 4: Slip st in first ch-7 sp, ch 1, in same sp work [sc, (ch 1, dc) 3 times, ch 2, (dc, ch 1) 3 times, sc], sc in next ch-3 sp, ★ in next ch-7 sp work [sc, (ch 1, dc) 3 times, ch 2, (dc, ch 1) 3 times, sc], sc in next ch-3 sp; repeat from ★ around; join with slip st to first sc.

Rnd 5: Slip st in next 2 sts and in next ch-1 sp, ch 1, sc in same sp, ch 3, sc in next ch-1 sp, ch 3, ★ † (sc, ch 5, sc) in next ch-2 sp, (ch 3, sc in next ch-1 sp) twice, ch 3, skip next 3 ch-1 sps, sc in next ch-1 sp, ch 3, (sc, ch 5, sc) in next ch-2 sp, ch 3, sc in next ch-1 sp, [skip next 4 ch-1 sps, sc in next ch-1 sp, ch 3, (sc, ch 5, sc) in next ch-2 sp, ch 3, sc in next ch-1 sp] across to next corner group, ch 3, skip next 3 ch-1 sps †, (sc in next ch-1 sp, ch 3) twice; repeat from ★ 2 times **more**, then repeat from † to † once; join with slip st to first sc, finish off.

IRISH PATCHWORK

The green hills and cloud-swept skies of the Emerald Isle are reproduced in this springtime granny. A perfect take-along project, the patchwork squares are easily whipstitched into a diamond pattern with the aid of a handy placement diagram.

Finished Size: 57" x 69"

MATERIALS
Worsted Weight Yarn:
  Green - 32 ounces, (910 grams, 2,010 yards)
  Cream - 22 ounces, (620 grams, 1,385 yards)
Crochet hook, size I (5.50 mm) **or** size needed
  for gauge
Yarn needle

GAUGE SWATCH: 3"
Work same as Square.

STITCH GUIDE

REVERSE SINGLE CROCHET
  (abbreviated reverse sc)
Working from **left** to **right**, insert hook in dc indicated to right of hook, YO and draw through, under, and to left of loop on hook (2 loops on hook), YO and draw through both loops on hook *(reverse sc made, Figs. 20a-d, page 142)*.

Referring to the Key, make the number of Squares specified in the colors indicated.

SQUARE
With color indicated, ch 4; join with slip st to form a ring.
Rnd 1 (Right side): Ch 3 **(counts as first dc, now and throughout)**, 2 dc in ring, ch 2, (3 dc in ring, ch 2) 3 times; join with slip st to first dc: 12 dc and 4 ch-2 sps.
Note: Loop a short piece of yarn around any stitch to mark Rnd 1 as **right** side.
Rnd 2: Slip st in next 2 dc and in next ch-2 sp, ch 3, (2 dc, ch 2, 3 dc) in same sp, ch 1, ★ (3 dc, ch 2, 3 dc) in next ch-2 sp, ch 1; repeat from ★ 2 times **more**; join with slip st to first dc, finish off: 24 dc and 8 sps.

ASSEMBLY
With matching color as desired, using Placement Diagram as a guide, and working through inside loops only, whipstitch Squares together *(Fig. 27a, page 143)*, forming 17 vertical strips of 21 Squares each, beginning in second ch of first corner ch-2 and ending in first ch of next corner ch-2; whipstitch strips together in same manner.

PLACEMENT DIAGRAM

KEY
■ - Green (Make 168)
□ - Cream (Make 189)

EDGING
Rnd 1: With **right** side facing, join Green with sc in any corner ch-2 sp *(see Joining With Sc, page 142)*; ★ † (sc in next 3 dc and in next sp) twice, hdc in joining, (sc in next sp and in next 3 dc) twice, [sc in next sp, hdc in joining, (sc in next sp and in next 3 dc) twice] across to next corner ch-2 sp †, (sc, ch 2, sc) in corner ch-2 sp; repeat from ★ 2 times **more**, then repeat from † to † once, sc in same sp as first sc, ch 1, sc in first sc to form last ch-2 sp: 756 sts and 4 ch-2 sps.

Rnd 2: Ch 3, dc in same sp and in each st across to next corner ch-2 sp, ★ (2 dc, ch 2, 2 dc) in corner ch-2 sp, dc in each st across to next corner ch-2 sp; repeat from ★ 2 times **more**, 2 dc in same sp as first dc, ch 1, sc in first dc to form last ch-2 sp: 772 dc and 4 ch-2 sps.

Rnd 3: Ch 3, dc in same sp, ch 1, skip next dc, (dc in next dc, ch 1, skip next dc) across to next corner ch-2 sp, ★ (2 dc, ch 2, 2 dc) in corner ch-2 sp, ch 1, skip next dc, (dc in next dc, ch 1, skip next dc) across to next corner ch-2 sp; repeat from ★ 2 times **more**, 2 dc in same sp as first dc, ch 1, sc in first dc to form last ch-2 sp: 400 dc and 392 sps.

Rnd 4: Ch 3, dc in same sp, dc in each dc and in each ch-1 sp across to next corner ch-2 sp, ★ (2 dc, ch 2, 2 dc) in corner ch-2 sp, dc in each dc and in each ch-1 sp across to next corner ch-2 sp; repeat from ★ 2 times **more**, 2 dc in same sp as first dc, ch 1, sc in first dc to form last ch-2 sp: 804 dc and 4 ch-2 sps.

Rnds 5 and 6: Repeat Rnds 3 and 4: 836 dc and 4 ch-2 sps.

Rnd 7: Ch 1, work reverse sc in same sp, ch 1, ★ † work reverse sc in next dc, ch 1, (skip next dc, work reverse sc in next dc, ch 1) across to next corner ch-2 sp †, work reverse sc in corner ch-2 sp; repeat from ★ 2 times **more**, then repeat from † to † once; join with slip st to first reverse sc, finish off.

SPRING RIPPLE

This colorful wrap reminds us of a countryside dotted with row upon row of spring blossoms. Black accents in the fringe and alternating ripples provide a dramatic contrast with the bright pastels.

Finished Size: 49" x 64"

MATERIALS
Worsted Weight Yarn:
Black - 21 ounces,
(600 grams, 1,190 yards)
Rose - 6 ounces,
(170 grams, 340 yards)
Lt Rose - 5¹/₂ ounces,
(160 grams, 310 yards)
Yellow - 5¹/₂ ounces,
(160 grams, 310 yards)
Blue - 5¹/₂ ounces,
(160 grams, 310 yards)
Green - 5¹/₂ ounces,
(160 grams, 310 yards)
Crochet hook, size I (5.50 mm) **or**
size needed for gauge

GAUGE: Each repeat from point to point =
3¹/₂"; 5 rows = 4"

Gauge Swatch: 7"w x 4"h
Ch 37 **loosely**.
Work same as Afghan for 5 rows.
Finish off.

STITCH GUIDE

DECREASE (uses next 5 sts)
YO, † insert hook in **next** st, YO and pull up a loop, YO and draw through 2 loops on hook †, YO, skip next 3 sts, repeat from † to † once, YO and draw through all 3 loops on hook **(counts as one dc)**.

ENDING DECREASE (uses last 4 sts)
YO, insert hook in next dc, YO and pull up a loop, YO and draw through 2 loops on hook, YO, skip next 2 sts, insert hook in top of turning ch, YO and pull up a loop, YO and draw through 2 loops on hook, YO and draw through all 3 loops on hook **(counts as one dc)**.

COLOR SEQUENCE

One row Black **(Fig. 24, page 143)**, 2 rows Rose, 1 row Black, ★ 2 rows Yellow, 1 row Black, 2 rows Blue, 1 row Black, 2 rows Lt Rose, 1 row Black, 2 rows Green, 1 row Black, 2 rows Rose, 1 row Black; repeat from ★ 4 times **more**.

AFGHAN BODY

With Black, ch 241 **loosely**.
Row 1 (Right side): Dc in fifth ch from hook, ch 1, skip next ch, (dc in next ch, ch 1, skip next ch) twice, 3 dc in next ch, ch 3, 3 dc in next ch, ch 1, (skip next ch, dc in next ch, ch 1) twice, ★ skip next ch, decrease, ch 1, skip next ch, (dc in next ch, ch 1, skip next ch) twice, 3 dc in next ch, ch 3, 3 dc in next ch, ch 1, (skip next ch, dc in next ch, ch 1) twice; repeat from ★ across to last 4 chs, † YO, skip next ch, insert hook in **next** ch, YO and pull up a loop, YO and draw through 2 loops on hook †, repeat from † to † once **more**, cut Black, with Rose, YO and draw through all 3 loops on hook **(counts as one dc)**: 155 dc.
Note: Loop a short piece of yarn around any stitch to mark Row 1 as **right** side.

Continued on page 47.

april

LILAC BOUQUET

Everything about this springtime throw is lovely, from its scalloped squares to the gently curved border. Delicate openwork joins squares stitched in soft shades of purple.

Finished Size: 50" x 66"

MATERIALS
Worsted Weight Yarn:
Lt Purple - 27 ounces, (770 grams, 1,850 yards)
Purple - 5 ounces, (140 grams, 345 yards)
Crochet hook, size I (5.50 mm) **or** size needed for gauge

GAUGE: Each Square = 8"

Gauge Swatch: 2³/4" in diameter
Work same as First Square Rnds 1 and 2.

STITCH GUIDE

DECREASE (uses next 2 sps)
Pull up a loop in next 2 sps, YO and draw through all 3 loops on hook.

FIRST SQUARE

Rnd 1 (Right side)**:** With Purple, ch 2, 12 sc in second ch from hook; join with slip st to first sc.
Note: Loop a short piece of yarn around any stitch to mark Rnd 1 as **right** side.
Rnd 2: Ch 1, sc in same st, 3 dc in next sc, (sc in next sc, 3 dc in next sc) around; join with slip st to first sc, finish off: 18 dc and 6 sc.
Rnd 3: With **right** side facing, join Lt Purple with sc in any sc **(see Joining With Sc, page 142)**; ch 3, skip next dc, ★ sc in next st, ch 3, skip next st; repeat from ★ around; join with slip st to first sc: 12 ch-3 sps.
Rnd 4: Slip st in first ch-3 sp, ch 1, sc in same sp, ch 5, sc in next ch-3 sp, 7 dc in next ch-3 sp, ★ sc in next ch-3 sp, ch 5, sc in next ch-3 sp, 7 dc in next ch-3 sp; repeat from ★ 2 times **more**; join with slip st to first sc: 28 dc and 4 ch-5 sps.

Rnd 5: Slip st in first ch-5 sp, ch 3 **(counts as first dc, now and throughout)**, 8 dc in same sp, skip next 2 sts, sc in next dc, (ch 3, skip next dc, sc in next dc) twice, skip next 2 sts, ★ 9 dc in next ch-5 sp, skip next 2 sts, sc in next dc, (ch 3, skip next dc, sc in next dc) twice, skip next 2 sts; repeat from ★ 2 times **more**; join with slip st to first dc: 36 dc and 8 ch-3 sps.
Rnd 6: Ch 1, sc in same st, ch 5, skip next 2 dc, sc in next dc, ch 7, skip next dc, sc in next dc, ch 5, skip next 2 dc, sc in next dc, ch 5, skip next sc, sc in next sc, ch 5, skip next sc, ★ sc in next dc, ch 5, skip next 2 dc, sc in next dc, ch 7, skip next dc, sc in next dc, ch 5, skip next 2 dc, sc in next dc, ch 5, skip next sc, sc in next sc, ch 5, skip next sc; repeat from ★ 2 times **more**; join with slip st to first sc: 20 sps.
Rnd 7: Slip st in next 2 chs and in same ch-5 sp, ch 1, sc in same sp, ch 5, (sc, ch 7, sc) in next corner ch-7 sp, ch 5, ★ (sc in next ch-5 sp, ch 5) 4 times, (sc, ch 7, sc) in next corner ch-7 sp, ch 5; repeat from ★ 2 times **more**, (sc in next ch-5 sp, ch 5) 3 times; join with slip st to first sc, finish off.

ADDITIONAL SQUARES

Work same as First Square through Rnd 6: 20 sps.
Rnd 7 (Joining rnd)**:** Work One or Two Side Joining, arranging Squares into 6 vertical rows of 8 Squares each.

ONE SIDE JOINING

When joining corners, always join into the same sp as previous joining.
Rnd 7 (Joining rnd)**:** Slip st in next 2 chs and in same ch-5 sp, ch 1, sc in same sp, ch 5, ★ (sc, ch 7, sc) in next corner ch-7 sp, ch 5, (sc in next ch-5 sp, ch 5) 4 times; repeat from ★ once **more**, sc in next corner ch-7 sp, ch 3, holding Squares with **wrong** sides together, sc in corresponding corner ch-7 sp on **adjacent Square** *(Fig. 26, page 143)*, ch 3, sc in same sp on **new Square**, ch 2, sc in next ch-5 sp on **adjacent Square**, ch 2, (sc in next ch-5 sp on **new Square**, ch 2, sc in next ch-5 sp on **adjacent Square**, ch 2) 4 times, sc in next corner ch-7 sp on **new Square**, ch 3, sc in corresponding corner ch-7 sp on **adjacent Square**, ch 3, sc in same sp on **new Square**, ch 5, (sc in next ch-5 sp, ch 5) 3 times; join with slip st to first sc, finish off.

Continued on page 47.

VIVACIOUS VIOLETS

Nosegays of vibrant violets dot this luscious coverlet. With their petals uplifted by chain loops worked behind them, the violets seem to be nestled in lacy doilies.

Finished Size: 45½" x 62"

MATERIALS
Worsted Weight Yarn:
    Ecru - 18 ounces, (510 grams, 1,140 yards)
    Green - 14½ ounces, (410 grams, 920 yards)
    Lavender - 14 ounces, (400 grams, 885 yards)
Crochet hook, size I (5.50 mm) **or** size needed
    for gauge

GAUGE: Each Square = 5½"

Gauge Swatch: 3" (petal to petal)
Work same as First Square through Rnd 2.

STITCH GUIDE

> **BACK POST SINGLE CROCHET** *(abbreviated BPsc)*
> Insert hook from **back** to **front** around post of st indicated *(Fig. 13, page 141)*, YO and pull up a loop, YO and draw through both loops on hook.
>
> **BEGINNING DECREASE** (uses next 3 dc)
> Ch 2, ★ YO, insert hook in **next** dc, YO and pull up a loop, YO and draw through 2 loops on hook; repeat from ★ 2 times **more**, YO and draw through all 4 loops on hook.
>
> **DECREASE** (uses next 4 dc)
> ★ YO, insert hook in **next** dc, YO and pull up a loop, YO and draw through 2 loops on hook; repeat from ★ 3 times **more**, YO and draw through all 5 loops on hook.
>
> **CLUSTER**
> ★ YO, insert hook in sp indicated, YO and pull up a loop, YO and draw through 2 loops on hook; repeat from ★ 2 times **more**, YO and draw through all 4 loops on hook *(Figs. 16a & b, page 141)*.

FIRST SQUARE

With Lavender, ch 4; join with slip st to form a ring.
Rnd 1 (Right side)**:** Ch 1, (sc in ring, ch 3) 5 times; join with slip st to first sc: 5 ch-3 sps.
Rnd 2: (Sc, dc, 3 tr, dc, sc, slip st) in each ch-3 sp around: 5 petals.
Rnd 3: Ch 1, working **behind** petals and around sc on Rnd 1, work BPsc around first sc, ch 4, (work BPsc around next sc, ch 4) around; join with slip st to first BPsc, finish off: 5 ch-4 sps.
Rnd 4: With **right** side facing, join Green with sc in any ch-4 sp *(see Joining With Sc, page 142)*; 3 sc in same sp and in each ch-4 sp around; join with slip st to first sc: 16 sc.
Rnd 5: Ch 3 **(counts as first dc, now and throughout)**, dc in next 3 sc, ch 4, (dc in next 4 sc, ch 4) around; join with slip st to first dc: 16 dc and 4 ch-4 sps.
Rnd 6: Work beginning decrease, ch 4, (dc, ch 4) twice in next ch-4 sp, ★ decrease, ch 4, (dc, ch 4) twice in next ch-4 sp; repeat from ★ 2 times **more**; join with slip st to beginning decrease, finish off: 12 ch-4 sps.
Rnd 7: With **right** side facing, join Ecru with sc in first ch of first ch-4; ch 5, (work Cluster, ch 5) 4 times in next ch-4 sp, skip next ch-4 sp, ★ sc in first ch of next ch-4, ch 5, (work Cluster, ch 5) 4 times in next ch-4 sp, skip next ch-4 sp; repeat from ★ 2 times **more**; join with slip st to first sc, finish off: 20 ch-5 sps.

ADDITIONAL SQUARES

Work same as First Square through Rnd 6: 12 ch-4 sps.
Rnd 7 (Joining rnd)**:** Work One or Two Side Joining, arranging Squares into 8 vertical rows of 11 Squares each.

Continued on page 48.

BUNNY TALES

Clusters of soft cottontails cover this comfy cuddle-up, which is perfect for baby's story-tale time. The puffy clusters make a pretty border for each square, as well as for the outer edges.

Finished Size: 38½" x 49½"

MATERIALS
Sport Weight Yarn:
    White - 20½ ounces, (580 grams, 1,935 yards)
    Pink - 4½ ounces, (130 grams, 425 yards)
    Yellow - 4½ ounces, (130 grams, 425 yards)
    Aqua - 4½ ounces, (130 grams, 425 yards)
Crochet hook, size H (5.00 mm) **or** size needed
    for gauge
Yarn needle

GAUGE: Each Square = 5½"

Gauge Swatch: 3¾"
Work same as Square through Rnd 5.

STITCH GUIDE

> **CLUSTER**
> Ch 3, YO, insert hook in third ch from hook, YO and pull up a loop, YO and draw through 2 loops on hook, YO, insert hook in same ch, YO and pull up a loop, YO and draw though 2 loops on hook, YO and draw through all 3 loops on hook *(Figs. 16a & b, page 141)*.

SQUARE (Make 48)

Rnd 1 (Right side)**:** With Yellow, ch 4, 2 dc in fourth ch from hook **(3 skipped chs count as first dc)**, ch 3, (3 dc in same ch, ch 3) 3 times; join with slip st to first dc: 12 dc and 4 ch-3 sps.
Note: Loop a short piece of yarn around any stitch to mark Rnd 1 as **right** side.
Rnd 2: Ch 1, turn; ★ (sc, work Cluster, ch 1, sc) in next ch-3 sp, work Cluster; repeat from ★ around; join with slip st to first sc, finish off: 8 Clusters and 8 sc.
Rnd 3: With **right** side facing, join White with sc in same st as joining *(see Joining With Sc, page 142)*; ★ † working **behind** next Cluster, dc in next 3 dc one rnd **below** Cluster, sc in next sc, working **behind** next corner Cluster, (dc, ch 3, dc) in ch-3 sp **before** next sc one rnd **below** Cluster †, sc in next sc; repeat from ★ 2 times **more**, then repeat from † to † once; join with slip st to first sc, finish off: 28 sts and 4 ch-3 sps.

Rnd 4: With **wrong** side facing, join Pink with sc in any corner ch-3 sp; work Cluster, ch 1, sc in same sp, work Cluster, skip next 3 sts, sc in next dc, work Cluster, skip next 3 sts, ★ (sc, work Cluster, ch 1, sc) in next corner ch-3 sp, work Cluster, skip next 3 sts, sc in next dc, work Cluster, skip next 3 sts; repeat from ★ 2 times **more**; join with slip st to first sc, finish off: 12 Clusters and 12 sc.
Rnd 5: With **right** side facing, join White with sc in first sc to left of any corner Cluster; ★ † (working **behind** next Cluster, dc in next 3 sts one rnd **below** Cluster, sc in next sc) twice, working **behind** corner Cluster, (dc, ch 3, dc) in ch-3 sp **before** next sc one rnd **below** Cluster †, sc in next sc; repeat from ★ 2 times **more**, then repeat from † to † once; join with slip st to first sc, finish off: 44 sts and 4 ch-3 sps.
Rnd 6: With **wrong** side facing, join Aqua with sc in any corner ch-3 sp; work Cluster, ch 1, sc in same sp, work Cluster, skip next 3 sts, (sc in next dc, work Cluster, skip next 3 sts) twice, ★ (sc, work Cluster, ch 1, sc) in next corner ch-3 sp, work Cluster, skip next 3 sts, (sc in next dc, work Cluster, skip next 3 sts) twice; repeat from ★ 2 times **more**; join with slip st to first sc, finish off: 16 Clusters and 16 sc.
Rnd 7: With **right** side facing, join White with sc in first sc to left of any corner Cluster; ★ † (working **behind** next Cluster, dc in next 3 sts one rnd **below** Cluster, sc in next sc) 3 times, working **behind** next corner Cluster, (dc, ch 3, dc) in ch-3 sp **before** next sc one rnd **below** Cluster †, sc in next sc; repeat from ★ 2 times **more**, then repeat from † to † once; join with slip st to first sc, do **not** finish off: 60 sts and 4 ch-3 sps.
Rnd 8: Slip st in next 2 dc, ch 3 **(counts as first dc)**, 2 dc in same st, ch 1, skip next 3 sts, (3 dc in next dc, ch 1, skip next 3 sts) twice, (3 dc, ch 3, 3 dc) in next corner ch-3 sp, ch 1, skip next 3 sts, ★ (3 dc in next dc, ch 1, skip next 3 sts) 3 times, (3 dc, ch 3, 3 dc) in next corner ch-3 sp, ch 1, skip next 3 sts; repeat from ★ 2 times **more**; join with slip st to first dc, finish off: 60 dc and 20 sps.

ASSEMBLY

With White and working through both loops, whipstitch Squares together *(Fig. 27b, page 143)*, forming 6 vertical strips of 8 Squares each, beginning in center ch of first corner ch-3 and ending in center ch of next corner ch-3; whipstitch strips together in same manner.

Continued on page 49.

TULIPS IN BLOOM

*Bursting with springtime color and vitality, our patchwork tulips
are made by arranging solid and two-color squares. Slip stitched
flower stems and a ruffly border are appealing finishes.*

Finished Size: 56" x 74"

MATERIALS
Worsted Weight Yarn:
　Cream - 52 ounces, (1,480 grams, 3,565 yards)
　Green - 5 ounces, (140 grams, 345 yards)
　Lt Blue - 1 ounce, (30 grams, 70 yards)
　Blue - 1 ounce, (30 grams, 70 yards)
　Lt Purple - 1 ounce, (30 grams, 70 yards)
　Purple - 1 ounce, (30 grams, 70 yards)
　Lt Mauve - 1 ounce, (30 grams, 70 yards)
　Mauve - 1 ounce, (30 grams, 70 yards)
　Lt Rose - 1 ounce, (30 grams, 70 yards)
　Rose - 1 ounce, (30 grams, 70 yards)
Crochet hook, size I (5.50 mm) **or** size needed
　for gauge
Yarn needle

GAUGE SWATCH: 3"
Work same as Square A.

Referring to the Key, page 46, make the number of Squares
specified in the colors indicated.

SQUARE A

With Cream, ch 4; join with slip st to form a ring.
Rnd 1 (Right side): Ch 3 **(counts as first dc, now and
throughout)**, 2 dc in ring, ch 2, (3 dc in ring, ch 2) 3 times;
join with slip st to first dc: 12 dc and 4 ch-2 sps.
Note: Loop a short piece of yarn around any stitch to mark
Rnd 1 as **right** side.
Rnd 2: Slip st in next 2 dc and in next ch-2 sp, ch 3, (2 dc,
ch 2, 3 dc) in same sp, ch 1, ★ (3 dc, ch 2, 3 dc) in next
ch-2 sp, ch 1; repeat from ★ 2 times **more**; join with slip st to
first dc, finish off: 24 dc and 8 sps.

SQUARE B

With first color indicated, ch 4; join with slip st to form a ring.
Rnd 1 (Right side): Ch 5 **(counts as first dc plus ch 2)**, 3 dc
in ring, cut first color, with second color indicated, YO and draw
through, ch 1, 3 dc in ring, ch 2, 3 dc in ring, cut second color,
with first color, YO and draw through, ch 1, 2 dc in ring; join
with slip st to first dc: 12 dc and 4 ch-2 sps.
Note: Mark Rnd 1 as **right** side.
Rnd 2: Slip st in first ch-2 sp, ch 3, (2 dc, ch 2, 3 dc) in same
sp, ch 1, 3 dc in next ch-2 sp, cut first color, with second color,
YO and draw through, ch 1, 3 dc in same sp, ch 1, (3 dc, ch 2,
3 dc) in next ch-2 sp, ch 1, 3 dc in next ch-2 sp, cut second
color, with first color, YO and draw through, ch 1, 3 dc in same
sp, ch 1; join with slip st to first dc, finish off: 24 dc and 8 sps.

ASSEMBLY

With matching color as desired and using Placement Diagram,
page 46, as a guide, and working through inside loops only,
whipstitch Squares together **(Fig. 27a, page 143)** forming
16 vertical strips of 22 Squares each, beginning in second ch of
first corner ch-2 and ending in first ch of next corner ch-2;
whipstitch strips together in same manner.

FINISHING

With Green and using Placement Diagram, page 46, as a guide,
beginning at base of flower and holding working yarn to back of
Afghan, slip st over whipstitch to form stems.

EDGING

Rnd 1: With **right** side facing, join Cream with sc in any corner
ch-2 sp **(see Joining With Sc, page 142)**; ch 2, sc in same
sp, sc in each dc and in each sp and joining across to next
corner ch-2 sp, ★ (sc, ch 2, sc) in corner ch-2 sp, sc in each
dc and in each sp and joining across to next corner ch-2 sp;
repeat from ★ 2 times **more**; join with slip st to first sc,
finish off: 756 sc and 4 ch-2 sps.

Continued on page 46.

Continued from page 44.

PLACEMENT DIAGRAM

Rnd 2: With **right** side facing, join Green with sc in any corner ch-2 sp; ch 2, sc in same sp, ch 1, skip next sc, (sc in next sc, ch 1, skip next sc) across to next corner ch-2 sp, ★ (sc, ch 2, sc) in corner ch-2 sp, ch 1, skip next sc, (sc in next sc, ch 1, skip next sc) across to next corner ch-2 sp; repeat from ★ 2 times **more**; join with slip st to first sc: 384 sc and 384 sps.

Rnd 3: Slip st in first corner ch-2 sp, ch 1, (sc, ch 2, sc) in same sp, ch 1, (sc in next ch-1 sp, ch 1) across to next corner ch-2 sp, ★ (sc, ch 2, sc) in corner ch-2 sp, ch 1, (sc in next ch-1 sp, ch 1) across to next corner ch-2 sp; repeat from ★ 2 times **more**; join with slip st to first sc, finish off: 388 sc and 388 sps.

Rnd 4: With **right** side facing, join Cream with slip st in any corner ch-2 sp; ch 6, dc in same sp, (dc, ch 2, dc) in each ch-1 sp across to next corner ch-2 sp, ★ (dc, ch 3, dc) in corner ch-2 sp, (dc, ch 2, dc) in each ch-1 sp across to next corner ch-2 sp; repeat from ★ 2 times **more**; join with slip st to third ch of beginning ch-6: 776 sts and 388 sps.

Rnd 5: Slip st in first corner ch-3 sp, ch 6, dc in same sp, (dc, ch 2, dc) in each ch-2 sp across to next corner ch-3 sp, ★ (dc, ch 3, dc) in corner ch-3 sp, (dc, ch 2, dc) in each ch-2 sp across to next corner ch-3 sp; repeat from ★ 2 times **more**; join with slip st to third ch of beginning ch-6.

Rnds 6 and 7: Slip st in first corner sp, ch 7, dc in same sp, (dc, ch 3, dc) in next sp and in each sp across to next corner sp, ★ (dc, ch 4, dc) in corner sp, (dc, ch 3, dc) in next sp and in each sp across to next corner sp; repeat from ★ 2 times **more**; join with slip st to third ch of beginning ch-7. Finish off.

KEY

Square A

 - Cream (Make 256)

Square B

- Cream & Green (Make 48)
- Cream & Lt Blue (Make 4)
- Cream & Blue (Make 4)
- Blue & Lt Blue (Make 4)
- Cream & Lt Purple (Make 4)
- Cream & Purple (Make 4)
- Purple & Lt Purple (Make 4)
- Cream & Lt Mauve (Make 4)
- Cream & Mauve (Make 4)
- Mauve & Lt Mauve (Make 4)
- Cream & Lt Rose (Make 4)
- Cream & Rose (Make 4)
- Rose & Lt Rose (Make 4)

SPRING RIPPLE Continued from page 36.

Row 2: Ch 3, turn; (dc in next dc, ch 1) 3 times, skip next 2 dc, (3 dc, ch 3, 3 dc) in next ch-3 sp, ch 1, skip next 2 dc, (dc in next dc, ch 1) twice, ★ skip next ch, decrease, ch 1, (dc in next dc, ch 1) twice, skip next 2 dc, (3 dc, ch 3, 3 dc) in next ch-3 sp, ch 1, skip next 2 dc, (dc in next dc, ch 1) twice; repeat from ★ across to last 5 sts, skip next ch, work ending decrease.
Rows 3-79: Repeat Row 2; at end of Row 79, do **not** change colors and do **not** finish off.

EDGING

Ch 2, do **not** turn; dc in top of last dc made; working in end of rows, (slip st, ch 2, dc) in top of each row across; working in sps and in free loops of beginning ch *(Fig. 22b, page 142)*, (slip st, ch 3, slip st) in first ch, ch 1, (slip st in next ch-1 sp, ch 1) 4 times, skip next ch, slip st in sp **before** next ch *(Fig. 25, page 143)*, ch 1, (slip st in next ch-1 sp, ch 1) 3 times, ★ (slip st, ch 3, slip st) in next ch-3 sp, ch 1, (slip st in next ch-1 sp, ch 1) 3 times, skip next ch, slip st in sp **before** next ch, ch 1, (slip st in next ch-1 sp, ch 1) 3 times; repeat from ★ across to last sp, skip next 2 chs, (slip st, ch 3, slip st, ch 2, dc) in next ch; working in end of rows, (slip st, ch 2, dc) in top of each row across to Row 79; working in sts on Row 79, slip st in first dc, ch 1, (slip st in next ch-1 sp, ch 1) 3 times, skip next dc, slip st in next dc, ch 1, (slip st, ch 3, slip st) in next ch-3 sp, ch 1, skip next dc, slip st in next dc, ch 1, † (slip st in next ch-1 sp, ch 1) 6 times, skip next dc, slip st in next dc, ch 1, (slip st, ch 3, slip st) in next ch-3 sp, ch 1, skip next dc, slip st in next dc, ch 1 †, repeat from † to † across to last 3 ch-1 sps, (slip st in next ch-1 sp, ch 1) 3 times; join with slip st at base of beginning ch-2, finish off.

Holding 12 strands of Black together, add fringe in each point across short edges of Afghan *(Figs. 28a & c, page 143)*.

LILAC BOUQUET Continued from page 38.

TWO SIDE JOINING

Rnd 7 (Joining rnd)**:** Slip st in next 2 chs and in same ch-5 sp, ch 1, sc in same sp, ch 5, (sc, ch 7, sc) in next corner ch-7 sp, ch 5, (sc in next ch-5 sp, ch 5) 4 times, sc in next corner ch-7 sp, ch 3, holding Squares with **wrong** sides together, sc in corresponding corner ch-7 sp on **adjacent Square**, † ch 3, sc in same sp on **new Square**, ch 2, sc in next ch-5 sp on **adjacent Square**, ch 2, (sc in next ch-5 sp on **new Square**, ch 2, sc in next ch-5 sp on **adjacent Square**, ch 2) 4 times, sc in next corner ch-7 sp on **new Square**, ch 3, sc in corresponding corner sp on **adjacent Square** †, skip next 2 joining sc, sc in corresponding corner sp on next **adjacent Square**, repeat from † to † once, ch 3, sc in same sp on **new Square**, ch 5, (sc in next ch-5 sp, ch 5) 3 times; join with slip st to first sc, finish off.

EDGING

With **right** side facing, join Lt Purple with slip st in first ch-5 sp to left of any corner ch-7 sp; ch 3, 8 dc in same sp, ★ † (sc in next ch-5 sp, 9 dc in next ch-5 sp) twice, [decrease, 9 dc in next ch-5 sp, (sc in next ch-5 sp, 9 dc in next ch-5 sp) twice] across to next corner ch-7 sp, (sc, 9 dc, sc) in corner ch-7 sp †, 9 dc in next ch-5 sp; repeat from ★ 2 times **more**, then repeat from † to † once; join with slip st to first dc, finish off.

ONE SIDE JOINING

When joining corners, always join into the same st as previous joining.

Rnd 7 (Joining rnd): With **right** side facing, join Ecru with sc in first ch of first ch-4; ch 5, ★ (work Cluster, ch 5) 4 times in next ch-4 sp, skip next ch-4 sp, sc in first ch of next ch-4, ch 5; repeat from ★ once **more**, work (Cluster, ch 5, Cluster) in next ch-4 sp, ch 2, holding Squares with **wrong** sides together, slip st in center ch of corresponding corner ch-5 on **adjacent Square** *(Fig. 26, page 143)*, ch 2, † work Cluster in same sp on **new Square**, ch 2, slip st in center ch of next ch-5 on **adjacent Square**, ch 2 †, repeat from † to † once **more**, skip next ch-4 sp on **new Square**, sc in first ch of next ch-4, ch 2, slip st in center ch of next ch-5 on **adjacent Square**, ch 2, work Cluster in next ch-4 sp on **new Square**, ch 2, slip st in center ch of next ch-5 on **adjacent Square**, ch 2, repeat from † to † once, (work Cluster in same sp on **new Square**, ch 5) twice; join with slip st to first sc, finish off.

TWO SIDE JOINING

Rnd 7 (Joining rnd): With **right** side facing, join Ecru with sc in first ch of first ch-4; ch 5, (work Cluster, ch 5) 4 times in next ch-4 sp, skip next ch-4 sp, sc in first ch of next ch-4, ch 5, work (Cluster, ch 5, Cluster) in next ch-4 sp, ch 2, holding Squares with **wrong** sides together, slip st in center ch of corresponding corner ch-5 on **adjacent Square**, ch 2, † work Cluster in same sp on **new Square**, ch 2, slip st in center ch of next ch-5 on **adjacent Square**, ch 2 †, repeat from † to † once **more**, skip next ch-4 sp on **new Square**, sc in first ch of next ch-4, ch 2, slip st in center ch of next ch-5 on **adjacent Square**, ch 2, work Cluster in next ch-4 sp on **new Square**, ch 2, slip st in center ch of next ch-5 on **adjacent Square**, ch 2, repeat from † to † 3 times, skip next ch-4 sp on **new Square**, sc in first ch of next ch-4, ch 2, slip st in center ch of next ch-5 on **adjacent Square**, ch 2, work Cluster in next ch-4 sp on **new Square**, ch 2, slip st in center ch of next ch-5 on **adjacent Square**, ch 2, repeat from † to † once, (work Cluster in same sp on **new Square**, ch 5) twice; join with slip st to first sc, finish off.

EDGING

With **right** side facing, join Ecru with sc in ch-5 sp to **right** of any corner 4-Cluster group; ch 6, slip st in fourth ch from hook, ch 2, ★ † work Cluster in next ch-5 sp, ch 6, slip st in fourth ch from hook, ch 2, work (Cluster, ch 6, slip st in fourth ch from hook, ch 2) 4 times in next ch-5 sp, work Cluster in next ch-5 sp, ch 6, slip st in fourth ch from hook, ch 2 †, (sc in next sp, ch 6, slip st in fourth ch from hook, ch 2) across to next corner 4-Cluster group; repeat from ★ 2 times **more**, then repeat from † to † once, (sc in next sp, ch 6, slip st in fourth ch from hook, ch 2) across; join with slip st to first sc, finish off.

EDGING

Rnd 1: With **wrong** side facing, join Yellow with sc in any corner ch-3 sp; work Cluster, ch 1, sc in same sp, work Cluster, ★ (sc in next sp, work Cluster) across to next corner ch-3 sp, (sc, work Cluster, ch 1, sc) in corner ch-3 sp, work Cluster; repeat from ★ 2 times **more**, (sc in next sp, work Cluster) across; join with slip st to first sc, finish off: 168 Clusters and 168 sc.

Rnd 2: With **right** side facing, join White with sc in first sc to left of any corner Cluster; ★ † (working **behind** next Cluster, dc in next 3 dc one rnd **below** Cluster, sc in next sc) 5 times, [working **behind** next Cluster in sts one rnd **below**, dc in same ch as joining on same Square, dc in joining and in same ch as joining on next Square, sc in next sc, (working **behind** next Cluster, dc in next 3 dc one rnd **below** Cluster, sc in next sc) 5 times] across to next corner Cluster, working **behind** corner Cluster, (dc, ch 3, dc) in ch-3 sp **before** next sc one rnd **below** Cluster †, sc in next sc; repeat from ★ 2 times **more**, then repeat from † to † once; join with slip st to first sc, finish off: 668 sts and 4 ch-3 sps.

Rnd 3: With **wrong** side facing, join Pink with sc in any corner ch-3 sp; work Cluster, ch 1, sc in same sp, work Cluster, ★ skip next 3 sts, (sc in next dc, work Cluster, skip next 3 sts) across to next corner ch-3 sp, (sc, work Cluster, ch 1, sc) in corner ch-3 sp, work Cluster; repeat from ★ 2 times **more**, skip next 3 sts, (sc in next dc, work Cluster, skip next 3 sts) across; join with slip st to first sc, finish off: 172 Clusters and 172 sc.

Rnd 4: With **right** side facing, join White with sc in first sc to left of any corner Cluster; ★ † (working **behind** next Cluster, dc in next 3 sts one rnd **below** Cluster, sc in next sc) across to next corner Cluster, working **behind** corner Cluster, (dc, ch 3, dc) in ch-3 sp **before** next sc one rnd **below** Cluster †, sc in next sc; repeat from ★ 2 times **more**, then repeat from † to † once; join with slip st to first sc, finish off: 684 sts and 4 ch-3 sps.

Rnd 5: With Aqua, repeat Rnd 3: 176 Clusters and 176 sc.

Rnd 6: Repeat Rnd 4: 700 sts and 4 ch-3 sps.

Rnds 7 and 8: Repeat Rnds 3 and 4: 716 sts and 4 ch-3 sps.

Rnd 9: With Yellow, repeat Rnd 3: 184 Clusters and 184 sc.

Rnd 10: Repeat Rnd 4; do **not** finish off: 732 sts and 4 ch-3 sps.

Rnd 11: Ch 1, **turn**; sc in same st, ch 1, skip next dc, (sc, ch 3, sc) in next corner ch-3 sp, ch 1, ★ skip next dc, (sc in next st, ch 1, skip next st) across to next corner ch-3 sp, (sc, ch 3, sc) in corner ch-3 sp, ch 1; repeat from ★ 2 times **more**, skip next dc, (sc in next st, ch 1, skip next st) across; join with slip st to first sc, do **not** finish off: 372 sc and 372 sps.

Rnd 12: Ch 1, turn; ★ (slip st in next ch-1 sp, ch 1) across to next corner ch-3 sp, (slip st, ch 1) twice in corner ch-3 sp; repeat from ★ around to last ch-1 sp, slip st in last ch-1 sp, ch 1; join with slip st to first slip st, finish off.

Mix the colors of your favorite flowers in a lively wrap that's as pleasant as a garden-fresh bouquet. With popcorn-stitch petals, this cover-up kindles a sense of fun.

STITCH GUIDE

BEGINNING POPCORN
Ch 3 (**counts as first dc, now and throughout**), 3 dc in sp indicated, drop loop from hook, insert hook in first dc of 4-dc group, hook dropped loop and draw through (***Fig. 18, page 141***).

POPCORN
4 Dc in sp indicated, drop loop from hook, insert hook in first dc of 4-dc group, hook dropped loop and draw through.

FRONT POST DOUBLE CROCHET
  (***abbreviated FPdc***)
YO, insert hook from **front** to **back** around post of st indicated, YO and pull up a loop (***Fig. 11, page 140***), (YO and draw through 2 loops on hook) twice.

SQUARE (Make 48)

With Off-White, ch 6; join with slip st to form a ring.
Rnd 1 (Right side): Work Beginning Popcorn in ring, ch 2, (work Popcorn in ring, ch 2) 7 times; join with slip st to top of Beginning Popcorn, finish off: 8 Popcorns and 8 ch-2 sps.
Note: Loop a short piece of yarn around any stitch to mark Rnd 1 as **right** side.
Rnd 2: With **right** side facing, join Green with slip st in any ch-2 sp; work (Beginning Popcorn, ch 2, Popcorn) in same sp, ch 2, (work Popcorn, ch 2) twice in each ch-2 sp around; join with slip st to top of Beginning Popcorn, finish off: 16 Popcorns and 16 ch-2 sps.
Rnd 3: With **right** side facing, join Peach with slip st in any ch-2 sp; work Beginning Popcorn in same sp, ch 2, (work Popcorn, ch 2) twice in next ch-2 sp, ★ work Popcorn in next ch-2 sp, ch 2, (work Popcorn, ch 2) twice in next ch-2 sp; repeat from ★ around; join with slip st to top of Beginning Popcorn, finish off: 24 Popcorns and 24 ch-2 sps.
Rnd 4: With **right** side facing, join Blue with slip st in any ch-2 sp, ch 3, 2 dc in same sp, 3 hdc in each of next 3 ch-2 sps, 3 dc in next ch-2 sp, (dc, 3 tr, dc) in next ch-2 sp (corner made), ★ 3 dc in next ch-2 sp, 3 hdc in each of next 3 ch-2 sps, 3 dc in next ch-2 sp, (dc, 3 tr, dc) in next ch-2 sp (corner made); repeat from ★ around; join with slip st to first dc, finish off: 80 sts.

Finished Size: 43" x 57"

MATERIALS
  Worsted Weight Yarn:
    Off-White - 18¹/₂ ounces,
      (530 grams, 1,080 yards)
    Peach - 12 ounces,
      (340 grams, 700 yards)
    Pink - 12 ounces,
      (340 grams, 700 yards)
    Blue - 10¹/₂ ounces,
      (300 grams, 610 yards)
    Green - 9 ounces,
      (260 grams, 525 yards)
  Crochet hook, size H (5.00 mm) **or** size needed for gauge
  Yarn needle

GAUGE: Each Square = 7"

Gauge Swatch: 4¹/₂"
Work same as Square through Rnd 3.

Rnd 5: With **right** side facing, join Pink with slip st in center tr of any corner 3-tr group; ch 4, 2 tr in same st, work FPdc around next tr, (dc in next 2 sts, work FPdc around next st) 6 times, ★ 3 tr in next tr, work FPdc around next tr, (dc in next 2 sts, work FPdc around next st) 6 times; repeat from ★ around; join with slip st to top of beginning ch-4, finish off: 88 sts.

Rnd 6: With **right** side facing, join Off-White with slip st in center tr of any corner 3-tr group; ch 3, 4 dc in same st, dc in next tr, work FPdc around next FPdc, (dc in next 2 dc, work FPdc around next FPdc) 6 times, dc in next tr, ★ 5 dc in next tr, dc in next tr, work FPdc around next FPdc, (dc in next 2 dc, work FPdc around next FPdc) 6 times, dc in next tr; repeat from ★ around; join with slip st to first dc, finish off: 104 sts.

ASSEMBLY

With Off-White and working through both loops, whipstitch Squares together *(Fig. 27b, page 143)*, forming 6 vertical strips of 8 Squares each, beginning in center dc of first 5-dc group and ending in center dc of next 5-dc group; whipstitch strips together in same manner.

EDGING

With **right** side facing, join Off-White with sc in any st *(see Joining With Sc, page 142)*; sc evenly around working 3 sc in center dc of each corner 5-dc group; join with slip st to first sc, finish off.

WINDOWPANE POSIES

This elegant throw has a unique look — ornate "windowpanes" highlighted with colorful posies made from scraps. The scalloped "sashing" and corner openwork are created with simple clusters.

Finished Size: 53" x 70"

MATERIALS
Worsted Weight Yarn:
    Green - 40 ounces, (1,140 grams, 2,745 yards)
    Ecru - 10½ ounces, (300 grams, 720 yards)
    Scraps - 11½ ounces, (330 grams, 790 yards) **total**
       Note: We used 9 different colors in shades of pink
       and purple.
Crochet hook, size G (4.00 mm) **or** size needed
    for gauge
Yarn needle

GAUGE: Each Square = 8½"

Gauge Swatch: 4"
Work same as Square through Rnd 3.

STITCH GUIDE

> **CLUSTER**
> ★ YO, insert hook in sp indicated, YO and pull up a loop, YO and draw through 2 loops on hook; repeat from ★ 4 times **more**, YO and draw through all 6 loops on hook *(Figs. 16a & b, page 141)*.
>
> **DECREASE**
> YO, insert hook in same st as joining on same Square, † YO and pull up a loop, YO and draw through 2 loops on hook †, YO, insert hook in same st as joining on next Square, repeat from † to † once, YO and draw through all 3 loops on hook **(counts as one dc)**.

SQUARE (Make 48)
With Scrap color desired, ch 6; join with slip st to form a ring.
Rnd 1 (Right side)**:** Ch 3 **(counts as first dc, now and throughout)**, 3 dc in ring, (ch 2, 4 dc in ring) 3 times, ch 1, sc in first dc to form last ch-2 sp: 16 dc and 4 ch-2 sps.
Note: Loop a short piece of yarn around any stitch to mark Rnd 1 as **right** side.
Rnd 2: Ch 3, 3 dc in same sp, (4 dc, ch 2, 4 dc) in next 3 ch-2 sps, 4 dc in same sp as first dc, ch 2; join with slip st to first dc, finish off: 32 dc and 4 ch-2 sps.

Rnd 3: With **right** side facing, skip first 4 dc and join Green with slip st in sp **before** next dc *(Fig. 25, page 143)*; ch 3, 4 dc in same sp, (4 dc, ch 2, 4 dc) in next ch-2 sp, skip next 4 dc, ★ 5 dc in sp **before** next dc, (4 dc, ch 2, 4 dc) in next ch-2 sp, skip next 4 dc; repeat from ★ 2 times **more**; join with slip st to first dc: 52 dc.
Rnd 4: Ch 3, dc in same st and in next 3 dc, 2 dc in next dc, (4 dc, ch 2, sc, ch 2, 4 dc) in next ch-2 sp, skip next 4 dc, ★ 2 dc in next dc, dc in next 3 dc, 2 dc in next dc, (4 dc, ch 2, sc, ch 2, 4 dc) in next ch-2 sp, skip next 4 dc; repeat from ★ 2 times **more**; join with slip st to first dc: 60 dc and 8 ch-2 sps.
Rnd 5: Ch 3, dc in same st and in next 5 dc, 2 dc in next dc, (4 dc, ch 3, sc) in next ch-2 sp, ch 5, (sc, ch 3, 4 dc) in next ch-2 sp, skip next 4 dc, ★ 2 dc in next dc, dc in next 5 dc, 2 dc in next dc, (4 dc, ch 3, sc) in next ch-2 sp, ch 5, (sc, ch 3, 4 dc) in next ch-2 sp, skip next 4 dc; repeat from ★ 2 times **more**; join with slip st to first dc: 68 dc and 12 sps.
Rnd 6: Ch 3, dc in same st and in next 7 dc, 2 dc in next dc, 4 dc in next ch-3 sp, ch 5, work Cluster in next ch-5 sp, ch 5, 4 dc in next ch-3 sp, skip next 4 dc, ★ 2 dc in next dc, dc in next 7 dc, 2 dc in next dc, 4 dc in next ch-3 sp, ch 5, work Cluster in next ch-5 sp, ch 5, 4 dc in next ch-3 sp, skip next 4 dc; repeat from ★ 2 times **more**; join with slip st to first dc: 76 dc, 4 Clusters, and 8 ch-5 sps.
Rnd 7: Ch 3, dc in same st and in next 9 dc, 2 dc in next dc, ch 7, sc in next ch-5 sp, ch 5, sc in next ch-5 sp, ch 7, skip next 4 dc, ★ 2 dc in next dc, dc in next 9 dc, 2 dc in next dc, ch 7, sc in next ch-5 sp, ch 5, sc in next ch-5 sp, ch 7, skip next 4 dc; repeat from ★ 2 times **more**; join with slip st to first dc, finish off: 52 dc, 8 sc, and 12 sps.
Rnd 8: With **right** side facing, join Ecru with slip st in same st as joining; ch 1, sc in same st and in next 12 dc, ★ † working in **front** of next ch-7 and in sp **before** next sc, (tr, 3 dc) in ch-5 sp one rnd **below** ch-7, (4 dc, ch 3, 4 dc) in next corner ch-5 sp, working in **front** of next ch-7 and in sp **after** next sc, (3 dc, tr) in ch-5 sp one rnd **below** ch-7 †, sc in next 13 dc; repeat from ★ 2 times **more**, then repeat from † to † once; join with slip st to first sc, finish off: 116 sts and 4 ch-3 sps.

ASSEMBLY

With Ecru, using photo as a guide for placement, and working through both loops, whipstitch Squares together *(Fig. 27b, page 143)*, forming 6 vertical strips of 8 Squares each, beginning in center ch of first corner ch-3 and ending in center ch of next corner ch-3; whipstitch strips together in same manner.

EDGING

Rnd 1: With **right** side facing, join Ecru with slip st in top right corner ch-3 sp; ch 3, (2 dc, ch 3, 3 dc) in same sp, ★ † skip next dc, dc in next 28 sts, [dc in next sp, decrease, dc in next sp, skip next dc, dc in next 28 sts] across to next corner ch-3 sp †, (3 dc, ch 3, 3 dc) in corner ch-3 sp; repeat from ★ 2 times **more**, then repeat from † to † once; join with slip st to first dc: 880 dc.

Rnd 2: Ch 1, sc in same st and in each dc around working 3 sc in each corner ch-3 sp; join with slip st to first sc, finish off.

MOTHER'S TREASURE

*This heirloom-quality wrap featuring gorgeous cascades of shells will show
Mother how much you care. Worked in puff stitches and dainty picots,
the sumptuous border adds luxury to a very feminine afghan.*

Finished Size: 43" x 60"

MATERIALS

Worsted Weight Yarn:
   48 ounces, (1,360 grams, 2,320 yards)
Crochet hook, size G (4.00 mm) **or** size needed
   for gauge

GAUGE: In pattern, one repeat = 2³/₄";
             7 rows = 4¹/₄"

Gauge Swatch: 6"w x 4¹/₄"h
Ch 30 **loosely**.
Work same as Afghan for 7 rows.
Finish off.

STITCH GUIDE

SHELL

 (2 Dc, ch 2, 2 dc) in st or sp indicated.

PICOT

Ch 4, slip st in top of last st made *(Fig. 23, page 142)*.

BEGINNING PUFF STITCH
 (abbreviated Beginning Puff St)

Ch 2, ★ YO, insert hook in sp indicated, YO and pull up a
loop even with loop on hook; repeat from ★ 2 times **more**,
YO and draw through all 7 loops on hook *(Fig. 19, page 142)*.

PUFF STITCH *(abbreviated Puff St)*

★ YO, insert hook in sp indicated, YO and pull up a loop
even with loop on hook; repeat from ★ 3 times **more**, YO
and draw through all 9 loops on hook.

AFGHAN BODY

Ch 150 **loosely**.

Row 1 (Right side)**:** 2 Dc in sixth ch from hook **(5 skipped
chs count as first dc plus ch 2)**, skip next 2 chs, dc in next
7 chs, ★ skip next 2 chs, work Shell in next ch, skip next 2 chs,
dc in next 7 chs; repeat from ★ across to last 3 chs, skip next
2 chs, (2 dc, ch 2, dc) in last ch: 134 dc and 13 ch-2 sps.

Row 2: Ch 4 **(counts as first tr, now and throughout)**,
turn; 3 tr in next ch-2 sp, skip next 5 dc, work Shell in next dc,
★ 7 tr in next ch-2 sp, skip next 5 dc, work Shell in next dc;
repeat from ★ across to last ch-2 sp, 3 tr in last ch-2 sp, tr in
last dc: 85 tr and 12 Shells.

Row 3: Ch 3 **(counts as first dc)**, turn; dc in next tr, (ch 1, dc
in next tr) twice, work Shell in next ch-2 sp, ★ skip next 2 dc,
dc in next tr, (ch 1, dc in next tr) 3 times, work Picot, (ch 1, dc
in next tr) 3 times, work Shell in next ch-2 sp; repeat from ★
across to last 6 sts, skip next 2 dc, (dc in next tr, ch 1) twice, dc
in last 2 tr: 133 dc and 11 Picots.

Row 4: Ch 5 **(counts as first dc plus ch 2, now and
throughout)**, turn; 2 dc in same st, 7 tr in next ch-2 sp, (work
Shell in next Picot, 7 tr in next ch-2 sp) across to last 6 dc, skip
next 5 dc, (2 dc, ch 2, dc) in last dc: 134 sts and 13 ch-2 sps.

Row 5: Ch 5, turn; 2 dc in next ch-2 sp, skip next 2 dc, dc in
next tr, (ch 1, dc in next tr) 3 times, work Picot, (ch 1, dc in
next tr) 3 times, ★ work Shell in next ch-2 sp, skip next 2 dc,
dc in next tr, (ch 1, dc in next tr) 3 times, work Picot, (ch 1, dc
in next tr) 3 times; repeat from ★ across to last ch-2 sp, 2 dc in
last ch-2 sp, ch 2, dc in last dc: 134 dc and 12 Picots.

Row 6: Ch 4, turn; 3 tr in next ch-2 sp, work Shell in next Picot,
(7 tr in next ch-2 sp, work Shell in next Picot) across to last
ch-2 sp, 3 tr in last ch-2 sp, tr in last dc: 85 tr and 12 Shells.

Rows 7-84: Repeat Rows 3-6, 19 times; then repeat Rows 3
and 4 once **more**; do **not** finish off.

Continued on page 61.

ROYAL VINEYARD

Latticework and grape clusters make a pleasing combination in nature — and on this cozy coverlet! Front and back post treble crochets and cluster stitches add texture to the trellis and plump fruit.

Finished Size: 47¹/₂" x 60¹/₂"

MATERIALS

Worsted Weight Yarn:

44 ounces, (1,250 grams, 3,015 yards)

Crochet hook, size H (5.00 mm) **or** size needed for gauge

GAUGE: In pattern, one repeat = 6¹/₂"; 7 rows = 3³/₄"

Gauge Swatch: 15"w x 4"h
Ch 68 **loosely.**
Work same as Afghan Body for 7 rows.
Finish off.

STITCH GUIDE

CLUSTER (uses one st)
★ YO, insert hook in st indicated, YO and pull up a loop, YO and draw through 2 loops on hook; repeat from ★ 4 times **more,** YO and draw through all 6 loops on hook. Push Cluster to **right** side *(Figs. 16a & b, page 141).*
BACK POST TREBLE CROCHET (abbreviated BPtr)
YO twice, insert hook from **back** to **front** around post of st indicated, YO and pull up a loop *(Fig. 15, page 141),* (YO and draw through 2 loops on hook) 3 times.
FRONT POST TREBLE CROCHET (abbreviated FPtr)
YO twice, insert hook from **front** to **back** around post of st indicated, YO and pull up a loop *(Fig. 12, page 141),* (YO and draw through 2 loops on hook) 3 times.

AFGHAN BODY

Ch 218 **loosely.**

Row 1 (Right side)**:** Sc in second ch from hook, ch 3, skip next ch, dc in next 2 chs, ★ † sc in next ch, ch 5, skip next 5 chs, sc in next ch, (ch 1, skip next ch, work Cluster in next ch, ch 1, skip next ch, sc in next ch) 4 times, ch 5, skip next 5 chs, sc in next ch †, (2 dc, ch 1, 2 dc) in next ch; repeat from ★ 5 times **more,** then repeat from † to † once, dc in next 2 chs, ch 3, skip next ch, sc in last ch: 107 sts and 78 sps.

Note: Loop a short piece of yarn around any stitch to mark Row 1 as **right** side.

Row 2: Ch 6 **(counts as first tr plus ch 2, now and throughout),** turn; sc in next ch-3 sp, ★ † ch 3, work BPtr around each of next 2 dc, sc in next ch-5 sp, ch 5, skip next sc, sc in next Cluster, (ch 1, work Cluster in next sc, ch 1, sc in next Cluster) 3 times, ch 5, skip next ch-1 sp, sc in next ch-5 sp, skip next sc, work BPtr around each of next 2 dc, ch 3 †, sc in next ch-1 sp; repeat from ★ 5 times **more,** then repeat from † to † once, sc in next ch-3 sp, ch 2, tr in last sc: 101 sts and 72 sps.

Row 3: Ch 1, turn; sc in first tr, ch 5, skip next ch-2 sp, ★ sc in next ch-3 sp, ch 3, work FPtr around each of next 2 BPtr, sc in next ch-5 sp, ch 5, skip next sc, sc in next Cluster, (ch 1, work Cluster in next sc, ch 1, sc in next Cluster) twice, ch 5, skip next ch-1 sp, sc in next ch-5 sp, skip next sc, work FPtr around each of next 2 BPtr, ch 3, sc in next ch-3 sp, ch 5; repeat from ★ across to last sc, skip last sc and next ch-2 sp, sc in last tr: 93 sts and 64 sps.

Row 4: Ch 6, turn; sc in next ch-5 sp, ch 5, sc in next ch-3 sp, ★ † ch 3, work BPtr around each of next 2 FPtr, sc in next ch-5 sp, ch 5, skip next sc, sc in next Cluster, ch 2, tr in next sc, ch 2, sc in next Cluster, ch 5, skip next ch-1 sp, sc in next ch-5 sp, skip next sc, work BPtr around each of next 2 FPtr, ch 3, sc in next ch-3 sp †, (ch 5, sc in next sp) twice; repeat from ★ 5 times **more,** then repeat from † to † once, ch 5, sc in next ch-5 sp, ch 2, tr in last sc: 87 sts and 58 sps.

Row 5: Ch 4 **(counts as first dc plus ch 1, now and throughout),** turn; work Cluster in same st, ch 1, skip next ch-2 sp, ★ † sc in next ch-5 sp, ch 5, sc in next ch-3 sp, ch 3, work FPtr around each of next 2 BPtr, sc in next ch-5 sp, ch 5, skip next sc, sc in next tr, ch 5, skip next ch-2 sp, sc in next ch-5 sp, skip next sc, work FPtr around each of next 2 BPtr, ch 3, sc in next ch-3 sp, ch 5, sc in next ch-5 sp, ch 1 †, work Cluster in next sc, ch 1; repeat from ★ 5 times **more,** then repeat from † to † once, skip next sc, (work Cluster, ch 1, dc) in last tr; do **not** finish off.

Continued on page 58.

ROYAL VINEYARD Continued from page 56.

Row 6: Ch 1, turn; sc in first dc, ch 1, skip next Cluster, ★ † work Cluster in next sc, ch 1, sc in next ch-5 sp, ch 5, sc in next ch-3 sp, ch 3, work BPtr around each of next 2 FPtr, sc in next ch-5 sp, ch 5, sc in next ch-5 sp, skip next sc, work BPtr around each of next 2 FPtr, ch 3, sc in next ch-3 sp, ch 5, sc in next ch-5 sp, ch 1, work Cluster in next sc, ch 1 †, sc in next Cluster, ch 1; repeat from ★ 5 times **more**, then repeat from † to † once, skip next Cluster, sc in last dc: 92 sts and 63 sps.

Row 7: Ch 4, turn; work Cluster in same st, ch 1, sc in next Cluster, ch 1, work Cluster in next sc, ch 1, ★ † sc in next ch-5 sp, ch 5, sc in next ch-3 sp, ch 3, work FPtr around each of next 2 BPtr, sc in next ch-5 sp, skip next sc, work FPtr around each of next 2 BPtr, ch 3, sc in next ch-3 sp, ch 5, sc in next ch-5 sp, ch 1, work Cluster in next sc, ch 1 †, (sc in next Cluster, ch 1, work Cluster in next sc, ch 1) twice; repeat from ★ 5 times **more**, then repeat from † to † once, sc in next Cluster, ch 1, (work Cluster, ch 1, dc) in last sc: 101 sts and 72 sps.

Row 8: Ch 1, turn; sc in first dc, ch 1, (sc in next Cluster, ch 1, work Cluster in next sc, ch 1) twice, ★ † sc in next ch-5 sp, ch 5, sc in next ch-3 sp, skip next 2 FPtr and next sc, work BPtr around each of next 2 FPtr, ch 1, working **behind** last 2 BPtr made, work BPtr around first skipped FPtr and around next skipped FPtr, sc in next ch-3 sp, ch 5, sc in next ch-5 sp, ch 1 †, work Cluster in next sc, ch 1, (sc in next Cluster, ch 1, work Cluster in next sc, ch 1) 3 times; repeat from ★ 5 times **more**, then repeat from † to † once, (work Cluster in next sc, ch 1, sc in next Cluster, ch 1) twice, sc in last dc: 108 sts and 79 sps.

Row 9: Ch 4, turn; work Cluster in next sc, ch 1, sc in next Cluster, ch 1, work Cluster in next sc, ch 1, sc in next Cluster, ★ † ch 5, skip next ch-1 sp, sc in next ch-5 sp, work FPtr around each of next 2 BPtr, ch 3, sc in next ch-1 sp, ch 3, work FPtr around each of next 2 BPtr, sc in next ch-5 sp, ch 5, skip next sc †, sc in next Cluster, (ch 1, work Cluster in next sc, ch 1, sc in next Cluster) 3 times; repeat from ★ 5 times **more**, then repeat from † to † once, (sc in next Cluster, ch 1, work Cluster in next sc, ch 1) twice, dc in last sc: 101 sts and 72 sps.

Row 10: Ch 1, turn; sc in first dc, ch 1, skip next Cluster, work Cluster in next sc, ch 1, sc in next Cluster, ★ † ch 5, skip next ch-1 sp, sc in next ch-5 sp, skip next sc, work BPtr around each of next 2 FPtr, ch 3, sc in next ch-3 sp, ch 5, sc in next ch-3 sp, ch 3, work BPtr around each of next 2 FPtr, sc in next ch-5 sp, ch 5, skip next sc, sc in next Cluster †, (ch 1, work Cluster in next sc, ch 1, sc in next Cluster) twice; repeat from ★ 5 times **more**, then repeat from † to † once, ch 1, work Cluster in next sc, ch 1, skip next Cluster, sc in last dc: 92 sts and 63 sps.

Row 11: Ch 6, turn; ★ † sc in next Cluster, ch 5, skip next ch-1 sp, sc in next ch-5 sp, skip next sc, work FPtr around each of next 2 BPtr, ch 3, sc in next ch-3 sp, (ch 5, sc in next sp) twice, ch 3, work FPtr around each of next 2 BPtr, sc in next ch-5 sp, ch 5, skip next sc, sc in next Cluster, ch 2, tr in next sc †, ch 2; repeat from ★ 5 times **more**, then repeat from † to † once: 85 sts and 56 sps.

Row 12: Ch 1, turn; sc in first tr, ★ ch 5, skip next ch-2 sp, sc in next ch-5 sp, skip next sc, work BPtr around each of next 2 FPtr, ch 3, sc in next ch-3 sp, ch 5, sc in next ch-5 sp, ch 1, work Cluster in next sc, ch 1, sc in next ch-5 sp, ch 5, sc in next ch-3 sp, ch 3, work BPtr around each of next 2 FPtr, sc in next ch-5 sp, ch 5, skip next sc, sc in next tr; repeat from ★ across.

Row 13: Ch 6, turn; ★ † sc in next ch-5 sp, skip next sc, work FPtr around each of next 2 BPtr, ch 3, sc in next ch-3 sp, ch 5, sc in next ch-5 sp, ch 1, work Cluster in next sc, ch 1, sc in next Cluster, ch 1, work Cluster in next sc, ch 1, sc in next ch-5 sp, ch 5, sc in next ch-3 sp, ch 3, work FPtr around each of next 2 BPtr, sc in next ch-5 sp †, ch 5; repeat from ★ 5 times **more**, then repeat from † to † once, ch 2, tr in last sc: 93 sts and 64 sps.

Row 14: Ch 1, turn; sc in first tr, ★ † skip next sc, work BPtr around each of next 2 FPtr, ch 3, sc in next ch-3 sp, ch 5, sc in next ch-5 sp, ch 1, work Cluster in next sc, ch 1, (sc in next Cluster, ch 1, work Cluster in next sc, ch 1) twice, sc in next ch-5 sp, ch 5, sc in next ch-3 sp, ch 3, work BPtr around each of next 2 FPtr †, sc in next ch-5 sp; repeat from ★ 5 times **more**, then repeat from † to † once, skip next sc, sc in last tr: 99 sts and 70 sps.

Row 15: Ch 6, turn; work FPtr around each of next 2 BPtr, ★ † sc in next ch-3 sp, ch 5, sc in next ch-5 sp, ch 1, work Cluster in next sc, ch 1, (sc in next Cluster, ch 1, work Cluster in next sc, ch 1) 3 times, sc in next ch-5 sp, ch 5, sc in next ch-3 sp †, skip next 2 BPtr and next sc, work FPtr around each of next 2 BPtr, ch 1, working in **front** of last 2 FPtr made, work FPtr around first skipped BPtr and around next skipped BPtr; repeat from ★ 5 times **more**, then repeat from † to † once, work FPtr around each of next 2 BPtr, ch 2, tr in last sc: 107 sts and 78 sps.

Row 16: Ch 6, turn; sc in next ch-2 sp, ★ † ch 3, work BPtr around each of next 2 FPtr, sc in next ch-5 sp, ch 5, skip next sc, sc in next Cluster, (ch 1, work Cluster in next sc, ch 1, sc in next Cluster) 3 times, ch 5, skip next ch-1 sp, sc in next ch-5 sp, skip next sc, work BPtr around each of next 2 FPtr, ch 3 †, sc in next ch-1 sp; repeat from ★ 5 times **more**, then repeat from † to † once, sc in next ch-2 sp, ch 2, tr in last tr: 101 sts and 72 sps.

Rows 17-98: Repeat Rows 3-16, 5 times; then repeat Rows 3-14 once **more**.

Row 99: Ch 3 (**counts and first dc, now and throughout**), turn; work FPtr around each of next 2 BPtr, ★ † sc in next ch-3 sp, ch 5, sc in next ch-5 sp, ch 1, work Cluster in next sc, ch 1, (sc in next Cluster, ch 1, work Cluster in next sc, ch 1) 3 times, sc in next ch-5 sp, ch 5, sc in next ch-3 sp †, skip next 2 BPtr and next sc, work FPtr around each of next 2 BPtr, ch 1, working in **front** of last 2 FPtr made, work FPtr around first skipped BPtr and around next skipped BPtr; repeat from ★ 5 times **more**, then repeat from † to † once, work FPtr around each of next 2 BPtr, dc in last sc; do **not** finish off: 107 sts and 76 sps.

TRIM
TOP
FIRST POINT

Row 1: Ch 3, turn; work BPtr around each of next 2 FPtr, sc in next ch-5 sp, ch 5, skip next sc, sc in next Cluster, ★ ch 1, work Cluster in next sc, ch 1, sc in next Cluster; repeat from ★ 2 times **more**, ch 5, skip next ch-1 sp, sc in next ch-5 sp, skip next sc, work BPtr around each of next 2 FPtr, dc in next ch-1 sp, place marker in same ch-1 sp as dc just made for st placement, leave remaining sts unworked: 15 sts and 8 sps.

Row 2: Ch 3, turn; work FPtr around each of next 2 BPtr, sc in next ch-5 sp, ch 5, skip next sc, sc in next Cluster, ★ ch 1, work Cluster in next sc, ch 1, sc in next Cluster; repeat from ★ once **more**, ch 5, skip next ch-1 sp, sc in next ch-5 sp, skip next sc, work FPtr around each of next 2 BPtr, dc in last dc: 13 sts and 6 sps.

Row 3: Ch 3, turn; work BPtr around each of next 2 FPtr, sc in next ch-5 sp, ch 5, skip next sc, sc in next Cluster, ch 2, tr in next sc, ch 2, sc in next Cluster, ch 5, skip next ch-1 sp, sc in next ch-5 sp, skip next sc, work BPtr around each of next 2 FPtr, dc in last dc: 11 sts and 4 sps.

Row 4: Ch 3, turn; work FPtr around each of next 2 BPtr, sc in next ch-5 sp, ch 5, skip next sc, sc in next tr, ch 5, skip next ch-2 sp, sc in next ch-5 sp, skip next sc, work FPtr around each of next 2 BPtr, dc in last dc: 9 sts and 2 ch-5 sps.

Row 5: Ch 3, turn; work BPtr around each of next 2 FPtr, sc in next ch-5 sp, ch 5, sc in next ch-5 sp, skip next sc, work BPtr around each of next 2 FPtr, dc in last dc: 8 sts and one ch-5 sp.

Row 6: Ch 3, turn; work FPtr around each of next 2 BPtr, sc in next ch-5 sp, skip next sc, work FPtr around each of next 2 BPtr, dc in last dc: 7 sts.

Row 7: Ch 3, turn; skip next 2 FPtr and next sc, work BPtr around each of next 2 FPtr, ch 1, working **behind** last 2 BPtr made, work BPtr around first skipped FPtr and around next skipped FPtr, dc in last dc; finish off: 6 sts and one ch-1 sp.

NEXT 5 POINTS

Row 1: With **wrong** side facing, join yarn with slip st in marked ch-1 sp, remove marker; ch 3, work BPtr around each of next 2 FPtr, sc in next ch-5 sp, ch 5, skip next sc, sc in next Cluster, ★ ch 1, work Cluster in next sc, ch 1, sc in next Cluster; repeat from ★ 2 times **more**, ch 5, skip next ch-1 sp, sc in next ch-5 sp, skip next sc, work BPtr around each of next 2 FPtr, dc in next ch-1 sp, place marker in same ch-1 sp as dc just made for st placement, leave remaining sts unworked: 15 sts and 8 sps.

Rows 2-7: Work same as Rows 2-7 of First Point.

LAST POINT

Row 1: With **wrong** side facing, join yarn with slip st in marked ch-1 sp, remove marker; ch 3, work BPtr around each of next 2 FPtr, sc in next ch-5 sp, ch 5, skip next sc, sc in next Cluster, ★ ch 1, work Cluster in next sc, ch 1, sc in next Cluster; repeat from ★ 2 times **more**, ch 5, skip next ch-1 sp, sc in next ch-5 sp, skip next sc, work BPtr around each of next 2 FPtr, dc in last dc: 15 sts and 8 sps.

Rows 2-7: Work same as Rows 2-7 of First Point.

Continued on page 60.

BOTTOM
FIRST POINT

Row 1: With **wrong** side facing, working in free loops of beginning ch *(Fig. 22b, page 142)* and around sts on Row 1, join yarn with slip st in ch at base of first sc; ch 3, work BPtr around each of next 2 dc, sc in next sp, ch 5, skip next 2 chs, sc in ch at base of next Cluster, ★ ch 1, skip next ch, work Cluster in ch at base of next sc, ch 1, skip next ch, sc in ch at base of next Cluster; repeat from ★ 2 times **more**, ch 5, skip next 2 chs, sc in next sp, skip first 2 dc of next 4-dc group, work BPtr around each of next 2 dc, dc in ch at base of 4-dc group, place marker in same ch as dc just made for st placement, leave remaining chs unworked: 15 sts and 8 sps.

Row 2: Ch 3, turn; work FPtr around each of next 2 BPtr, sc in next ch-5 sp, ch 5, skip next sc, sc in next Cluster, ★ ch 1, work Cluster in next sc, ch 1, sc in next Cluster; repeat from ★ once **more**, ch 5, skip next ch-1 sp, sc in next ch-5 sp, skip next sc, work FPtr around each of next 2 BPtr, dc in last dc: 13 sts and 6 sps.

Row 3: Ch 3, turn; work BPtr around each of next 2 FPtr, sc in next ch-5 sp, ch 5, skip next sc, sc in next Cluster, ch 1, work Cluster in next sc, ch 1, sc in next Cluster, ch 5, skip next ch-1 sp, sc in next ch-5 sp, skip next sc, work BPtr around each of next 2 FPtr, dc in last dc: 11 sts and 4 sps.

Row 4: Ch 3, turn; work FPtr around each of next 2 BPtr, sc in next ch-5 sp, ch 5, skip next sc, sc in next Cluster, ch 5, skip next ch-1 sp, sc in next ch-5 sp, skip next sc, work FPtr around each of next 2 BPtr, dc in last dc: 9 sts and 2 ch-5 sps.

Row 5: Ch 3, turn; work BPtr around each of next 2 FPtr, sc in next ch-5 sp, ch 5, sc in next ch-5 sp, skip next sc, work BPtr around each of next 2 FPtr, dc in last dc: 8 sts and one ch-5 sp.

Row 6: Ch 3, turn; work FPtr around each of next 2 BPtr, sc in next ch-5 sp, skip next sc, work FPtr around each of next 2 BPtr, dc in last dc: 7 sts.

Row 7: Ch 3, turn; skip next 2 FPtr and next sc, work BPtr around each of next 2 FPtr, ch 1, working **behind** last 2 BPtr made, work BPtr around first skipped FPtr and around next skipped FPtr, dc in last dc; finish off: 6 sts and one ch-1 sp.

NEXT 5 POINTS

Row 1: With **wrong** side facing, working in free loops of beginning ch and around sts on Row 1, join yarn with slip st in marked ch, remove marker; ch 3, working in **front** of last 2 BPtr on previous Point, work BPtr around first skipped dc and around next skipped dc, sc in next sp, ch 5, skip next 2 chs, sc in ch at base of next Cluster, ★ ch 1, skip next ch, work Cluster in ch at base of next sc, ch 1, skip next ch, sc in ch at base of next Cluster; repeat from ★ 2 times **more**, ch 5, skip next 2 chs, sc in next sp, skip first 2 dc of next 4-dc group, work BPtr around each of next 2 dc, dc in ch at base of 4-dc group, place marker in same ch as dc just made for st placement, leave remaining chs unworked: 15 sts and 8 sps.

Rows 2-7: Work same as Rows 2-7 of Bottom First Point.

LAST POINT

Row 1: With **wrong** side facing, working in free loops of beginning ch and around sts on Row 1, join yarn with slip st in marked ch, remove marker; ch 3, working in **front** of last 2 BPtr on previous Point, work BPtr around first skipped dc and around next skipped dc, sc in next sp, ch 5, skip next 2 chs, sc in ch at base of next Cluster, ★ ch 1, skip next ch, work Cluster in ch at base of next sc, ch 1, skip next ch, sc in ch at base of next Cluster; repeat from ★ 2 times **more**, ch 5, skip next 2 chs, sc in next sp, skip ch at base of next sc, work BPtr around each of next 2 dc, skip next ch, dc in last ch: 15 sts and 8 sps.

Rows 2-7: Work same as Rows 2-7 of Bottom First Point.

EDGING

With **right** side facing, working across Points and in end of rows, join yarn with sc in any st *(see Joining With Sc, page 142)*; sc evenly around entire Afghan increasing or decreasing as necessary to keep piece lying flat; join with slip st to first sc, finish off.

EDGING

Rnd 1: Ch 1, turn; sc in first dc, ch 5, skip next 2 dc, (sc in next tr, ch 5, skip next 2 sts) 3 times, ★ sc in next ch-2 sp, ch 5, skip next 2 dc, (sc in next tr, ch 5, skip next 2 sts) 3 times; repeat from ★ across to last ch-2 sp, skip last ch-2 sp, sc in last dc, ch 5; working in end of rows, skip first row, (sc in next row, ch 5) across; working in free loops of beginning ch *(Fig. 22b, page 142)*, sc in first ch, ch 5, (skip next 2 chs, sc in next ch, ch 5) 48 times; working in end of rows, sc in first row, ch 5, (sc in next row, ch 5) across to last row, skip last row; join with slip st to first sc: 264 ch-5 sps.

Rnd 2: Slip st in next 2 chs, ch 1, sc in same ch-5 sp, (ch 5, sc in next ch-5 sp) around, ch 2, dc in first sc to form last ch-5 sp.

Rnd 3: Work (Beginning Puff St, ch 2, Puff St) in same sp, ch 2, (dc, ch 1) twice in next 2 ch-5 sps, (dc, ch 1, dc) in next ch-5 sp, ch 2, ★ (work Puff St, ch 2) twice in next ch-5 sp, (dc, ch 1) twice in next 2 ch-5 sps, (dc, ch 1, dc) in next ch-5 sp, ch 2; repeat from ★ around; join with slip st to top of Beginning Puff St: 132 Puff Sts and 396 dc.

Rnd 4: Slip st in first ch-2 sp, work (Beginning Puff St, ch 2, Puff St) in same sp, ch 2, skip next ch-2 sp, dc in next ch-1 sp, (ch 1, dc in next ch-1 sp) twice, (ch 1, dc in same sp) 3 times, (ch 1, dc in next ch-1 sp) twice, ch 2, skip next ch-2 sp, ★ (work Puff St, ch 2) twice in next ch-2 sp, skip next ch-2 sp, dc in next ch-1 sp, (ch 1, dc in next ch-1 sp) twice, (ch 1, dc in same sp) 3 times, (ch 1, dc in next ch-1 sp) twice, ch 2, skip next ch-2 sp; repeat from ★ around; join with slip st to top of Beginning Puff St.

Rnd 5: Slip st in first ch-2 sp, work Beginning Puff St in same sp, ch 2, (work Puff St in same sp, ch 2) twice, ★ † skip next dc, (dc in next dc, ch 1) twice, dc in next ch-1 sp, ch 1, (dc, ch 1) 4 times in next ch-1 sp, dc in next ch-1 sp, (ch 1, dc in next dc) twice, ch 2, skip next ch-1 sp and next ch-2 sp, [(work Puff St, ch 2) twice in next ch-2 sp, skip next dc, (dc in next dc, ch 1) twice, dc in next ch-1 sp, ch 1, (dc, ch 1) 4 times in next ch-1 sp, dc in next ch-1 sp, (ch 1, dc in next dc) twice, ch 2, skip next ch-1 sp and next ch-2 sp] across to next corner ch-2 sp †, (work Puff St, ch 2) 3 times in corner ch-2 sp; repeat from ★ 2 times **more**, then repeat from † to † once; join with slip st to top of Beginning Puff St.

Rnd 6: Slip st in first ch-2 sp, work (Beginning Puff St, ch 2, Puff St) in same sp, ch 2, (work Puff St, ch 2) twice in next ch-2 sp, ★ † skip next dc, (dc in next dc, ch 1) 3 times, skip next ch-1 sp, (dc, ch 1) 4 times in next ch-1 sp, skip next dc, dc in next dc, (ch 1, dc in next dc) twice, ch 2, skip next ch-1 sp and next ch-2 sp, [(work Puff St, ch 2) twice in next ch-2 sp, skip next dc, (dc in next dc, ch 1) 3 times, skip next ch-1 sp, (dc, ch 1) 4 times in next ch-1 sp, skip next dc, dc in next dc, (ch 1, dc in next dc) twice, ch 2, skip next ch-1 sp and next ch-2 sp] across to next corner 3-Puff St group †, (work Puff St, ch 2) twice in next 2 ch-2 sps; repeat from ★ 2 times **more**, then repeat from † to † once; join with slip st to top of Beginning Puff St.

Rnd 7: Slip st in first ch-2 sp, work (Beginning Puff St, ch 2, Puff St) in same sp, ch 2, (work Puff St, ch 2) twice in next 2 ch-2 sps, ★ † skip next dc, (dc in next dc, ch 1) 3 times, skip next ch-1 sp, (dc, ch 1) 4 times in next ch-1 sp, skip next dc, dc in next dc, (ch 1, dc in next dc) twice, ch 2, skip next ch-1 sp and next ch-2 sp, [(work Puff St, ch 2) twice in next ch-2 sp, skip next dc, (dc in next dc, ch 1) 3 times, skip next ch-1 sp, (dc, ch 1) 4 times in next ch-1 sp, skip next dc, dc in next dc, (ch 1, dc in next dc) twice, ch 2, skip next ch-1 sp and next ch-2 sp] across to next corner 4-Puff St group †, (work Puff St, ch 2) twice in next 3 ch-2 sps; repeat from ★ 2 times **more**, then repeat from † to † once; join with slip st to top of Beginning Puff St.

Rnd 8: Slip st in first ch-2 sp, work Beginning Puff St in same sp, (ch 2, work Puff St in next ch-2 sp) twice, work Picot, ch 2, (work Puff St in next ch-2 sp, ch 2) twice, ★ † skip next dc, (dc in next dc, work Picot, ch 1) 3 times, skip next ch-1 sp, dc in next ch-1 sp, work Picot, ch 1, skip next dc, dc in next dc, work Picot, (ch 1, dc in next dc, work Picot) twice, ch 2, skip next ch-1 sp and next ch-2 sp, [(work Puff St, ch 2) twice in next ch-2 sp, skip next dc, (dc in next dc, work Picot, ch 1) 3 times, skip next ch-1 sp, dc in next ch-1 sp, work Picot, ch 1, skip next dc, dc in next dc, work Picot, (ch 1, dc in next dc, work Picot) twice, ch 2, skip next ch-1 sp and next ch-2 sp] across to next corner 6-Puff St group †, work Puff St in next ch-2 sp, (ch 2, work Puff St in next ch-2 sp) twice, work Picot, ch 2, (work Puff St in next ch-2 sp, ch 2) twice; repeat from ★ 2 times **more**, then repeat from † to † once; join with slip st to top of Beginning Puff St, finish off.

LADYLIKE CHARM

Soft and ladylike, this romantic throw will be a summertime favorite with its light, lacy look. The latticed openwork is formed with simple chain and shell stitches.

STITCH GUIDE

SHELL
Dc in st indicated, (ch 1, dc in same st) twice.

AFGHAN BODY

Ch 150 **loosely**.

Row 1 (Right side)**:** Sc in second ch from hook, skip next ch, work Shell in next ch, skip next ch, sc in next ch, ★ (ch 5, skip next 3 chs, sc in next ch) twice, skip next ch, work Shell in next ch, skip next ch, sc in next ch; repeat from ★ across: 13 Shells and 24 ch-5 sps.

Row 2: Ch 4 **(counts as first dc plus ch 1, now and throughout)**, turn; dc in same st, sc in center dc of next Shell, ★ work Shell in next sc, sc in next ch-5 sp, ch 5, sc in next ch-5 sp, work Shell in next sc, sc in center dc of next Shell; repeat from ★ across to last sc, (dc, ch 1, dc) in last sc: 24 Shells and 12 ch-5 sps.

Row 3: Ch 1, turn; sc in first dc, ch 5, ★ sc in center dc of next Shell, work Shell in next sc, sc in next ch-5 sp, work Shell in next sc, sc in center dc of next Shell, ch 5; repeat from ★ across to last sc, skip next sc and next dc, sc in last dc: 24 Shells and 13 ch-5 sps.

Row 4: Ch 5 **(counts as first dc plus ch 2, now and throughout)**, turn; sc in first ch-5 sp, ★ ch 5, sc in center dc of next Shell, work Shell in next sc, sc in center dc of next Shell, ch 5, sc in next ch-5 sp; repeat from ★ across to last sc, ch 2, dc in last sc: 12 Shells and 24 ch-5 sps.

Row 5: Ch 1, turn; sc in first dc, ch 5, ★ sc in next ch-5 sp, work Shell in next sc, sc in center dc of next Shell, work Shell in next sc, sc in next ch-5 sp, ch 5; repeat from ★ across to last sc, skip last sc, sc in last dc: 24 Shells and 13 ch-5 sps.

Row 6: Ch 4, turn; dc in same st, sc in next ch-5 sp, ★ work Shell in next sc, sc in center dc of next Shell, ch 5, sc in center dc of next Shell, work Shell in next sc, sc in next ch-5 sp; repeat from ★ across to last sc, (dc, ch 1, dc) in last sc: 24 Shells and 12 ch-5 sps.

Row 7: Ch 1, turn; sc in first dc, work Shell in next sc, ★ sc in center dc of next Shell, ch 5, sc in next ch-5 sp, ch 5, sc in center dc of next Shell, work Shell in next sc; repeat from ★ across to last 2 dc, skip next dc, sc in last dc: 13 Shells and 24 ch-5 sps.

Rows 8-127: Repeat Rows 2-7, 20 times; do **not** finish off.

Finished Size: 47¹⁄₂" x 64¹⁄₂"

MATERIALS

Worsted Weight Yarn:
  34 ounces, (970 grams, 2,330 yards)
Crochet hook, size H (5.00 mm) **or** size
  needed for gauge

GAUGE: In pattern, one repeat = 3³⁄₄";
      8 rows = 4"

Gauge Swatch: 9"w x 4"h
Ch 30 **loosely**.
Work same as Afghan for 8 rows.
Finish off.

EDGING

Rnd 1: Ch 1, do **not** turn; working in end of rows, skip first row, (2 sc in next row, sc in next row) across; working in free loops of beginning ch *(Fig. 22b, page 142)*, 3 sc in first ch, sc in next 147 chs, 3 sc in next ch; working in end of rows, skip first row, (2 sc in next row, sc in next row) across; working in sts and in ch-5 sps across Row 127, 3 sc in first sc, sc in next 3 dc, ★ sc in next sc, (3 sc in next ch-5 sp, sc in next sc) twice, sc in next 3 dc; repeat from ★ across to last sc, 3 sc in last sc; join with slip st to first sc: 684 sc.

Rnd 2: Ch 1, (sc, ch 1, dc, ch 1, sc) in same st, skip next sc, ★ (sc, ch 1, dc, ch 1, sc) in next sc, skip next sc; repeat from ★ around; join with slip st to first sc, finish off.

CAREFREE PLEASURES

*Subtle rose and spruce colors give a carefree, tranquil air
to this garden-inspired wrap. Front post treble crochets
add interest to the mile-a-minute panels.*

Finished Size: 52" x 66"

MATERIALS

Worsted Weight Yarn:
- Spruce - 28¹/₂ ounces, (810 grams, 1,610 yards)
- Rose - 22 ounces, (620 grams, 1,245 yards)
- Crochet hook, size I (5.50 mm) **or** size needed for gauge

GAUGE: Each Strip = 4" wide

Gauge Swatch: 4"w x 7¹/₂"h
Work same as Center for 7 rows.
Finish off.
Work Border.

STITCH GUIDE

> **FRONT POST TREBLE CROCHET** *(abbreviated FPtr)*
> YO twice, insert hook from **front** to **back** around post of st indicated, YO and pull up a loop *(Fig. 12, page 141)*, (YO and draw through 2 loops on hook) 3 times.

STRIP A
CENTER

With Spruce, ch 7 **loosely**.

Row 1 (Right side): Dc in fourth ch from hook **(3 skipped chs count as first dc)** and in each ch across: 5 dc.

Note: Loop a short piece of yarn around any stitch to mark Row 1 as **right** side and bottom edge.

Row 2: Ch 3 **(counts as first dc, now and throughout)**, turn; dc in next dc, ch 1, skip next dc, dc in last 2 dc: 4 dc.

Row 3: Ch 3, turn; dc in next dc and in next ch, dc in last 2 dc: 5 dc.

Rows 4-99: Repeat Rows 2 and 3, 48 times.
Finish off.

BORDER

Rnd 1: With **right** side facing and working in end of rows, join Rose with slip st in last row; ch 3, † (2 dc, ch 1, 2 dc) in next row, dc in next row †, repeat from † to † across; working in free loops of beginning ch *(Fig. 22b, page 142)*, skip first 2 chs, (4 dc, ch 2, 4 dc) in next ch; working in end of rows, dc in first row, repeat from † to † across; working in sts on last row of Center, skip first 2 dc, (4 dc, ch 2, 4 dc) in next dc; join with slip st to first dc, finish off: 508 dc and 100 sps.

Rnd 2: With **right** side facing, join Spruce with slip st in first ch-1 sp to **left** of joining; ch 3, 4 dc in same sp, skip next 2 dc, work FPtr around next dc, ★ (5 dc in next ch-1 sp, skip next 2 dc, work FPtr around next dc) across to next 4-dc group, skip next 2 dc, 5 dc in sp **before** next dc and in next ch-2 sp *(Fig. 25, page 143)*, skip next 2 dc, 5 dc in sp **before** next dc, skip next 2 dc, work FPtr around next dc; repeat from ★ once **more**; join with slip st to first dc, finish off.

STRIP B
CENTER

With Rose, ch 7 **loosely**.

Row 1 (Right side): Dc in fourth ch from hook **(3 skipped chs count as first dc)** and in each ch across: 5 dc.

Note: Mark Row 1 as **right** side and bottom edge.

Row 2: Ch 3, turn; dc in next dc, ch 1, skip next dc, dc in last 2 dc: 4 dc.

Row 3: Ch 3, turn; dc in next dc and in next ch, dc in last 2 dc: 5 dc.

Rows 4-99: Repeat Rows 2 and 3, 48 times; do **not** finish off.

Continued on page 73.

PEACEFUL GARDEN

Beautifully textured rosettes bloom on this airy throw.
Front post clusters give texture to the peaceful squares, and
a gently scalloped border makes a feminine finish.

Finished Size: 51" x 68"

MATERIALS
  Worsted Weight Yarn:
    43 ounces, (1,220 grams, 2,950 yards)
  Crochet hook, size H (5.00 mm) **or** size needed
    for gauge
  Yarn needle

GAUGE: Each Square = 5³/4"

Gauge Swatch: 2¹/2" diameter
Work same as Square through Rnd 2.

STITCH GUIDE

FRONT POST CLUSTER
  (abbreviated FP Cluster)
★ YO twice, insert hook from **front** to **back** around post of
dc indicated *(Fig. 9, page 140)*, YO and pull up a loop, (YO
and draw through 2 loops on hook) twice; repeat from ★
once **more**, YO and draw through all 3 loops on hook
(Figs. 16a & b, page 141).

SQUARE (Make 88)

Rnd 1 (Right side)**:** Ch 5, dc in fifth ch from hook **(4 skipped**
chs count as first dc plus ch 1), ch 1, (dc in same ch,
ch 1) 6 times; join with slip st to first dc: 8 dc and 8 ch-1 sps.
Note: Loop a short piece of yarn around any stitch to mark
Rnd 1 as **right** side.
Rnd 2: Slip st in first ch-1 sp, ch 3 **(counts as first dc, now**
and throughout), dc in same sp, work FP Cluster around next
dc, (2 dc in next ch-1 sp, work FP Cluster around next dc)
around; join with slip st to first dc: 8 FP Clusters and 16 dc.
Rnd 3: Ch 4 **(counts as first dc plus ch 1, now and**
throughout), skip next dc, dc in next FP Cluster, ch 1, skip next
dc, (tr, ch 5, tr) in next dc, ch 1, skip next FP Cluster, ★ (dc in
next st, ch 1, skip next dc) twice, (tr, ch 5, tr) in next dc, ch 1,
skip next FP Cluster; repeat from ★ 2 times **more**; join with
slip st to first dc: 16 sts and 16 sps.

Rnd 4: Ch 3, (dc in next ch-1 sp and in next st) twice, (3 dc,
ch 3, 3 dc) in next ch-5 sp, dc in next tr, ★ (dc in next ch-1 sp
and in next st) 3 times, (3 dc, ch 3, 3 dc) in next ch-5 sp, dc in
next tr; repeat from ★ 2 times **more**, dc in last ch-1 sp; join
with slip st to first dc: 52 dc and 4 ch-3 sps.
Rnd 5: Slip st in next dc, ch 4, skip next dc, dc in next dc, ch 1,
skip next dc, dc in next 3 dc, ch 1, (dc, ch 3, dc) in next
ch-3 sp, ch 1, dc in next 3 dc, ch 1, skip next dc, ★ (dc in next
dc, ch 1, skip next dc) 3 times, dc in next 3 dc, ch 1, (dc, ch 3,
dc) in next ch-3 sp, ch 1, dc in next 3 dc, ch 1, skip next dc;
repeat from ★ 2 times **more**, dc in next dc, ch 1, skip last st;
join with slip st to first dc, finish off: 44 dc and 28 sps.

ASSEMBLY
Working through both loops, whipstitch Squares together
(Fig. 27b, page 143), forming 8 vertical strips of 11 Squares
each, beginning in center ch of first corner ch-3 and ending in
center ch of next corner ch-3; whipstitch strips together in same
manner.

EDGING
Rnd 1: With **right** side facing, join yarn with slip st in any
corner ch-3 sp; ch 6 **(counts as first dc plus ch 3)**, dc in
same sp, ★ † ch 1, dc in next dc, ch 1, dc in next 3 dc, ch 1,
(dc in next dc, ch 1) 3 times, dc in next 3 dc, ch 1, dc in next
dc, [ch 2, dc in next joining, ch 2, dc in next dc, ch 1, dc in next
3 dc, ch 1, (dc in next dc, ch 1) 3 times, dc in next 3 dc, ch 1,
dc in next dc] across to next corner ch-3 sp, ch 1 †, (dc, ch 3,
dc) in corner ch-3 sp; repeat from ★ 2 times **more**, then
repeat from † to † once; join with slip st to first dc, do **not**
finish off: 460 dc and 308 sps.

Continued on page 74.

SWEET DREAMS

This heirloom baby blanket is a beautiful blend of stitchery. Sweet shells in the center panel are surrounded by appealing openwork that's edged with a fancy trim of clusters and picots.

Finished Size: 32" x 40"

MATERIALS
  Sport Weight Yarn:
    14 ounces, (400 grams, 1,400 yards)
  Crochet hook, size H (5.00 mm) **or** size needed
    for gauge

GAUGE: 11 dc = 3"; 7 rows = 4"

Gauge Swatch: 7¼"w x 4"h
Ch 30 **loosely**.
Work same as Afghan Body for 7 rows.
Finish off.

STITCH GUIDE

CLUSTER (uses one st or sp)
★ YO, insert hook in st or sp indicated, YO and pull up a loop, YO and draw through 2 loops on hook; repeat from ★ 2 times **more**, YO and draw through all 4 loops on hook *(Figs. 16a & b, page 141)*.
PICOT
Ch 5, sc in fifth ch from hook.

AFGHAN BODY
Ch 90 **loosely**, place marker in fourth ch from hook for st placement.
Row 1: Dc in sixth ch from hook, ★ ch 1, skip next ch, dc in next ch; repeat from ★ across: 43 dc and 43 sps.
Row 2 (Right side)**:** Ch 4 (**counts as first dc plus ch 1, now and throughout**), turn; ★ dc in next dc, (dc in next ch-1 sp and in next dc) 5 times, ch 1; repeat from ★ across to last sp, skip next ch, dc in next ch: 79 dc and 8 ch-1 sps.
Row 3: Ch 4, turn; ★ dc in next 3 dc, ch 2, skip next 2 dc, (sc, ch 3, sc) in next dc, ch 2, skip next 2 dc, dc in next 3 dc, ch 1; repeat from ★ across to last dc, dc in last dc: 44 dc and 29 sps.

Row 4: Ch 4, turn; dc in next 3 dc, ch 1, skip next ch-2 sp, work (Cluster, ch 3, Cluster) in next ch-3 sp, ch 1, ★ (dc in next 3 dc, ch 1) twice, skip next ch-2 sp, work (Cluster, ch 3, Cluster) in next ch-3 sp, ch 1; repeat from ★ across to last 4 dc, dc in next 3 dc, ch 1, dc in last dc.
Row 5: Ch 4, turn; ★ dc in next 3 dc, ch 3, skip next ch-1 sp, sc in next ch-3 sp, ch 3, skip next Cluster, dc in next 3 dc, ch 1; repeat from ★ across to last dc, dc in last dc: 51 sts and 22 sps.
Row 6: Ch 4, turn; ★ dc in next 3 dc, 2 dc in next ch-3 sp, dc in next sc, 2 dc in next ch-3 sp, dc in next 3 dc, ch 1; repeat from ★ across to last dc, dc in last dc: 79 dc and 8 ch-1 sps.
Row 7: Ch 4, turn; dc in next dc, ★ ch 1, (skip next dc, dc in next dc, ch 1) 5 times, dc in next dc; repeat from ★ across: 44 dc and 43 ch-1 sps.
Row 8: Ch 4, turn; dc in next dc, (dc in next ch-1 sp and in next dc) 5 times, ch 1, dc in next dc, ★ skip next dc, 5 dc in next dc, skip next dc, (dc, ch 2, dc) in next dc; repeat from ★ 6 times **more**, dc in next dc, ch 1, dc in next dc, (dc in next ch-1 sp and in next dc) 5 times, ch 1, dc in last dc: 75 dc and 11 sps.
Row 9: Ch 4, turn; dc in next 3 dc, ch 2, skip next 2 dc, (sc, ch 3, sc) in next dc, ch 2, skip next 2 dc, dc in next 3 dc, ch 1, dc in next dc, ★ 5 dc in next ch-2 sp, skip next 3 dc, (dc, ch 2, dc) in next dc; repeat from ★ 6 times **more**, skip next 2 dc, dc in next dc, ch 1, dc in next 3 dc, ch 2, skip next 2 dc, (sc, ch 3, sc) in next dc, ch 2, skip next 2 dc, dc in next 3 dc, ch 1, dc in last dc: 65 dc and 17 sps.
Row 10: Ch 4, turn; dc in next 3 dc, ch 1, skip next ch-2 sp, work (Cluster, ch 3, Cluster) in next ch-3 sp, ch 1, dc in next 3 dc, ch 1, dc in next dc, ★ 5 dc in next ch-2 sp, skip next 3 dc, (dc, ch 2, dc) in next dc; repeat from ★ 6 times **more**, skip next 2 dc, dc in next dc, ch 1, dc in next 3 dc, ch 1, skip next ch-2 sp, work (Cluster, ch 3, Cluster) in next ch-3 sp, ch 1, dc in next 3 dc, ch 1, dc in last dc.
Row 11: Ch 4, turn; dc in next 3 dc, ch 3, skip next ch-1 sp, sc in next ch-3 sp, ch 3, skip next Cluster, dc in next 3 dc, ch 1, dc in next dc, ★ 5 dc in next ch-2 sp, skip next 3 dc, (dc, ch 2, dc) in next dc; repeat from ★ 6 times **more**, skip next 2 dc, dc in next dc, ch 1, dc in next 3 dc, ch 3, skip next ch-1 sp, sc in next ch-3 sp, ch 3, skip next Cluster, dc in next 3 dc, ch 1, dc in last dc; do **not** finish off: 67 sts and 15 sps.

68

Continued on page 75.

DAISY DELIGHT

With all the charm of wildflower meadows in June, our daisy-dotted afghan captures the breezy look of blue skies and summer sunshine. Bright-eyed daisies alternate with soft two-tone squares on this warm-weather rendition of granny's favorite throw.

Finished Size: 46" x 64"

MATERIALS

Worsted Weight Yarn:

Blue - 30 ounces, (850 grams, 1,955 yards)

White - 10¹/₂ ounces, (300 grams, 685 yards)

Yellow - 8¹/₂ ounces, (240 grams, 555 yards)

Crochet hook, size H (5.00 mm) **or** size needed for gauge

Yarn needle

GAUGE SWATCH: 4¹/₂"

Work same as Square A or B.

SQUARE A (Make 59)

Rnd 1 (Right side): With Yellow, ch 4, 11 dc in fourth ch from hook **(3 skipped chs count as first dc)**; join with slip st to first dc, finish off: 12 dc.

Note: Loop a short piece of yarn around any stitch to mark Rnd 1 as **right** side.

Rnd 2: With **right** side facing, join White with slip st in Front Loop Only of same st as joining *(Fig. 21, page 142)*; ch 5 **loosely,** sc in second ch from hook, dc in next 2 chs, sc in last ch **(Petal made),** ★ slip st in Front Loop Only of next dc, ch 5 **loosely,** sc in second ch from hook, dc in next 2 chs, sc in last ch; repeat from ★ around; join with slip st to first slip st, finish off: 12 Petals.

Rnd 3: With **right** side facing, working **behind** Petals in free loops of dc on Rnd 1 *(Fig. 22a, page 142)*, join Blue with sc in any dc *(see Joining With Sc, page 142)*; sc in same st, 2 sc in each dc around; join with slip st to **both** loops of first sc: 24 sc.

Rnd 4: Ch 1, working in both loops, sc in same st, ch 1, skip next sc, hdc in next sc, (dc, ch 3, dc) in next sc, hdc in next sc, ch 1, skip next sc, ★ sc in next sc, ch 1, skip next sc, hdc in next sc, (dc, ch 3, dc) in next sc, hdc in next sc, ch 1, skip next sc; repeat from ★ 2 times **more;** join with slip st to first sc: 12 sps.

Rnd 5: Ch 3 **(counts as first dc, now and throughout),** sc in tip of First Petal (in unworked ch), dc in same st on Rnd 4, ch 1, in next ch-3 sp work (dc, sc in tip of next Petal, dc, ch 3, dc, sc in tip of next Petal, dc), ch 1, ★ skip next ch-1 sp, (dc, sc in tip of next Petal, dc) in next sc, ch 1, in next ch-3 sp work (dc, sc in tip of next Petal, dc, ch 3, dc, sc in tip of next Petal, dc), ch 1; repeat from ★ 2 times **more;** join with slip st to first dc.

Rnd 6: Slip st in next 2 sts and in next ch-1 sp, ch 3, 2 dc in same sp, ch 1, (3 dc, ch 3, 3 dc) in next ch-3 sp, ch 1, ★ (3 dc in next ch-1 sp, ch 1) twice, (3 dc, ch 3, 3 dc) in next ch-3 sp, ch 1; repeat from ★ 2 times **more,** 3 dc in last ch-1 sp, ch 1; join with slip st to first dc, finish off: 48 dc and 16 sps.

SQUARE B (Make 58)

Rnd 1 (Right side): With Yellow, ch 4, 2 dc in fourth ch from hook **(3 skipped chs count as first dc),** ch 3, (3 dc in same ch, ch 3) 3 times; join with slip st to first dc, finish off: 12 dc.

Note: Mark Rnd 1 as **right** side.

Rnd 2: With **right** side facing, join Blue with slip st in any ch-3 sp; ch 3, (2 dc, ch 3, 3 dc) in same sp, ch 1, ★ (3 dc, ch 3, 3 dc) in next ch-3 sp, ch 1; repeat from ★ 2 times **more;** join with slip st to first dc, finish off: 8 sps.

Rnd 3: With **right** side facing, join Yellow with slip st in any corner ch-3 sp; ch 3, (2 dc, ch 3, 3 dc) in same sp, ch 1, 3 dc in next ch-1 sp, ch 1, ★ (3 dc, ch 3, 3 dc) in next corner ch-3 sp, ch 1, 3 dc in next ch-1 sp, ch 1; repeat from ★ 2 times **more;** join with slip st to first dc, finish off: 12 sps.

Rnd 4: With **right** side facing, join Blue with slip st in any corner ch-3 sp; ch 3, (2 dc, ch 3, 3 dc) in same sp, ch 1, (3 dc in next ch-1 sp, ch 1) twice, ★ (3 dc, ch 3, 3 dc) in next corner ch-3 sp, ch 1, (3 dc in next ch-1 sp, ch 1) twice; repeat from ★ 2 times **more;** join with slip st to first dc, finish off: 48 dc and 16 sps.

Continued on page 72.

ASSEMBLY

With Blue, using Placement Diagram as a guide, and working through both loops, whipstitch Squares together *(Fig. 27b, page 143)*, forming 9 vertical strips of 13 Squares each, beginning in center ch of first corner ch-3 and ending in center ch of next corner ch-3; whipstitch strips together in same manner.

PLACEMENT DIAGRAM

A	B	A	B	A	B	A	B	A
B	A	B	A	B	A	B	A	B
A	B	A	B	A	B	A	B	A
B	A	B	A	B	A	B	A	B
A	B	A	B	A	B	A	B	A
B	A	B	A	B	A	B	A	B
A	B	A	B	A	B	A	B	A
B	A	B	A	B	A	B	A	B
A	B	A	B	A	B	A	B	A
B	A	B	A	B	A	B	A	B
A	B	A	B	A	B	A	B	A
B	A	B	A	B	A	B	A	B
A	B	A	B	A	B	A	B	A

EDGING

Rnd 1: With **right** side facing, join Blue with sc in any corner ch-3 sp; ch 2, sc in same sp, ★ † ch 1, skip next dc, sc in next dc, ch 1, (sc in next ch-1 sp, ch 1, skip next dc, sc in next dc, ch 1) 3 times, [(sc in next sp, ch 1) twice, skip next dc, sc in next dc, ch 1, (sc in next ch-1 sp, ch 1, skip next dc, sc in next dc, ch 1) 3 times] across to next corner ch-3 sp †, (sc, ch 2, sc) in corner ch-3 sp; repeat from ★ 2 times **more**, then repeat from † to † once; join with slip st to first sc: 396 sps.

Rnd 2: Slip st in first ch-2 sp, ch 1, (sc, ch 2, sc) in same sp, ch 1, (sc in next ch-1 sp, ch 1) across to next corner ch-2 sp, ★ (sc, ch 2, sc) in corner ch-2 sp, ch 1, (sc in next ch-1 sp, ch 1) across to next corner ch-2 sp; repeat from ★ 2 times **more**; join with slip st to first sc: 400 sps.

Rnd 3: Slip st in first ch-2 sp, ch 3, (2 dc, ch 3, 3 dc) in same sp, ch 1, skip next ch-1 sp, (3 dc in next ch-1 sp, ch 1, skip next ch-1 sp) across to next corner ch-2 sp, ★ (3 dc, ch 3, 3 dc) in corner ch-2 sp, ch 1, skip next ch-1 sp, (3 dc in next ch-1 sp, ch 1, skip next ch-1 sp) across to next corner ch-2 sp; repeat from ★ 2 times **more**; join with slip st to first dc, finish off.

Rnd 4: With **right** side facing, join White with slip st in any corner ch-3 sp; ch 3, (2 dc, ch 3, 3 dc) in same sp, ch 1, (3 dc in next ch-1 sp, ch 1) across to next corner ch-3 sp, ★ (3 dc, ch 3, 3 dc) in corner ch-3 sp, ch 1, (3 dc in next ch-1 sp, ch 1) across to next corner ch-3 sp; repeat from ★ 2 times **more**; join with slip st to first dc.

Rnd 5: Slip st in next 2 dc and in next ch-3 sp, ch 3, (2 dc, ch 3, 3 dc) in same sp, ch 1, (3 dc in next ch-1 sp, ch 1) across to next corner ch-3 sp, ★ (3 dc, ch 3, 3 dc) in corner ch-3 sp, ch 1, (3 dc in next ch-1 sp, ch 1) across to next corner ch-3 sp; repeat from ★ 2 times **more**; join with slip st to first dc.

Rnd 6: Slip st in next 2 dc, ★ (slip st, ch 3, dc in third ch from hook, ch 1, slip st) in next corner ch-3 sp, ch 3, dc in third ch from hook, (slip st in next ch-1 sp, ch 3, dc in third ch from hook) across to next corner ch-3 sp; repeat from ★ around; join with slip st to slip st at base of beginning ch-3, finish off.

BORDER

Rnd 1: Do **not** turn; working in end of rows, slip st in first row, ch 3, † (2 dc, ch 1, 2 dc) in next row, dc in next row †, repeat from † to † across; working in free loops of beginning ch, skip first 2 chs, (4 dc, ch 2, 4 dc) in next ch; working in end of rows, dc in first row, repeat from † to † across; working in sts on last row of Center, skip first 2 dc, (4 dc, ch 2, 4 dc) in next dc; join with slip st to first dc, finish off: 508 dc and 100 sps.

Rnd 2 (Joining rnd)**:** With **right** side facing, join Spruce with slip st in first ch-1 sp to **left** of joining; ch 3, 4 dc in same sp, skip next 2 dc, work FPtr around next dc, (5 dc in next ch-1 sp, skip next 2 dc, work FPtr around next dc) across to next 4-dc group; skip next 2 dc, 5 dc in sp **before** next dc and in next ch-2 sp, skip next 2 dc, 5 dc in sp **before** next dc, skip next 2 dc, work FPtr around next dc, ★ 3 dc in next ch-1 sp, holding Strips with **wrong** sides together and bottom edges at same end, slip st in center dc of corresponding 5-dc group on **previous Strip** *(Fig. 26, page 143)*, slip st in top of last dc made *(Fig. 23, page 142)*, 2 dc in same sp on **new Strip**, skip next 2 dc, work FPtr around next dc; repeat from ★ across to next 4-dc group, skip next 2 dc, 5 dc in sp **before** next dc and in next ch-2 sp, skip next 2 dc, 5 dc in sp **before** next dc, skip next 2 dc, work FPtr around next dc; join with slip st to first dc, finish off.

STRIP C

CENTER

With Spruce, ch 7 **loosely**.

Row 1 (Right side)**:** Dc in fourth ch from hook **(3 skipped chs count as first dc)** and in each ch across: 5 dc.
Note: Mark Row 1 as **right** side and bottom edge.

Row 2: Ch 3, turn; dc in next dc, ch 1, skip next dc, dc in last 2 dc: 4 dc.

Row 3: Ch 3, turn; dc in next dc and in next ch, dc in last 2 dc: 5 dc.

Rows 4-99: Repeat Rows 2 and 3, 48 times.
Finish off.

BORDER

Rnd 1: With **right** side facing and working in end of rows, join Rose with slip st in last row; ch 3, † (2 dc, ch 1, 2 dc) in next row, dc in next row †, repeat from † to † across; working in free loops of beginning ch, skip first 2 chs, (4 dc, ch 2, 4 dc) in next ch; working in end of rows, dc in first row, repeat from † to † across; working in sts on last row of Center, skip first 2 dc, (4 dc, ch 2, 4 dc) in next dc; join with slip st to first dc, finish off: 508 dc and 100 sps.

Rnd 2 (Joining rnd)**:** With **right** side facing, join Spruce with slip st in first ch-1 sp to **left** of joining; ch 3, 4 dc in same sp, skip next 2 dc, work FPtr around next dc, (5 dc in next ch-1 sp, skip next 2 dc, work FPtr around next dc) across to next 4-dc group, skip next 2 dc, 5 dc in sp **before** next dc and in next ch-2 sp, skip next 2 dc, 5 dc in sp **before** next dc, skip next 2 dc, work FPtr around next dc, ★ 3 dc in next ch-1 sp, holding Strips with **wrong** sides together and bottom edges at same end, slip st in center dc of corresponding 5-dc group on **previous Strip**, slip st in top of last dc made, 2 dc in same sp on **new Strip**, skip next 2 dc, work FPtr around next dc; repeat from ★ across to next 4-dc group, skip next 2 dc, 5 dc in sp **before** next dc and in next ch-2 sp, skip next 2 dc, 5 dc in sp **before** next dc, skip next 2 dc, work FPtr around next dc; join with slip st to first dc, finish off.

REMAINING 10 STRIPS

Repeat Strip B and Strip C, 5 times.

Rnd 2: Ch 4, (dc, ch 3, dc) in next corner ch-3 sp, ch 1, (dc in next dc, ch 1) twice, dc in next 3 dc and in next ch-1 sp, (dc in next dc and in next ch-1 sp) 3 times, dc in next 3 dc, ch 1, ★ † dc in next dc, (ch 2, dc in next dc) twice, ch 1, dc in next 3 dc and in next ch-1 sp, (dc in next dc and in next ch-1 sp) 3 times, dc in next 3 dc, ch 1 †, repeat from † to † across to within 2 dc of next corner ch-3 sp, (dc in next dc, ch 1) twice, (dc, ch 3, dc) in corner ch-3 sp, ch 1, (dc in next dc, ch 1) twice, dc in next 3 dc and in next ch-1 sp, (dc in next dc and in next ch-1 sp) 3 times, dc in next 3 dc, ch 1; repeat from ★ 2 times **more**, then repeat from † to † across to last dc, dc in last dc, ch 1; join with slip st to first dc: 620 dc and 164 sps.

Rnd 3: Ch 4, dc in next dc, ch 1, (dc, ch 3, dc) in next corner ch-3 sp, ch 1, (dc in next dc, ch 1) 4 times, (skip next dc, dc in next dc, ch 1) 6 times, ★ † dc in next dc, ch 1, (dc in next ch-2 sp, ch 1) twice, (dc in next dc, ch 1) twice, (skip next dc, dc in next dc, ch 1) 6 times †, repeat from † to † across to within 3 dc of next corner ch-3 sp, (dc in next dc, ch 1) 3 times, (dc, ch 3, dc) in corner ch-3 sp, ch 1, (dc in next dc, ch 1) 4 times, (skip next dc, dc in next dc, ch 1) 6 times; repeat from ★ 2 times **more**, then repeat from † to † across to last dc, dc in last dc, ch 1; join with slip st to first dc: 434 dc and 434 sps.

Rnd 4: Ch 1, (sc in next ch-1 sp, ch 1) twice, (sc, ch 3, sc) in next corner ch-3 sp, ch 1, ★ (sc in next ch-1 sp, ch 1) across to next corner ch-3 sp, (sc, ch 3, sc) in corner ch-3 sp, ch 1; repeat from ★ 2 times **more**, (sc in next ch-1 sp, ch 1) across; join with slip st to first sc: 438 sps.

Rnd 5: Slip st in first ch-1 sp, ch 5, dc in same sp, sc in next ch-1 sp, † ch 2, (dc, ch 2) twice in next corner ch-3 sp, sc in next ch-1 sp, [(dc, ch 2, dc) in next ch-1 sp, sc in next ch-1 sp] across to within one ch-1 sp of next corner ch-3 sp, ch 2, skip next ch-1 sp, (dc, ch 2) twice in corner ch-3 sp, sc in next ch-1 sp †, ★ (dc, ch 2, dc) in next ch-1 sp, sc in next ch-1 sp; repeat from ★ across to next corner ch-3 sp, repeat from † to † once, [(dc, ch 2, dc) in next ch-1 sp, sc in next ch-1 sp] across; join with slip st to third ch of beginning ch-5, finish off.

Row 12: Ch 4, turn; dc in next 3 dc, 2 dc in next ch-3 sp, dc in next sc, 2 dc in next ch-3 sp, dc in next 3 dc, ch 1, dc in next dc, ★ 5 dc in next ch-2 sp, skip next 3 dc, (dc, ch 2, dc) in next dc; repeat from ★ 6 times **more**, skip next 2 dc, dc in next dc, ch 1, dc in next 3 dc, 2 dc in next ch-3 sp, dc in next sc, 2 dc in next ch-3 sp, dc in next 3 dc, ch 1, dc in last dc: 75 dc and 11 sps.

Row 13: Ch 4, turn; dc in next dc, ch 1, (skip next dc, dc in next dc, ch 1) 5 times, dc in next dc, ★ 5 dc in next ch-2 sp, skip next 3 dc, (dc, ch 2, dc) in next dc; repeat from ★ 6 times **more**, skip next 2 dc, (dc in next dc, ch 1) twice, (skip next dc, dc in next dc, ch 1) 5 times, dc in last dc: 65 dc and 21 sps.

Row 14: Ch 4, turn; dc in next dc, (dc in next ch-1 sp and in next dc) 5 times, ch 1, dc in next dc, ★ 5 dc in next ch-2 sp, skip next 3 dc, (dc, ch 2, dc) in next dc; repeat from ★ 6 times **more**, skip next 2 dc, dc in next dc, ch 1, dc in next dc, (dc in next ch-1 sp and in next dc) 5 times, ch 1, dc in last dc: 75 dc and 11 sps.

Rows 15-48: Repeat Rows 9-14, 5 times; then repeat Rows 9-12 once **more**.

Row 49: Ch 4, turn; dc in next dc, ch 1, (skip next dc, dc in next dc, ch 1) 5 times, (dc in next dc, ch 1) 3 times, ★ (skip next dc, dc in next dc, ch 1) 3 times, dc in next dc, ch 1; repeat from ★ 6 times **more**, (skip next dc, dc in next dc, ch 1) 5 times, dc in last dc: 44 dc and 43 ch-1 sps.

Row 50: Ch 4, turn; dc in next dc, ★ (dc in next ch-1 sp and in next dc) 5 times, ch 1, dc in next dc; repeat from ★ across: 79 dc and 8 ch-1 sps.

Rows 51-55: Repeat Rows 3-7; do **not** finish off.

EDGING

Rnd 1: Ch 1, turn; sc in first dc, (sc in next ch-1 sp and in next dc) across; 2 sc in end of each row across; working in sps and in free loops of beginning ch *(Fig. 22b, page 142)*, sc in marked ch, remove marker, place marker around sc just made for st placement, (sc in next ch-1 sp and in next ch) across; 2 sc in end of each row across; join with slip st to first sc: 394 sc.

Rnd 2: Ch 3 **(counts as first dc)**, do **not** turn; 2 dc in same st and in next sc, dc in next 83 sc, 2 dc in next sc, 5 dc in next sc, 2 dc in next sc, dc in each sc across to marked sc, 5 dc in marked sc, 2 dc in next sc, dc in next 83 sc, 2 dc in next sc, 5 dc in next sc, 2 dc in next sc, dc in each sc across, 2 dc in same st as first dc; join with slip st to first dc: 416 dc.

Rnd 3: Ch 4, dc in same st, ch 1, ★ skip next dc, (dc in next dc, ch 1, skip next dc) across to center dc of next 5-dc group, (dc, ch 1) 3 times in center dc; repeat from ★ 2 times **more**, skip next dc, (dc in next dc, ch 1, skip next dc) across, dc in same st as first dc, ch 1; join with slip st to first dc: 216 dc.

Rnd 4: Ch 1, sc in same st, ch 3, skip next dc, (work Cluster, ch 3) twice in next dc, skip next dc, ★ sc in next dc, ch 3, skip next dc, (work Cluster, ch 3) twice in next dc, skip next dc; repeat from ★ around; join with slip st to first sc: 162 ch-3 sps.

Rnd 5: Ch 1, sc in same st, (sc, dc) in next ch-3 sp, dc in next Cluster, 5 dc in next ch-3 sp, dc in next Cluster, (dc, sc) in next ch-3 sp, ★ sc in next sc, (sc, dc) in next ch-3 sp, dc in next Cluster, 5 dc in next ch-3 sp, dc in next Cluster, (dc, sc) in next ch-3 sp; repeat from ★ around; join with slip st to first sc: 648 sts.

Rnd 6: Ch 1, (sc, ch 3, sc) in same st, † skip next sc, sc in next dc, (ch 3, skip next dc, sc in next dc) 4 times, [skip next 3 sc, sc in next dc, (ch 3, skip next dc, sc in next dc) 4 times] 11 times, skip next sc, (sc, ch 3, sc) in next sc, skip next sc, sc in next dc, (ch 3, skip next dc, sc in next dc) 4 times, [skip next 3 sc, sc in next dc, (ch 3, skip next dc, sc in next dc) 4 times] 14 times, skip next sc †, (sc, ch 3, sc) in next sc, repeat from † to † once; join with slip st to first sc: 220 ch-3 sps.

Rnd 7: Slip st in first corner ch-3 sp, ch 1, (sc, work 3 Picots, sc in ch at base of third Picot from hook, sc) in same ch-3 sp, ★ † (work Picot, sc in next ch-3 sp) twice, work 3 Picots, sc in ch at base of third Picot from hook, (sc in next ch-3 sp, work Picot, sc in next 2 ch-3 sps, work Picot, sc in next ch-3 sp, work 3 Picots, sc in ch at base of third Picot from hook) across to within 2 ch-3 sps of next corner ch-3 sp, (sc in next ch-3 sp, work Picot) twice †, (sc, work 3 Picots, sc in ch at base of third Picot from hook, sc) in corner ch-3 sp; repeat from ★ 2 times **more**, then repeat from † to † once; join with slip st to first sc, finish off.

PEACEFUL PROMENADE

As cool and refreshing as a picnic in a shaded garden, our summer wrap uses turquoise and variegated yarns to create the look of heather. Luxurious fringe completes this quick-to-make Q-hook afghan, which is crocheted holding two strands of yarn.

Finished Size: 44" x 61"

MATERIALS
Worsted Weight Yarn:
    Turquoise - 36 ounces,
      (1,020 grams, 1,950 yards)
    Variegated - 16³/4 ounces,
      (480 grams, 970 yards)
Crochet hook, size Q (15.00 mm)

Each row is worked across length of Afghan holding two strands of yarn together.

GAUGE: In pattern, 7 sts = 5";
      Rows 1-6 = 5¹/2"

Gauge Swatch: 5"w x 5¹/2"h
Ch 8 **loosely**.
Work same as Afghan for 6 rows.
Finish off.

Holding one strand of Turquoise and one strand of Variegated together, ch 86 **loosely**.

Row 1 (Right side): Working in back ridges of ch *(Fig. 2b, page 139)*, sc in second ch from hook, ★ skip next ch, (dc, sc) in next ch; repeat from ★ across: 85 sts.

Note: Loop a short piece of yarn around any stitch to mark Row 1 as **right** side.

Rows 2-6: Ch 1, turn; sc in first sc, ★ skip next dc, (dc, sc) in next sc; repeat from ★ across.
Finish off.

Row 7: With **right** side facing and holding two strands of Turquoise together, join yarn with sc in first sc *(see Joining With Sc, page 142)*; sc in next dc and in each st across.

Rows 8-12: Ch 1, turn; sc in each sc across.
Finish off.

Row 13: With **right** side facing and holding one strand of Turquoise and one strand of Variegated together, join yarn with sc in first sc; ★ skip next sc, (dc, sc) in next sc; repeat from ★ across.

Rows 14-24: Ch 1, turn; sc in first sc, ★ skip next dc, (dc, sc) in next sc; repeat from ★ across.
Finish off.

Rows 25-49: Repeat Rows 7-24 once, then repeat Rows 7-13 once **more**.

Rows 50-54: Ch 1, turn; sc in first sc, ★ skip next dc, (dc, sc) in next sc; repeat from ★ across.
Finish off.

Holding 6 strands of Turquoise together, add fringe in each row across short edges of Afghan *(Figs. 28b & d, page 143)*.

AMERICAN HERITAGE

Hooray for the red, white, and blue! Salute our country's colors on an interesting afghan underscored with a lush blue fringe. This patriotic throw features shell-like stitches in alternating rows of all-American hues.

Finished Size: 44" x 61"

MATERIALS

Worsted Weight Yarn:

Blue - 27 ounces, (770 grams, 1,525 yards)

Aran - 22 ounces, (620 grams, 1,245 yards)

Burgundy - 21 ounces, (600 grams, 1,190 yards)

Crochet hook, size I (5.50 mm) **or** size needed for gauge

GAUGE: In pattern, (2 dc, ch 1, 2 dc) 3 times = 4¼";
         11 rows = 4⅛"

Gauge Swatch: 4½"w x 4⅛"h
With Blue, ch 18 **loosely**.
Work same as Afghan for 11 rows.
Finish off.

With Blue, ch 158 **loosely**.
Row 1 (Right side)**:** Working in back ridges of beginning ch, (2 dc, ch 1, 2 dc) in fifth ch from hook, ★ skip next 4 chs, (2 dc, ch 1, 2 dc) in next ch; repeat from ★ across to last 3 chs, skip next 2 chs, hdc in last ch changing to Aran *(Fig. 24, page 143)*: 124 dc and 31 ch-1 sps.
Note: Loop a short piece of yarn around any stitch to mark Row 1 as **right** side.
Row 2: Ch 2 **(counts as first hdc, now and throughout)**, turn; working **around** Row 1 and in back ridge of skipped chs of beginning ch, skip first ch-2, (2 dc, ch 1, 2 dc) in second ch of each skipped ch-4 across to last sp *(Fig. 1)*, hdc in top of beginning ch changing to Burgundy: 120 dc and 30 ch-1 sps.

Fig. 1

Row 3: Ch 2, turn; working **around** previous row, (2 dc, ch 1, 2 dc) in each ch-1 sp on row **below** previous row *(Fig. 2)*, hdc in last hdc on previous row changing to Blue: 124 dc and 31 ch-1 sps.

Fig. 2

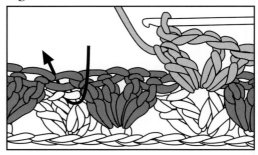

Row 4: Ch 2, turn; working **around** previous row, (2 dc, ch 1, 2 dc) in each ch-1 sp on row **below** previous row, hdc in last hdc on previous row changing to Aran: 120 dc and 30 ch-1 sps.
Row 5: Ch 2, turn; working **around** previous row, (2 dc, ch 1, 2 dc) in each ch-1 sp on row **below** previous row, hdc in last hdc on previous row changing to Burgundy: 124 dc and 31 ch-1 sps.
Rows 6-163: Repeat Rows 3-5, 52 times; then repeat Rows 3 and 4 once **more**; at end of Row 163, do **not** change colors, finish off.

Holding 8 strands of Blue together, add fringe evenly across short edges of Afghan *(Figs. 28a & c, page 143)*.

HOMEGROWN GOODNESS

Resembling carefully plotted rows in a vegetable garden, these deep green mile-a-minute strips have the rich appeal of mid-summer foliage. Working single crochets around loops in previous rows creates the interesting openwork.

Finished Size: 51" x 63"

MATERIALS
Worsted Weight Yarn:
    Green - 42 ounces, (1,190 grams, 2,640 yards)
    Grey - 7 ounces, (200 grams, 440 yards)
Crochet hook, size H (5.00 mm) **or** size needed
    for gauge
Yarn needle

GAUGE: Each Strip = 7¼" wide
          16 sc and 16 rows = 4"

Gauge Swatch: 5¼"w x 3"h
Work same as Strip Center through Row 12.

STRIP (Make 7)
CENTER
With Green, ch 22 **loosely**.
Row 1 (Right side)**:** Sc in second ch from hook and in each ch across: 21 sc.
Note: Loop a short piece of yarn around any stitch to mark Row 1 as **right** side and bottom edge.
Row 2: Ch 1, turn; sc in first 3 sc, ★ ch 8, skip next 6 sc, sc in next 3 sc; repeat from ★ once **more**: 9 sc and 2 loops.
Rows 3-5: Ch 1, turn; sc in first 3 sc, (ch 8, sc in next 3 sc) twice.
Row 6: Ch 1, turn; sc in first 3 sc, ★ ch 4, working **around** loops of **previous** 4 rows, sc in loop 4 rows **below**, ch 4, sc in next 3 sc; repeat from ★ once **more**: 11 sc and 4 ch-4 sps.
Row 7: Ch 1, turn; sc in first 3 sc, ★ ch 8, skip next 2 ch-4 sps, sc in next 3 sc; repeat from ★ once **more**: 9 sc and 2 loops.
Rows 8-241: Repeat Rows 3-7, 46 times; then repeat Rows 3-6 once **more**.
Row 242: Ch 1, turn; sc in first 3 sc, ★ ch 6, skip next 2 ch-4 sps, sc in next 3 sc; repeat from ★ once **more**: 9 sc and 2 loops.
Row 243: Ch 1, turn; sc in each sc and in each ch across; do **not** finish off: 21 sc.

BORDER
Rnd 1: Ch 1, do **not** turn; 2 sc in last sc on Row 243; sc in end of each row across; working in free loops of beginning ch *(Fig. 22b, page 142)*, 3 sc in first ch, skip next ch, sc in next 18 chs, 3 sc in next ch; sc in end of each row across; 3 sc in first sc on Row 243, skip next sc, sc in next 18 sc and in same st as first sc; join with slip st to first sc: 534 sc.
Rnd 2: Ch 1, sc in same st, ch 3, skip next 2 sc, ★ sc in next sc, ch 3, skip next 2 sc; repeat from ★ around; join with slip st to first sc, finish off: 178 ch-3 sps.
Rnd 3: With **right** side facing, join Grey with slip st in first ch-3 sp; ch 1, (sc, dc, 2 sc, dc, sc) in same sp, † (sc, dc, sc) in each of next 80 ch-3 sps, (sc, dc, 2 sc, dc, sc) in each of next 2 ch-3 sps, (sc, dc, sc) in each of next 5 ch-3 sps †, (sc, dc, 2 sc, dc, sc) in each of next 2 ch-3 sps, repeat from † to † once, (sc, dc, 2 sc, dc, sc) in last ch-3 sp; join with slip st to first sc, finish off: 558 sts.
Rnd 4: With **right** side facing, join Green with slip st in same st as joining; ch 3 **(counts as first hdc plus ch 1)**, hdc in same st, ch 1, † skip next 2 sts, hdc in next sc, place marker around hdc just made for joining placement, ch 1, hdc in same st, ch 1, ★ skip next 2 sts, (hdc, ch 1) twice in next sc; repeat from ★ 81 times **more**, place marker around last hdc made for joining placement †, [skip next 2 sts, (hdc, ch 1) twice in next sc] 10 times, repeat from † to † once, skip next 2 sts, [(hdc, ch 1) twice in next sc, skip next 2 sts] across; join with slip st to first hdc, finish off: 372 hdc.

ASSEMBLY
Place two Strips with **wrong** sides together and bottom edges at the same end. With Green and working through inside loops only, whipstitch Strips together *(Fig. 27a, page 143)*, beginning in first marked hdc and ending in next marked hdc.

ALL-AMERICAN STARS

This summertime throw celebrates our nation's heritage with patriotic colors and star-centered squares. Five cluster stitches give each star its distinctive shape, and simple slip stitches and chains join the squares as you go.

Finished Size: 48" x 63"

MATERIALS
Worsted Weight Yarn:
Blue - 25 ounces, (710 grams, 1,570 yards)
Red - 17 ounces, (480 grams, 1,070 yards)
Ecru - 6 ounces, (170 grams, 375 yards)
Crochet hook, size I (5.50 mm) **or** size needed for gauge

GAUGE: Each Square = 7³/₄"

Gauge Swatch: 3¹/₂" diameter
Work same as Square through Rnd 3.

STITCH GUIDE

BEGINNING CLUSTER (uses next 2 dc)
Ch 2, ★ YO, insert hook in **next** dc, YO and pull up a loop, YO and draw through 2 loops on hook; repeat from ★ once **more**, YO and draw through all 3 loops on hook *(Figs. 17a & b, page 141)*.

CLUSTER (uses next 3 dc)
★ YO, insert hook in **next** dc, YO and pull up a loop, YO and draw through 2 loops on hook; repeat from ★ 2 times **more**, YO and draw through all 4 loops on hook.

DECREASE (uses next 2 sts)
★ YO, insert hook in **next** st, YO and pull up a loop, YO and draw through 2 loops on hook; repeat from ★ once **more**, YO and draw through all 3 loops on hook **(counts as one dc)**.

SQUARE (Make 48)
With Red, ch 4; join with slip st to form a ring.
Rnd 1 (Right side)**:** Ch 3 **(counts as first dc, now and throughout)**, 14 dc in ring; join with slip st to first dc: 15 dc.
Note: Loop a short piece of yarn around any stitch to mark Rnd 1 as **right** side.

Rnd 2: Work Beginning Cluster, ch 5, work Cluster, place marker around Cluster just made to mark top of Square, ch 5, (work Cluster, ch 5) 3 times; join with slip st to top of Beginning Cluster, finish off: 5 Clusters and 5 ch-5 sps.
Rnd 3: With **right** side facing, join Blue with slip st in first ch-5 sp to left of joining; ch 3, 6 dc in same sp, dc in next Cluster, (7 dc in next ch-5 sp, dc in next Cluster) around; join with slip st to first dc: 40 dc.
Rnd 4: Ch 3, dc in next dc, decrease, (dc in next 2 dc, 2 dc in next dc) twice, ★ dc in next 2 dc, decrease, (dc in next 2 dc, 2 dc in next dc) twice; repeat from ★ 2 times **more**; join with slip st to first dc, finish off: 44 dc.
Rnd 5: With **right** side facing, join Ecru with slip st in second dc to left of joining; ch 4 **(counts as first tr)**, (2 dc, ch 3, 2 dc, tr) in same st, dc in next 2 dc, hdc in next 2 dc, sc in next 2 dc, hdc in next 2 dc, dc in next 2 dc, ★ (tr, 2 dc, ch 3, 2 dc, tr) in next dc, dc in next 2 dc, hdc in next 2 dc, sc in next 2 dc, hdc in next 2 dc, dc in next 2 dc; repeat from ★ 2 times **more**; join with slip st to first tr, finish off: 64 sts and 4 ch-3 sps.
Rnd 6: With **right** side facing, join Red with sc in first ch-3 sp to left of joining *(see Joining With Sc, page 142)*; 2 sc in same sp, ★ sc in each st across to next ch-3 sp, 3 sc in ch-3 sp; repeat from ★ 2 times **more**, sc in each st across; join with slip st to first sc: 76 sc.
Rnd 7: Slip st in next sc, ch 2, 2 dc in same st, ch 2, ★ (slip st in next sc, ch 2, decrease, ch 2) 6 times, (slip st, ch 2, 2 dc) in next sc, ch 2; repeat from ★ 2 times **more**, (slip st in next sc, ch 2, decrease, ch 2) across; join with slip st to first slip st, finish off: 32 dc.
Rnd 8: With **right** side facing, join Blue with slip st in first dc to left of joining; ch 3, 2 dc in same st and in next slip st, (sc in next dc, 2 dc in next slip st) 6 times, ★ 3 dc in next dc, 2 dc in next slip st, (sc in next dc, 2 dc in next slip st) 6 times; repeat from ★ 2 times **more**; join with slip st to first dc: 92 sts.
Rnd 9: Ch 1, sc in same st, 3 sc in next dc, ★ sc in each st across to center dc of next corner 3-dc group, 3 sc in center dc; repeat from ★ 2 times **more**, sc in each st across; join with slip st to first sc, finish off: 100 sc.

ASSEMBLY

Afghan is assembled by joining Squares together, forming
6 vertical strips of 8 Squares each.

Join Squares as follows: With **wrong** sides together, matching
top edge of one Square to bottom edge of next Square, and
working through inside loops on **both** pieces, join Blue with
slip st in center sc of first corner 3-sc group; ch 1, (slip st in
next sc, ch 1) across to center sc of next corner 3-sc group,
slip st in center sc; finish off.

Join strips together in same manner.

EDGING

With **right** side facing and working in Back Loops Only
(Fig. 21, page 142), join Blue with slip st in any sc; ch 1,
(slip st in next sc, ch 1) around; join with slip st to first slip st,
finish off.

BUTTERCUPS AND BLUEBELLS

*Displaying the shades of creamy buttercups and delightful bluebells,
this summery coverlet has a natural, breezy charm. A combination
of clusters and decreases achieves the rippling effect.*

Finished Size: 52" x 71"

MATERIALS
Worsted Weight Yarn:
Yellow - 23 ounces,
(650 grams, 1,510 yards)
Blue - 13 ounces,
(370 grams, 855 yards)
Lt Blue - 10 ounces,
(280 grams, 655 yards)
Crochet hook, size I (5.50 mm) **or** size
needed for gauge

GAUGE: Each repeat from point
to point = 3¹/₄"

Gauge Swatch: 6³/₄"w x 4³/₄"h
Ch 26 **loosely**.
Work same as Afghan for 7 rows.
Finish off.

STITCH GUIDE

CLUSTER (uses one tr)
★ YO twice, insert hook in tr indicated, YO and pull up a
loop, (YO and draw through 2 loops on hook) twice; repeat
from ★ once **more**, YO and draw through all 3 loops on hook
(Figs. 16a & b, page 141).
DECREASE (uses next 3 sc)
★ YO 3 times, insert hook in **next** sc, YO and pull up a loop,
(YO and draw through 2 loops on hook) 3 times; repeat from
★ 2 times **more**, YO and draw through all 4 loops on hook.
ENDING DECREASE (uses next 2 sc)
★ YO 3 times, insert hook in **next** sc, YO and pull up a loop,
(YO and draw through 2 loops on hook) 3 times; repeat from
★ once **more**, YO and draw through all 3 loops on hook.

AFGHAN BODY

With Blue, ch 194 **loosely**.
Row 1 (Right side)**:** Sc in second ch from hook, (ch 1, skip
next ch, sc in next ch) across changing to Lt Blue in last sc
(Fig. 24, page 143): 97 sc.
Row 2: Ch 1, turn; sc in first sc, ch 1, sc in next sc, ★ † ch 1,
skip next sc, (tr, ch 1) 5 times in next sc, skip next sc, sc in next
sc †, (ch 1, sc in next sc) twice; repeat from ★ 14 times **more**,
then repeat from † to † once, ch 1, sc in last sc changing to
Yellow: 129 sts and 128 ch-1 sps.
Row 3: Ch 5, turn; dtr in next sc **(ch 5 plus dtr counts as
first decrease, now and throughout)**, ★ † ch 1, work
Cluster in next tr, ch 1, dc in next tr, ch 1, sc in next tr, ch 1, dc
in next tr, ch 1, work Cluster in next tr, ch 1 †, decrease; repeat
from ★ 14 times **more**, then repeat from † to † once, work
ending decrease.
Row 4: Ch 1, turn; sc in first ending decrease, ★ ch 1, sc in
next Cluster, ch 1, skip next dc, (tr, ch 1) 5 times in next sc,
skip next dc, sc in next Cluster, ch 1, sc in next decrease; repeat
from ★ across changing to Blue in last sc.

Row 5: Ch 5, turn; dtr in next sc, ★ † ch 1, work Cluster in next tr, ch 1, dc in next tr, ch 1, sc in next tr, ch 1, dc in next tr, ch 1, work Cluster in next tr, ch 1 †, decrease; repeat from ★ 14 times **more**, then repeat from † to † once, work ending decrease changing to Lt Blue.

Row 6: Ch 1, turn; sc in first ending decrease, ★ ch 1, sc in next Cluster, ch 1, skip next dc, (tr, ch 1) 5 times in next sc, skip next dc, sc in next Cluster, ch 1, sc in next decrease; repeat from ★ across changing to Yellow in last sc.

Repeat Rows 3-6 until Afghan Body measures approximately 70" from beginning ch, ending by working Row 5, do **not** change colors or finish off.

EDGING

Rnd 1: Do **not** turn; working in end of rows, slip st in first row, (ch 2, slip st in next row) across, ch 3; working over beginning ch, sc in first ch-1 sp, (ch 1, sc in next ch-1 sp) across, ch 3; working in end of rows, slip st in first row, (ch 2, slip st in next row) across, ch 3; working across last row, sc in first decrease, (ch 1, sc in next ch-1 sp) across, ch 3; join with slip st to first slip st.

Rnd 2: (Slip st in next sp, ch 2) around working (slip st, ch 2) twice in each corner ch-3 sp; join with slip st to first slip st, finish off.

85

PAW PRINTS

The striking blue eyes of our feline friend are reflected in soothing shades on this sophisticated cover-up. Clusters and double crochets stitched behind previous rows create the textured circles that resemble paw prints.

Finished Size: 51" x 68"

MATERIALS
Worsted Weight Yarn:
   Lt Blue - 43 ounces, (1,220 grams, 2,080 yards)
   Blue - 23 ounces, (650 grams, 1,115 yards)
Crochet hook, size I (5.50 mm) **or** size needed
   for gauge
Yarn needle

GAUGE: Sc, (ch 1, sc) 7 times = 4"
         Each Strip = 3" wide

Gauge Swatch: 3"w x 4"h
Ch 16 **loosely**.
Work same as Strip.

Each Strip is worked across length of Afghan. When joining yarn and finishing off, leave an 8" length to be worked into fringe.

STITCH GUIDE

> **CLUSTER**
> Ch 3, dc in third ch from hook.

STRIP (Make 17)
FIRST HALF
With Blue, ch 236 **loosely**.
Row 1 (Wrong side)**:** Sc in second ch from hook and in next ch, ch 1, ★ skip next ch, sc in next ch, ch 1; repeat from ★ across to last 3 chs, skip next ch, sc in last 2 chs; finish off: 119 sc and 116 ch-1 sps.
Note: Loop a short piece of yarn around the **back** of any stitch to mark **right** side.
Row 2: With **right** side facing, join Lt Blue with sc in first sc *(see Joining With Sc, page 142)*; ch 1, skip next sc, (sc in next ch-1 sp, ch 1) across to last 2 sc, skip next sc, sc in last sc; finish off: 117 ch-1 sps.

Row 3: With **wrong** side facing, join Blue with sc in first sc; working **behind** next ch-1, dc in skipped sc one row **below** ch-1, ★ work Cluster, skip next ch-1 sp, working **behind** next ch-1, dc in skipped sc one row **below** ch-1; repeat from ★ across to last sc, sc in last sc; finish off: 58 Clusters.
Row 4: With **right** side facing, join Lt Blue with sc in first sc; ★ sc in next dc, ch 1, working **behind** next Cluster, dc in skipped ch-1 sp one row **below** Cluster, ch 1; repeat from ★ across to last 2 sts, sc in last 2 sts; finish off.
Row 5: With **wrong** side facing, join Lt Blue with sc in first sc; ★ sc in next sc, ch 1, sc in next dc, ch 1; repeat from ★ across to last 2 sc, sc in last 2 sc; finish off.

SECOND HALF
Row 1: With **right** side facing and working in sps and in free loops of beginning ch *(Fig. 22b, page 142)*, join Lt Blue with sc in first ch; ch 1, ★ skip next ch, sc in next sp, ch 1; repeat from ★ across to last 2 chs, skip next ch, sc in last ch; finish off: 117 ch-1 sps.
Row 2: With **wrong** side facing, join Blue with sc in first sc; working **behind** next ch-1, dc in free loop of skipped ch one row **below** ch-1, ★ work Cluster, skip next ch-1 sp, working **behind** next ch-1, dc in free loop of skipped ch one row **below** ch-1; repeat from ★ across to last sc, sc in last sc; finish off: 58 Clusters.
Row 3: With **right** side facing, join Lt Blue with sc in first sc; ★ sc in next dc, ch 1, working **behind** next Cluster, dc in skipped ch-1 sp one row **below** Cluster, ch 1; repeat from ★ across to last 2 sts, sc in last 2 sts; finish off.
Row 4: With **wrong** side facing, join Lt Blue with sc in first sc; ★ sc in next sc, ch 1, sc in next dc, ch 1; repeat from ★ across to last 2 sc, sc in last 2 sc; finish off.

ASSEMBLY
With Lt Blue and working through both loops, whipstitch Strips together *(Fig. 27b, page 143)*, beginning in first sc and ending in last sc.

EDGING
FIRST SIDE
With **right** side facing and working across long edge, join
Lt Blue with slip st in first sc; ch 1, ★ skip next sc, slip st in next
ch-1 sp, ch 1; repeat from ★ across to last 2 sc, skip next sc,
slip st in last sc; finish off.

SECOND SIDE
Work same as First Side.

Holding 2 strands of corresponding color together, add fringe in
each row across short edges of Afghan *(Figs. 28b & d,
page 143)*.

SUMMER ABLAZE

A good use for colorful scraps, this granny variation offers tradition with a twist by using rectangles instead of squares. Double crochet clusters make up the centers of the rectangles, and long fringe accents the ends of the afghan.

Finished Size: 45" x 57"

MATERIALS
Worsted Weight Yarn:
Black - 28 ounces, (800 grams, 1,585 yards)
Scraps - 29 ounces, (820 grams, 1,640 yards) **total**
Note: We used 15 different colors.
Foundation Row plus Rnd 1 requires 8 yards.
Rnd 2 requires 7 yards.
Crochet hook, size I (5.50 mm) **or** size needed
for gauge
Yarn needle

GAUGE SWATCH: 3³⁄₄"w x 6¹⁄₄"h
Work same as Rectangle.

STITCH GUIDE

3-DC CLUSTER (uses one st)
★ YO, insert hook in ch indicated, YO and pull up a loop, YO and draw through 2 loops on hook; repeat from ★ 2 times **more**, YO and draw through all 4 loops on hook *(Figs. 16a & b, page 141)*.
4-DC CLUSTER (uses one st)
★ YO, insert hook in st indicated, YO and pull up a loop, YO and draw through 2 loops on hook; repeat from ★ 3 times **more**, YO and draw through all 5 loops on hook.

RECTANGLE (Make 108)
Foundation Row: With Scrap color desired, ch 2, work 3-dc Cluster in second ch from hook, (ch 3, work 3-dc Cluster in second ch from hook) 4 times: 5 3-dc Clusters.
Rnd 1 (Right side): Ch 5, skip first 3-dc Cluster, work 4-dc Cluster in ch **before** next 3-dc Cluster, (ch 3, skip next 3-dc Cluster, work 4-dc Cluster in ch **before** next 3-dc Cluster) 3 times, ch 5; working in free loops of chs *(Fig. 22b, page 142)*, slip st in ch at base of last 3-dc Cluster, ch 5, skip first 3-dc Cluster, work 4-dc Cluster in next ch (same ch as 4-dc Cluster), (ch 3, skip next 3-dc Cluster, work 4-dc Cluster in next ch) 3 times, ch 5; join with slip st to base of beginning ch-5, finish off: 10 sps.

Note: Loop a short piece of yarn around any stitch to mark Rnd 1 as **right** side.
Rnd 2: With **right** side facing, join Scrap color desired with slip st in last ch-5 sp made; ch 3 **(counts as first dc, now and throughout)**, (2 dc, ch 3, 3 dc) in same sp, ch 1, (3 dc, ch 3, 3 dc) in next ch-5 sp, ch 1, (3 dc in next ch-3 sp, ch 1) 3 times, [(3 dc, ch 3, 3 dc) in next ch-5 sp, ch 1] twice, (3 dc in next ch-3 sp, ch 1) 3 times; join with slip st to first dc, finish off: 42 dc and 14 sps.
Rnd 3: With **right** side facing, join Black with slip st in first ch-3 sp to left of joining; ch 3, (2 dc, ch 3, 3 dc) in same sp, † ch 1, 3 dc in next ch-1 sp, ch 1, (3 dc, ch 3, 3 dc) in next ch-3 sp, ch 1, (3 dc in next ch-1 sp, ch 1) 4 times †, (3 dc, ch 3, 3 dc) in next ch-3 sp, repeat from † to † once; join with slip st to first dc, finish off: 54 dc and 18 sps.

ASSEMBLY
With Black and working through inside loops only, whipstitch short edges of Rectangles together *(Fig. 27a, page 143)*, forming 12 vertical strips of 9 Rectangles each, beginning in center ch of first corner ch-3 and ending in center ch of next corner ch-3; whipstitch strips together in same manner.

EDGING
With **right** side of short edge facing, join Black with slip st in right corner ch-3 sp; ch 3, (2 dc, ch 3, 3 dc) in same sp, † ch 1, (3 dc in next ch-1 sp, ch 1) twice, [(2 dc in next sp, ch 1) twice, (3 dc in next ch-1 sp, ch 1) twice] across to next corner ch-3 sp, (3 dc, ch 3, 3 dc) in corner ch-3 sp, ch 1, (3 dc in next ch-1 sp, ch 1) 5 times, [(2 dc in next sp, ch 1) twice, (3 dc in next ch-1 sp, ch 1) 5 times] across to next corner ch-3 sp †, (3 dc, ch 3, 3 dc) in corner ch-3 sp, repeat from † to † once; join with slip st to first dc, finish off.

Holding 10 strands of Black together, add fringe in every other sp across short edges of Afghan *(Figs. 28a & c, page 143)*.

BLUSHING SEASHELLS

Seashells and romantic evenings by the shore inspired this gorgeous throw.
The shell-strewn afghan ends elegantly in scallops trimmed with picots.

Finished Size: 47" x 62"

MATERIALS
Worsted Weight Yarn:
37 ounces, (1,050 grams, 1,790 yards)
Crochet hook, size I (5.50 mm) **or** size needed
for gauge

GAUGE: In pattern, 2 repeats = 4"; 7 rows = 4¼"

Gauge Swatch: 4"w x 4¼"h
Ch 15 **loosely.**
Work same as Afghan Body for 7 rows.
Finish off.

STITCH GUIDE

SHELL
Dc in st or sp indicated, (ch 1, dc in same st or sp) twice.
PICOT
Ch 3, slip st in third ch from hook.

AFGHAN BODY

Ch 120 **loosely.**
Row 1 (Right side)**:** Sc in second ch from hook, skip next
2 chs, work Shell in next ch, skip next 2 chs, sc in next ch,
★ ch 3, sc in next ch, skip next 2 chs, work Shell in next ch,
skip next 2 chs, sc in next ch; repeat from ★ across: 17 Shells
and 16 ch-3 sps.
Row 2: Ch 7 **(counts as first tr plus ch 3)**, turn; (sc, ch 3)
twice in center dc of next Shell, ★ dc in next ch-3 sp, ch 3, (sc,
ch 3) twice in center dc of next Shell; repeat from ★ across, tr
in last sc: 52 sts and 51 ch-3 sps.
Row 3: Ch 1, turn; sc in first tr, skip next ch-3 sp, work Shell in
next ch-3 sp, skip next sc, ★ (sc, ch 3, sc) in next dc, skip next
ch-3 sp, work Shell in next ch-3 sp, skip next sc; repeat from ★
across to last tr, sc in last tr: 17 Shells and 16 ch-3 sps.
Rows 4-81: Repeat Rows 2 and 3, 39 times; do **not** finish off.

EDGING

Rnd 1: Ch 1, do **not** turn; 2 sc in last sc on Row 81; † working
in end of rows, skip first row, 4 sc in next row, (sc in next row,
3 sc in next row) across to last row, skip last row †; working in
free loops of beginning ch *(Fig. 22b, page 142)*, 3 sc in first
ch, sc in next 8 chs, skip next ch, (sc in next 9 chs, skip next
ch) 10 times, sc in next 8 chs, 3 sc in next ch; repeat from
† to † once; working across Row 81, 3 sc in first sc, (sc in next
3 dc, 3 sc in next ch-3 sp) twice, ★ sc in next dc, 2 sc in next
dc, sc in next dc, 3 sc in next ch-3 sp, sc in next 3 dc, 3 sc in
next ch-3 sp; repeat from ★ 6 times **more**, sc in next 3 dc and
in same st as first sc; join with slip st to first sc: 544 sc.
Rnd 2: Ch 8 **(counts as first dc plus ch 5, now and**
throughout), skip next sc, sc in next sc, ch 5, (skip next 2 sc,
sc in next sc, ch 5) across to next corner 3-sc group, skip next
sc, ★ (dc, ch 5) twice in corner sc, skip next sc, sc in next sc,
ch 5, (skip next 2 sc, sc in next sc, ch 5) across to next corner
3-sc group, skip next sc; repeat from ★ 2 times **more**, dc in
same st as first dc, ch 2, dc in first dc to form last ch-5 sp:
188 ch-5 sps.
Rnd 3: Ch 1, sc in same sp, 8 dc in next ch-5 sp, ★ (sc in next
ch-5 sp, ch 5, sc in next ch-5 sp, 8 dc in next ch-5 sp) across to
next corner ch-5 sp, sc in corner ch-5 sp, 8 dc in next ch-5 sp;
repeat from ★ 2 times **more**, (sc in next ch-5 sp, ch 5, sc in
next ch-5 sp, 8 dc in next ch-5 sp) across; join with slip st to
first sc: 64 8-dc groups.
Rnd 4: Slip st in first dc, ch 6, slip st in third ch from hook
(counts as first dc plus Picot), dc in next dc, (work Picot, dc
in next dc) 6 times, ★ [sc in next ch-5 sp, dc in next dc, (work
Picot, dc in next dc) 7 times] across to next corner sc, ch 5,
skip corner sc, dc in next dc, (work Picot, dc in next dc) 7
times; repeat from ★ 2 times **more**, [sc in next ch-5 sp, dc in
next dc, (work Picot, dc in next dc) 7 times] across, ch 2, dc in
first dc to form last ch-5 sp: 448 Picots.

Rnd 5: Ch 8, (skip next Picot, sc in next Picot, ch 5) 3 times, ★ [skip next 2 Picots, sc in next Picot, ch 5, (skip next Picot, sc in next Picot, ch 5) twice] across to next corner ch-5 sp, (dc, ch 5) twice in corner ch-5 sp, (skip next Picot, sc in next Picot, ch 5) 3 times; repeat from ★ 2 times **more**, [skip next 2 Picots, sc in next Picot, ch 5, (skip next Picot, sc in next Picot, ch 5) twice] across, dc in same sp as first dc, ch 2, dc in first dc to form last ch-5 sp: 200 ch-5 sps.

Rnds 6-10: Repeat Rnds 3-5 once; then repeat Rnds 3 and 4 once **more**; at end of Rnd 10, finish off.

DELICATE DIAMONDS

Delicate diamonds in pale green and tan exude fine wisps of splendor on this airy coverlet. The lovely design is worked in panels with lacy triple crochet borders surrounding each strip of diamonds.

Finished Size: 47" x 66"

MATERIALS

Worsted Weight Yarn:
- Cream - 27¹/₂ ounces, (780 grams, 1,690 yards)
- Green - 8 ounces, (230 grams, 490 yards)
- Tan - 6 ounces, (170 grams, 370 yards)
- Crochet hook, size J (6.00 mm) **or** size needed for gauge

GAUGE: Each Diamond = 2"w x 1³/₄"h x 2³/₄" diagonally
Each Strip = 4¹/₄" wide

Gauge Swatch: 2"w x 1³/₄"h x 2³/₄" diagonally
Work same as Strip A Diamond Center for 6 rows.

STRIP A

DIAMOND CENTER

With Green, ch 7 **loosely**, place marker in seventh ch from hook for st placement and to mark bottom edge.

Row 1: Sc in back ridge of second ch from hook and each ch across *(Fig. 2b, page 139)*: 6 sc.

Row 2 (Right side)**:** Ch 1, turn; sc in each sc across.

Note: Loop a short piece of yarn around any stitch to mark Row 2 as **right** side. Mark **right** side on **each** Diamond as they are made as Diamonds may twist.

Rows 3-6: Ch 1, turn; sc in each sc across.

Row 7: Ch 7 **loosely**, turn; sc in back ridge of second ch from hook and each ch across: 6 sc.

Repeat Rows 2-7 until 23 Diamonds are complete, ending by working Row 6; finish off.

BORDER

Work into Diamonds with **right** side of each Diamond facing you at all times.

Rnd 1: With **right** side facing, join Cream with sc in marked ch *(see Joining With Sc, page 142)*; 2 sc in same st, working in end of rows, skip first row, sc in next 4 rows; 3 sc in next corner sc, sc in next 4 sc, † skip next sc, sc **around** joining of Diamonds *(Fig. 1a)*; working in end of rows, skip first row on next Diamond, sc in next 4 rows; 3 sc in next corner sc, sc in next 4 sc †, repeat from † to † 21 times **more**, 3 sc in next sc; working in end of rows, skip first row, sc in next 4 rows, skip next row; working in free loops of beginning ch *(Fig. 22b, page 142)*, 3 sc in ch at base of first sc, sc in next 4 chs, ★ skip next ch, working **between** legs of next sc, sc **around** next joining *(Fig. 1b)*; working in end of rows, skip first row, sc in next 4 rows, skip next row; working in free loops of beginning ch, 3 sc in ch at base of first sc, sc in next 4 chs; repeat from ★ across; join with slip st to first sc: 556 sc.

Fig. 1a	Fig. 1b
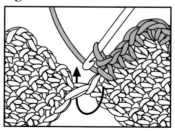	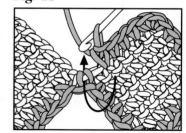

Rnd 2: Ch 5, (tr, ch 1) twice in same st, (tr, ch 1) 3 times in next 2 sc, skip next 4 sc, sc in next sc, ch 1, skip next sc, sc in next sc, ch 1, † skip next 4 sc, (tr, ch 1) 4 times in next sc, skip next 4 sc, sc in next sc, ch 1, skip next sc, sc in next sc, ch 1 †, repeat from † to † 21 times **more**, skip next 4 sc, (tr, ch 1) 3 times in next 3 sc, skip next 4 sc, sc in next sc, ch 1, skip next sc, sc in next sc, ch 1, repeat from † to † 22 times, skip last 4 sc; join with slip st to fourth ch of beginning ch-5: 286 ch-1 sps.

Rnd 3: Slip st in first ch-1 sp, ch 1, (sc, ch 3, sc) in same sp and in next 7 ch-1 sps, sc in next 3 ch-1 sps, † (sc, ch 3, sc) in next 3 ch-1 sps, sc in next 3 ch-1 sps †, repeat from † to † 21 times **more**, (sc, ch 3, sc) in next 8 ch-1 sps, sc in next 3 ch-1 sps, repeat from † to † across; join with slip st to first sc, finish off.

STRIP B

DIAMOND CENTER

With Tan, work same as Strip A.

BORDER

Work same as Border of Strip A, through Rnd 2: 286 ch-1 sps.

Rnd 3 (Joining rnd): Slip st in first ch-1 sp, ch 1, (sc, ch 3, sc) in same sp and in next 6 ch-1 sps, sc in next ch-1 sp, ch 1, holding Strips with **wrong** sides together and bottom edges at same end, sc in corresponding ch-3 sp on **previous Strip** *(Fig. 26, page 143)*, ch 1, sc in same sp on **new Strip**, sc in next 4 ch-1 sps, ch 1, sc in next ch-3 sp on **previous Strip**, ch 1, sc in same sp on **new Strip**, ★ (sc in next ch-1 sp, ch 1, sc in next ch-3 sp on **previous Strip**, ch 1, sc in same sp on

new Strip) twice, sc in next 4 ch-1 sps, ch 1, sc in next ch-3 sp on **previous Strip**, ch 1, sc in same sp on **new Strip**; repeat from ★ 21 times **more**, (sc, ch 3, sc) in next 7 ch-1 sps, sc in next 3 ch-1 sps, † (sc, ch 3, sc) in next 3 ch-1 sps, sc in next 3 ch-1 sps †, repeat from † to † across; join with slip st to first sc, finish off.

STRIP C

Work same as Strip A, through Rnd 2 of Border: 286 ch-1 sps.

Rnd 3 (Joining rnd): Work same as Strip B.

Repeat Strips B and C, 4 times: 11 Strips.

HOME ON THE RANGE

As cozy as a campfire on the open range, our snuggly throw is highlighted with rich burgundy and teal. The mile-a-minute strips are textured with front post double crochets.

Finished Size: 47" x 67"

MATERIALS
Worsted Weight Yarn:
Black - 32^1/$_2$ ounces,
  (920 grams, 1,835 yards)
Burgundy - 15^1/$_2$ ounces,
  (440 grams, 875 yards)
Dk Teal - 12^1/$_2$ ounces,
  (360 grams, 710 yards)
Crochet hook, size I (5.50 mm) **or** size
  needed for gauge
Yarn needle

GAUGE: Each Strip = 4^1/$_4$" wide

Gauge Swatch: 4^1/$_4$"w x 7^1/$_2$"h
Work same as Strip A Center for 7 rows.
Finish off.
Work Border.

STITCH GUIDE

> **FRONT POST DOUBLE CROCHET**
> *(abbreviated FPdc)*
> YO, insert hook from **front** to **back** around post of st indicated, YO and pull up a loop even with last st made *(Fig. 11, page 140)*, (YO and draw through 2 loops on hook) twice.

STRIP A (Make 6)
CENTER
With Burgundy, ch 13 **loosely**.
Row 1 (Wrong side)**:** Dc in fourth ch from hook **(3 skipped chs count as first dc)** and in each ch across: 11 dc.
Note: Loop a short piece of yarn around back of center dc to mark **right** side and bottom edge.
Row 2: Ch 3 **(counts as first dc, now and throughout)**, turn; work FPdc around each of next 3 dc, ch 3, skip next 3 dc, work FPdc around each of next 3 dc, dc in last dc: 6 FPdc.
Row 3: Ch 3, turn; dc in next FPdc and in each st and in each ch across: 11 dc.
Rows 4-111: Repeat Rows 2 and 3, 54 times.
Finish off.

BORDER
Rnd 1: With **right** side facing and working in end of rows, join Black with slip st in Row 1; ch 3, 2 dc in same row, † working in **front** of first dc on next row, dtr around third FPdc, dc around first dc on same row, dtr around same FPdc as last dtr made, ★ 2 dc in next row, working in **front** of first dc on next row, dtr around third FPdc, dc around first dc on same row, dtr around same FPdc as last dtr made; repeat from ★ across to last row, 3 dc in last row †; working in sts on last row of Center, skip first 5 dc, (4 dtr, ch 2, 4 dtr) in next dc; working in end of rows, 3 dc in first row, repeat from † to † once; working in free loop of beginning ch *(Fig. 22b, page 142)*, (4 dtr, ch 2, 4 dtr) in ch at base of marked dc; join with slip st to first dc: 574 sts and 2 ch-2 sps.

Rnd 2: Ch 1, working in Back Loops Only *(Fig. 21, page 142)*, sc in same st, † place marker around sc just made for joining placement, sc in each st across to next 4-dtr group, place marker around last sc made for joining placement, 2 sc in each of next 4 dtr and in each of next 2 chs, 2 sc in each of next 4 dtr †, sc in next dc, repeat from † to † once; join with slip st to **both** loops of first sc, finish off: 598 sc.

STRIP B (Make 5)

Work same as Strip A working Center with Dk Teal.

ASSEMBLY

Place two Strips with **wrong** sides together and bottom edges at the same end. With Black and working through inside loops only, whipstitch Strips together *(Fig. 27a, page 143)* in the following order: Strip A, (Strip B, Strip A) 5 times, beginning in first marked sc and ending in next marked sc.

COUNTRY RIPPLE

This cozy autumn coverlet captures the effect of daylight dancing over rippling water. The appearance of movement and reflected light is created by alternating between single and double crochets in each row.

Finished Size: 49" x 68"

MATERIALS

Worsted Weight Yarn:
Ecru - 21½ ounces, (610 grams, 1,400 yards)
Dk Blue - 10½ ounces, (300 grams, 685 yards)
Blue - 10½ ounces, (300 grams, 685 yards)
Crochet hook, size I (5.50 mm) **or** size needed for gauge

GAUGE: Each repeat from point to point = 3¼";
8 rows = 4"

Gauge Swatch: 9¾"w x 4"h
Ch 46 **loosely**.
Work same as Afghan for 8 rows.

STITCH GUIDE

> **DECREASE** (uses last 3 sts)
> YO, insert hook in next st, YO and pull up a loop, YO and draw through 2 loops on hook, YO, skip next st, insert hook in last st, YO and pull up a loop, YO and draw through 2 loops on hook, YO and draw through all 3 loops on hook **(counts as one dc)**.

AFGHAN BODY

With Ecru, ch 214 **loosely**.

Row 1 (Right side)**:** Dc in fifth ch from hook **(4 skipped chs count as first dc plus one skipped ch)** and in next 5 chs, ch 3, ★ dc in next 6 chs, skip next 2 chs, sc in next 6 chs, ch 2, sc in next 6 chs, skip next 2 chs, dc in next 6 chs, ch 3; repeat from ★ across to last 8 chs, dc in next 5 chs, decrease; finish off: 181 sts and 15 sps.
Note: Loop a short piece of yarn around any stitch to mark Row 1 as **right** side.

Row 2: With **wrong** side facing, join Dk Blue with sc in first dc **(see Joining With Sc, page 142)**; sc in next 5 dc, (sc, ch 2, sc) in next ch-3 sp, sc in next 5 dc, ★ skip next 2 sts, dc in next 5 sc, (dc, ch 3, dc) in next ch-2 sp, dc in next 5 sc, skip next 2 sts, sc in next 5 dc, (sc, ch 2, sc) in next ch-3 sp, sc in next 5 dc; repeat from ★ across to last 2 dc, skip next dc, sc in last dc; finish off: 182 sts and 15 sps.

Row 3: With **right** side facing, join Ecru with slip st in first sc; ch 3 **(counts as first dc, now and throughout)**, skip next sc, dc in next 5 sc, (dc, ch 3, dc) in next ch-2 sp, ★ dc in next 5 sc, skip next 2 sts, sc in next 5 dc, (sc, ch 2, sc) in next ch-3 sp, sc in next 5 dc, skip next 2 sts, dc in next 5 sc, (dc, ch 3, dc) in next ch-2 sp; repeat from ★ across to last 7 sc, dc in next 4 sc, decrease; finish off: 181 sts and 15 sps.

Row 4: With **wrong** side facing, join Blue with sc in first dc; sc in next 5 dc, (sc, ch 2, sc) in next ch-3 sp, sc in next 5 dc, ★ skip next 2 sts, dc in next 5 sc, (dc, ch 3, dc) in next ch-2 sp, dc in next 5 sc, skip next 2 sts, sc in next 5 dc, (sc, ch 2, sc) in next ch-3 sp, sc in next 5 dc; repeat from ★ across to last 2 dc, skip next dc, sc in last dc; finish off: 182 sts and 15 sps.

Row 5: With **right** side facing, join Ecru with slip st in first sc; ch 3, skip next sc, dc in next 5 sc, (dc, ch 3, dc) in next ch-2 sp, ★ dc in next 5 sc, skip next 2 sts, sc in next 5 dc, (sc, ch 2, sc) in next ch-3 sp, sc in next 5 dc, skip next 2 sts, dc in next 5 sc, (dc, ch 3, dc) in next ch-2 sp; repeat from ★ across to last 7 sc, dc in next 4 sc, decrease; finish off: 181 sts and 15 sps.

Rows 6-135: Repeat Rows 2-5, 32 times; then repeat Rows 2 and 3 once **more**; at end of Row 135, do **not** finish off.

EDGING

Ch 1, do **not** turn; working in end of rows, slip st in first row, (ch 3, skip next row, slip st in next row) across, ch 1; working in sps and in free loops of beginning ch **(Fig. 22b, page 142)**, slip st in first ch, ch 2, (slip st in next ch, ch 2, skip next ch) 3 times, slip st in next 2 chs, ch 2, ★ skip next ch, (slip st in next ch, ch 2, skip next ch) twice, (slip st, ch 2) twice in next ch-2 sp, skip next ch, (slip st in next ch, ch 2, skip next ch) twice, slip st in next 2 chs, ch 2; repeat from ★ 13 times **more**, (skip next ch, slip st in next ch, ch 2) 3 times, slip st in next ch, ch 1; working in end of rows, slip st in first row, (ch 3, skip next row, slip st in next row) across, ch 2; working in sts on Row 135, skip first dc, (slip st in next dc, ch 2, skip next dc) 3 times, (slip st, ch 2) twice in next sp, † skip next st, (slip st in next st, ch 2, skip next st) twice, slip st in next 2 sts, ch 2, skip next st, (slip st in next st, ch 2, skip next st) twice, (slip st, ch 2) twice in next sp †, repeat from † to † across to last 6 dc, (skip next dc, slip st in next dc, ch 2) across; join with slip st to first slip st, finish off.

SOUTHWESTERN STRIPES

Softly curving ripples on this striking throw produce a Southwestern-style accent. Popcorn stitches in contrasting colors are worked into the afghan as you go.

Finished Size: 44" x 58"

MATERIALS

Worsted Weight Yarn:
Dk Green - 22 ounces, (620 grams, 1,245 yards)
Lt Rose - 19½ ounces, (550 grams, 1,100 yards)
Med Rose - 6½ ounces, (180 grams, 365 yards)
Crochet hook, size I (5.50 mm) **or** size needed
for gauge

GAUGE: Each repeat from point to point and 7 rows = 4"

Gauge Swatch: 8"w x 4"h
With Dk Green, ch 32 **loosely**.
Work same as Afghan for 7 rows.
Finish off.

STITCH GUIDE

> **DECREASE** (uses next 3 sts)
> ★ YO, insert hook in **next** st, YO and pull up a loop, YO and draw through 2 loops on hook; repeat from ★ 2 times **more**, YO and draw though all 4 loops on hook **(counts as one dc)**.
> **POPCORN**
> Work 5 dc in st indicated, drop loop from hook, insert hook in first dc of 5-dc group, hook dropped loop and draw through **(Fig. 18, page 141)**.

With Dk Green, ch 158 **loosely**.
Row 1 (Right side)**:** Working in back ridge of chs **(Fig. 2b, page 139)**, dc in fourth ch from hook **(3 skipped chs count as first dc)** and in next 5 chs, decrease, dc in next 5 chs, ★ 3 dc in next ch, dc in next 5 chs, decrease, dc in next 5 chs; repeat from ★ across to last ch, 2 dc in last ch: 155 dc.
Note: Loop a short piece of yarn around any stitch to mark Row 1 as **right** side.
Row 2: Ch 3 **(counts as first dc, now and throughout)**, turn; dc in same st and in next 5 dc, decrease, dc in next 5 dc, ★ 3 dc in next dc, dc in next 5 dc, decrease, dc in next 5 dc; repeat from ★ across to last dc, 2 dc in last dc.

Row 3: Ch 3, turn; ★ † dc in same st and in next 5 dc changing to Lt Rose in last dc **(Fig. 24, page 143)**, skip next dc, work Popcorn in next dc changing to Dk Green, cut Lt Rose, skip next dc †, dc in next 6 dc changing to Lt Rose in last dc, work Popcorn in same st changing to Dk Green, cut Lt Rose; repeat from ★ 9 times **more**, then repeat from † to † once, dc in next 5 dc, 2 dc in last dc: 21 Popcorns.
Row 4: Ch 3, turn; dc in same st and in next 5 dc, decrease, dc in next 5 dc, ★ 3 dc in next Popcorn, dc in next 5 dc, decrease, dc in next 5 dc; repeat from ★ across to last dc, 2 dc in last dc: 155 dc.
Row 5: Ch 3, turn; dc in same st and in next 5 dc, decrease, dc in next 5 dc, ★ 3 dc in next dc, dc in next 5 dc, decrease, dc in next 5 dc; repeat from ★ across to last dc, 2 dc in last dc; finish off.
Row 6: With **wrong** side facing, join Med Rose with slip st in first dc; ch 3, dc in same st and in next 5 dc, decrease, dc in next 5 dc, ★ 3 dc in next dc, dc in next 5 dc, decrease, dc in next 5 dc; repeat from ★ across to last dc, 2 dc in last dc; finish off.
Row 7: With **right** side facing, join Lt Rose with slip st in first dc; ch 3, dc in same st and in next 5 dc, decrease, dc in next 5 dc, ★ 3 dc in next dc, dc in next 5 dc, decrease, dc in next 5 dc; repeat from ★ across to last dc, 2 dc in last dc.
Row 8: Ch 3, turn; dc in same st and in next 5 dc, decrease, dc in next 5 dc, ★ 3 dc in next dc, dc in next 5 dc, decrease, dc in next 5 dc; repeat from ★ across to last dc, 2 dc in last dc.
Row 9: Ch 3, turn; ★ † dc in same st and in next 5 dc changing to Dk Green in last dc, skip next dc, work Popcorn in next dc changing to Lt Rose, cut Dk Green, skip next dc †, dc in next 6 dc changing to Dk Green in last dc, work Popcorn in same st changing to Lt Rose, cut Dk Green; repeat from ★ 9 times **more**, then repeat from † to † once, dc in next 5 dc, 2 dc in last dc: 21 Popcorns.
Rows 10-12: Repeat Rows 4-6.
Rows 13 and 14: With Dk Green repeat Rows 7 and 8.
Rows 15-101: Repeat Rows 3-14, 7 times; then repeat Rows 3-5 once **more**.

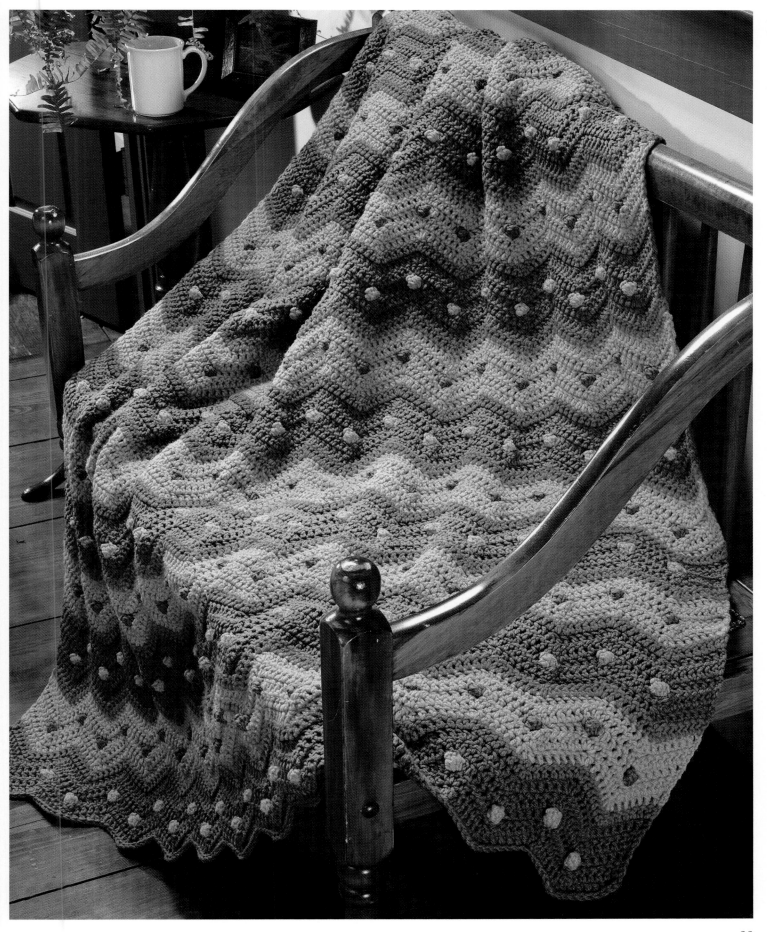

JEWELED DIAMONDS

Resplendent hues and distinctive patterning combine in this handsome variegated wrap. Worked with two strands of yarn and a jumbo hook, the afghan features three panels of texture-rich post stitches. Puff stitches form the diamond centers.

Finished Size: 48" x 61"

MATERIALS

Worsted Weight Yarn:

66 ounces, (1,870 grams, 3,830 yards)

Crochet hook, size P (10.00 mm) **or** size needed for gauge

Yarn needle

Entire Afghan is worked holding two strands of a variegated yarn together.

GAUGE: In pattern, 7 sts and 8 rows = 4"

Center = 12½" wide

Each Panel = 16" wide

Gauge Swatch: 4" square

Ch 8 **loosely**.

Row 1 (Right side)**:** Sc in second ch from hook and in each ch across: 7 sc.

Row 2: Ch 1, turn; sc in Front Loop Only of each sc across *(Fig. 21, page 142)*.

Row 3: Ch 1, turn; sc in both loops of each sc across.

Rows 4-8: Repeat Rows 2 and 3 twice, then repeat Row 2 once **more**.

Finish off.

STITCH GUIDE

FRONT POST DOUBLE CROCHET

  (abbreviated FPdc)

YO, insert hook from **front** to **back** around post of st indicated, YO and pull up a loop even with last st made *(Fig. 11, page 140)*, (YO and draw through 2 loops on hook) twice. Skip sc behind FPdc.

SPLIT FRONT POST DOUBLE CROCHET

  (abbreviated Split FPdc) (uses next 2 FPdc)

YO, insert hook from **front** to **back** around post of first FPdc one row **below** *(Fig. 9, page 140)*, YO and pull up a loop, YO and draw through 2 loops on hook, YO, insert hook from **front** to **back** around post of next FPdc one row **below**, YO and pull up a loop, YO and draw through 2 loops on hook, YO and draw through all 3 loops on hook. Skip sc behind Split FPdc.

PUFF STITCH (abbreviated Puff St)

YO, insert hook in free loop of sc one row or round **below** next sc *(Fig. 22a, page 142)*, YO and pull up a loop even with loop on hook, (YO, insert hook in same st, YO and pull up a loop even with loop on hook) twice, YO and draw through all 7 loops on hook, ch 1 to close. Skip sc behind Puff St *(Fig. 19, page 142)*.

PANEL (Make 3)
CENTER

Ch 24 **loosely**.

Row 1 (Wrong side)**:** Sc in second ch from hook and in each ch across: 23 sc.

Note: Loop a short piece of yarn around **back** of any stitch to mark **right** side and bottom edge.

Row 2: Ch 1, turn; sc in first 12 sc, place marker around last sc made for st placement, sc in each sc across.

Row 3: Ch 1, turn; sc in Front Loop Only of each sc across *(Fig. 21, page 142)*.

Row 4: Ch 1, turn; working in both loops, sc in first 10 sc, work FPdc around marked sc one row **below**, sc in next sc, work FPdc around same st as last FPdc, sc in last 10 sc; do **not** finish off.

Continued on page 106.

SCHOOL DAYS SILHOUETTES

Delightful silhouettes of school-yard playmates add charm to a snuggly throw. Worked in primary colors with a "built-in" fringe, the coverlet is highlighted with puffy white clusters that depict children as paper-doll cutouts.

Finished Size: 39" x 55"

MATERIALS

Worsted Weight Yarn:
   White - 22 ounces, (620 grams, 1,435 yards)
   Red - 10 ounces, (280 grams, 650 yards)
   Blue - 4 ounces, (110 grams, 260 yards)
   Green - 4 ounces, (110 grams, 260 yards)
Crochet hook, size I (5.50 mm) **or** size needed
   for gauge

GAUGE: Sc, (ch 1, sc) 7 times and 15 rows = 4"

Gauge Swatch: 4"w x 4"h
Ch 16.
Row 1: Sc in second ch from hook, (ch 1, skip next ch, sc in next ch) across: 8 sc and 7 ch-1 sps.
Rows 2-15: Ch 1, turn; sc in first sc, (ch 1, skip next ch, sc in next sc) across.
Finish off.

Each row is worked across length of Afghan. When joining yarn and finishing off, always leave an 8" length to be worked into fringe.

STITCH GUIDE

> **CLUSTER**
> Ch 3, ★ YO, insert hook in third ch from hook, YO and pull up a loop, YO and draw through 2 loops on hook; repeat from ★ 2 times **more**, YO and draw through all 4 loops on hook *(Figs. 16a & b, page 141)*.

With White, ch 208.
Row 1 (Wrong side)**:** Sc in second from hook, (ch 1, skip next ch, sc in next ch) across; finish off: 104 sc.
Note: Loop a short piece of yarn around the **back** of any stitch to mark last row as **right** side.
Row 2: With **right** side facing, join Red with sc in first sc *(see Joining With Sc, page 142)*; (ch 1, skip next ch, sc in next sc) across; finish off.

Row 3: With **wrong** side facing, join White with sc in first sc; (ch 1, skip next ch, sc in next st) 13 times, work Cluster, ch 1, skip next ch, skip next sc and next ch, sc in next st, ★ (ch 1, skip next ch, sc in next st) 23 times, work Cluster, ch 1, skip next ch, skip next sc and next ch, sc in next st; repeat from ★ 2 times **more**, (ch 1, skip next ch, sc in next sc) 13 times; finish off: 100 sc and 4 Clusters.
Row 4: With **right** side facing, join Blue with sc in first sc; ch 1, skip next ch, (sc in next sc, ch 1, skip next ch) 13 times, working **behind** next Cluster, dc in center sc of skipped sts one row **below** Cluster, ch 1, ★ (sc in next sc, ch 1, skip next ch) 24 times, working **behind** next Cluster, dc in center sc of skipped sts one row **below** Cluster, ch 1; repeat from ★ 2 times **more**, sc in next sc, (ch 1, skip next ch, sc in next sc) 13 times; finish off.
Row 5: With **wrong** side facing, join White with sc in first sc; (ch 1, skip next ch, sc in next st) 12 times, work Cluster, ch 1, skip next ch, skip next sc and next ch, sc in next st, ★ (ch 1, skip next ch, sc in next st) 23 times, work Cluster, ch 1, skip next ch, skip next sc and next ch, sc in next st; repeat from ★ 2 times **more**, (ch 1, skip next ch, sc in next sc) 14 times; finish off.
Row 6: With **right** side facing, join Red with sc in first sc; ch 1, skip next ch, (sc in next sc, ch 1, skip next ch) 14 times, working **behind** next Cluster, dc in center sc of skipped sts one row **below** Cluster, ch 1, ★ (sc in next sc, ch 1, skip next ch) 24 times, working **behind** next Cluster, dc in center sc of skipped sts one row **below** Cluster, ch 1; repeat from ★ 2 times **more**, sc in next sc, (ch 1, skip next ch, sc in next sc) 12 times; finish off.
Row 7: With **wrong** side facing, join White with sc in first sc; (ch 1, skip next ch, sc in next st) 11 times, work Cluster, ch 1, skip next ch, skip next sc and next ch, sc in next st, ★ (ch 1, skip next ch, sc in next st) 23 times, work Cluster, ch 1, skip next ch, skip next sc and next ch, sc in next st; repeat from ★ 2 times **more**, (ch 1, skip next ch, sc in next sc) 15 times; finish off.

Continued on page 104.

Row 8: With **right** side facing, join Green with sc in first sc; ch 1, skip next ch, (sc in next sc, ch 1, skip next ch) 15 times, working **behind** next Cluster, dc in center sc of skipped sts one row **below** Cluster, ch 1, ★ (sc in next sc, ch 1, skip next ch) 24 times, working **behind** next Cluster, dc in center sc of skipped sts one row **below** Cluster, ch 1; repeat from ★ 2 times **more**, sc in next sc, (ch 1, skip next ch, sc in next sc) 11 times; finish off.

Row 9: With **wrong** side facing, join White with sc in first sc; (ch 1, skip next ch, sc in next st) 10 times, work Cluster, ch 1, skip next ch, skip next sc and next ch, sc in next dc, ★ (ch 1, skip next ch, sc in next st) 23 times, work Cluster, ch 1, skip next ch, skip next sc and next ch, sc in next dc; repeat from ★ 2 times **more**, (ch 1, skip next ch, sc in next st) 16 times; finish off.

Row 10: With **right** side facing, join Red with sc in first sc; ch 1, skip next ch, (sc in next st, ch 1, skip next ch) 16 times, working **behind** next Cluster, dc in center sc of skipped sts one row **below** Cluster, ch 1, ★ (sc in next sc, ch 1, skip next ch) 24 times, working **behind** next Cluster, dc in center sc of skipped sts one row **below** Cluster, ch 1; repeat from ★ 2 times **more**, sc in next sc, (ch 1, skip next ch, sc in next st) 10 times; finish off.

Row 11: With **wrong** side facing, join White with sc in first sc; ★ (ch 1, skip next ch, sc in next st) 4 times, (work Cluster, ch 1, skip next ch, skip next sc and next ch, sc in next st) twice, ch 1, skip next ch, sc in next sc, (work Cluster, ch 1, skip next ch, skip next sc and next ch, sc in next st) 4 times, (ch 1, skip next ch, sc in next st) 6 times, work Cluster, ch 1, skip next ch, skip next sc and next ch, sc in next sc; repeat from ★ 3 times **more**, (ch 1, skip next ch, sc in next sc) 3 times; finish off.

Row 12: With **right** side facing, join Blue with sc in first sc; ch 1, skip next ch, (sc in next sc, ch 1, skip next ch) 3 times, ★ † working **behind** next Cluster, dc in center st of skipped sts one row **below** Cluster, ch 1, (sc in next sc, ch 1, skip next ch) 7 times, working **behind** next Cluster, dc in center st of skipped sts one row **below** Cluster, ch 1, (sc in next sc, ch 1, skip next ch, working **behind** next Cluster, dc in center st of skipped sts one row **below** Cluster, ch 1) 3 times, (sc in next sc, ch 1, skip next ch) twice, working **behind** next Cluster, dc in center st of skipped sts one row **below** Cluster, ch 1, sc in next sc, ch 1, working **behind** next Cluster, dc in center sc of skipped sts one row **below** Cluster, ch 1 †, (sc in next sc, ch 1, skip next ch) 5 times; repeat from ★ 2 times **more**, then repeat from † to † once, sc in next sc, (ch 1, skip next ch, sc in next sc) 4 times; finish off.

Row 13: With **wrong** side facing, join White with sc in first sc; (ch 1, skip next ch, sc in next st) 3 times, ★ (work Cluster, ch 1, skip next ch, skip next st and next ch, sc in next st) 11 times, (ch 1, skip next ch, sc in next st) 3 times; repeat from ★ across; finish off.

Row 14: With **right** side facing, join Red with sc in first sc; ch 1, skip next ch, (sc in next sc, ch 1, skip next ch) 3 times, ★ † working **behind** next Cluster, dc in center dc of skipped sts one row **below** Cluster, ch 1, (sc in next sc, ch 1, skip next ch, working **behind** next Cluster, dc in center st of skipped sts one row **below** Cluster, ch 1) 10 times †, (sc in next st, ch 1, skip next ch) 4 times; repeat from ★ 2 times **more**, then repeat from † to † once, sc in next sc, (ch 1, skip next ch, sc in next sc) 3 times; finish off.

Row 15: Repeat Row 13.

Row 16: With Green, repeat Row 14.

Row 17: Repeat Row 11.

Row 18: With Red, repeat Row 12.

Row 19: Repeat Row 9.

Row 20: With Blue, repeat Row 10.

Row 21: Repeat Row 7.

Row 22: With Red, repeat Row 8.

Row 23: Repeat Row 5.

Row 24: With Green, repeat Row 6.

Row 25: Repeat Row 3.

Row 26: With Red, repeat Row 4.

Rows 27-30: Repeat Rows 3-6.

Row 31: With **wrong** side facing, join White with sc in first sc; (ch 1, skip next ch, sc in next sc) 11 times, ★ † work Cluster, ch 1, skip next ch, skip next sc and next ch, sc in next st, (ch 1, skip next ch, sc in next st) twice, work Cluster, ch 1, skip next ch, skip next sc and next ch, sc in next st †, (ch 1, skip next ch, sc in next st) 19 times; repeat from ★ 2 times **more**, then repeat from † to † once, (ch 1, skip next ch, sc in next sc) 11 times; finish off.

Row 32: With **right** side facing, join Green with sc in first sc; ch 1, skip next ch, (sc in next sc, ch 1, skip next ch) 11 times, ★ † working **behind** next Cluster, dc in center sc of skipped sts one row **below** Cluster, ch 1, (sc in next sc, ch 1, skip next ch) 3 times, working **behind** next Cluster, dc in center sc of skipped sts one row **below** Cluster, ch 1 †, (sc in next sc, ch 1, skip next ch) 20 times; repeat from ★ 2 times **more**, then repeat from † to † once, sc in next sc, (ch 1, skip next ch, sc in next sc) 11 times; finish off.

Row 33: With **wrong** side facing, join White with sc in first sc; (ch 1, skip next ch, sc in next st) 10 times, ★ † work Cluster, ch 1, skip next ch, skip next sc and next ch, sc in next dc, (ch 1, skip next ch, sc in next st) twice, (work Cluster, ch 1, skip next ch, skip next sc and next ch, sc in next st) twice †, (ch 1, skip next ch, sc in next st) 17 times; repeat from ★ 2 times **more**, then repeat from † to † once, (ch 1, skip next ch, sc in next st) 10 times; finish off.

Row 34: With **right** side facing, join Red with sc in first sc; ch 1, skip next ch, (sc in next sc, ch 1, skip next ch) 10 times, ★ † working **behind** next Cluster, dc in center sc of skipped sts one row **below** Cluster, ch 1, sc in next sc, ch 1, working **behind** next Cluster, dc in center sc of skipped sts one row **below** Cluster, ch 1, (sc in next sc, ch 1, skip next ch) 3 times, working **behind** next Cluster, dc in center sc of skipped sts one row **below** Cluster, ch 1 †, (sc in next st, ch 1, skip next ch) 18 times; repeat from ★ 2 times **more**, then repeat from † to † once, sc in next sc, (ch 1, skip next ch, sc in next sc) 10 times; finish off.

Row 35: With **wrong** side facing, join White with sc in first sc; (ch 1, skip next ch, sc in next st) 4 times, ★ † (work Cluster, ch 1, skip next ch, skip next sc and next ch, sc in next sc) twice, ch 1, skip next ch, sc in next sc, (work Cluster, ch 1, skip next ch, skip next st and next ch, sc in next st) 5 times, (ch 1, skip next ch, sc in next st) 4 times, work Cluster, ch 1, skip next ch, skip next st and next ch, sc in next sc †, (ch 1, skip next ch, sc in next st) 4 times; repeat from ★ 2 times **more**, then repeat from † to † once, (ch 1, skip next ch, sc in next sc) 3 times; finish off.

Row 36: With **right** side facing, join Blue with sc in first sc; ch 1, skip next ch, (sc in next sc, ch 1, skip next ch) 3 times, ★ † working **behind** next Cluster, dc in center st of skipped sts one row **below** Cluster, ch 1, (sc in next sc, ch 1, skip next ch) 5 times, working **behind** next Cluster, dc in center sc of skipped sts one row **below** Cluster, ch 1, (sc in next sc, ch 1, working **behind** next Cluster, dc in center st of skipped sts one row **below** Cluster, ch 1) 4 times, (sc in next sc, ch 1, skip next ch) twice, working **behind** next Cluster, dc in center sc of skipped sts one row **below** Cluster, ch 1, sc in next sc, ch 1, working **behind** next Cluster, dc in center sc of skipped sts one row **below** Cluster, ch 1 †, (sc in next sc, ch 1, skip next ch) 5 times; repeat from ★ 2 times **more**, then repeat from † to † once, sc in next sc, (ch 1, skip next ch, sc in next sc) 4 times; finish off.

Rows 37-39: Repeat Rows 13 and 14 once, then repeat Row 13 once **more**.

Row 40: With Green, repeat Row 14.

Row 41: Repeat Row 35.

Row 42: With Red, repeat Row 36.

Row 43: Repeat Row 33.

Row 44: With Blue, repeat Row 34.

Row 45: Repeat Row 31.

Row 46: With Red, repeat Row 32.

Row 47: Repeat Row 5.

Row 48: With Green, repeat Row 6.

Row 49: Repeat Row 3.

Row 50: With Red, repeat Row 4.

Rows 51-146: Repeat Rows 3-50 twice.

Row 147: With **wrong** side facing, join White with sc in first sc; ★ ch 1, skip next ch, sc in next st; repeat from ★ across; finish off.

Using one 17" length of corresponding color, add additional fringe in each row across short edges of Afghan *(Figs. 28b & d, page 143)*.

Row 5: Ch 1, turn; sc in Front Loop Only of each st across.

Row 6: Ch 1, turn; working in both loops, sc in first 9 sc, work FPdc around first FPdc one row **below**, sc in next 3 sc, work FPdc around next FPdc one row **below**, sc in last 9 sc.

Row 7: Ch 1, turn; sc in Front Loop Only of each st across.

Row 8: Ch 1, turn; working in both loops, sc in first 8 sc, work FPdc around first FPdc one row **below**, sc in next 5 sc, work FPdc around next FPdc one row **below**, sc in last 8 sc.

Row 9: Ch 1, turn; sc in Front Loop Only of each st across.

Row 10: Ch 1, turn; working in both loops, sc in first 7 sc, work FPdc around first FPdc one row **below**, sc in next 3 sc, work Puff St, sc in next 3 sc, work FPdc around next FPdc one row **below**, sc in last 7 sc.

Row 11: Ch 1, turn; working in Front Loops Only, sc in first 11 sts, sc in next Puff St and in last 11 sts.

Row 12: Ch 1, turn; working in both loops, sc in first 6 sc, work FPdc around first FPdc one row **below**, sc in next 3 sc, work Puff St, sc in next sc, work Puff St, sc in next 3 sc, work FPdc around next FPdc one row **below**, sc in last 6 sc.

Row 13: Ch 1, turn; working in Front Loops Only, sc in first 10 sts, sc in next Puff St and in next sc, sc in next Puff St and in last 10 sts.

Row 14: Ch 1, turn; working in both loops, sc in first 5 sc, work FPdc around first FPdc one row **below**, sc in next 3 sc, work Puff St, (sc in next sc, work Puff St) twice, sc in next 3 sc, work FPdc around next FPdc one row **below**, sc in last 5 sc.

Row 15: Ch 1, turn; working in Front Loops Only, sc in first 9 sts and in next Puff St, (sc in next sc and in next Puff St) twice, sc in last 9 sts.

Row 16: Ch 1, turn; working in both loops, sc in first 4 sc, work FPdc around first FPdc one row **below**, sc in next 3 sc, work Puff St, (sc in next sc, work Puff St) 3 times, sc in next 3 sc, work FPdc around next FPdc one row **below**, sc in last 4 sc.

Row 17: Ch 1, turn; working in Front Loops Only, sc in first 8 sts and in next Puff St, (sc in next sc and in next Puff St) 3 times, sc in last 8 sts.

Row 18: Ch 1, turn; working in both loops, sc in first 5 sc, work FPdc around first FPdc one row **below**, sc in next 3 sc, work Puff St, (sc in next sc, work Puff St) twice, sc in next 3 sc, work FPdc around next FPdc one row **below**, sc in last 5 sc.

Row 19: Ch 1, turn; working in Front Loops Only, sc in first 9 sts and in next Puff St, (sc in next sc and in next Puff St) twice, sc in last 9 sts.

Row 20: Ch 1, turn; working in both loops, sc in first 6 sc, work FPdc around first FPdc one row **below**, sc in next 3 sc, work Puff St, sc in next sc, work Puff St, sc in next 3 sc, work FPdc around next FPdc one row **below**, sc in last 6 sc.

Row 21: Ch 1, turn; working in Front Loops Only, sc in first 10 sts, sc in next Puff St and in next sc, sc in next Puff St and in last 10 sts.

Row 22: Ch 1, turn; working in both loops, sc in first 7 sc, work FPdc around first FPdc one row **below**, sc in next 3 sc, work Puff St, sc in next 3 sc, work FPdc around next FPdc one row **below**, sc in last 7 sc.

Row 23: Ch 1, turn; working in Front Loops Only, sc in first 11 sts, sc in next Puff St and in last 11 sts.

Row 24: Ch 1, turn; working in both loops, sc in first 8 sc, work FPdc around first FPdc one row **below**, sc in next 5 sc, work FPdc around next FPdc one row **below**, sc in last 8 sc.

Row 25: Ch 1, turn; sc in Front Loop Only of each st across.

Row 26: Ch 1, turn; working in both loops, sc in first 9 sc, work FPdc around first FPdc one row **below**, sc in next 3 sc, work FPdc around next FPdc one row **below**, sc in last 9 sc.

Row 27: Ch 1, turn; sc in Front Loop Only of each st across.
Row 28: Ch 1, turn; working in both loops, sc in first 10 sc, work FPdc around first FPdc one row **below**, sc in next sc, work FPdc around next FPdc one row **below**, sc in last 10 sc.
Row 29: Ch 1, turn; sc in Front Loop Only of each st across.
Row 30: Ch 1, turn; working in both loops, sc in first 11 sc, work Split FPdc, sc in last 11 sc.
Row 31: Ch 1, turn; sc in Front Loop Only of each st across.
Row 32: Ch 1, turn; working in both loops, sc in first 10 sc, work FPdc around next Split FPdc one row **below**, sc in next sc, work FPdc around same st as last FPdc, sc in last 10 sc.
Rows 33-115: Repeat Rows 5-32 twice, then repeat Rows 5-31 once **more**; do **not** finish off.

BORDER

Rnd 1: Ch 1, turn; working in both loops, 2 sc in first sc, sc in each sc across to last sc, 3 sc in last sc; † working in end of rows, skip first row, sc in each row across to last row, skip last row †; working in free loops of beginning ch *(Fig. 22b, page 142)*, 3 sc in ch at base of first sc, sc in each ch across to last ch, 3 sc in last ch; repeat from † to † once, sc in same st as first sc; join with slip st to Back Loop Only of first sc: 280 sc.

Rnd 2: Ch 1, turn; working in Front Loops Only, sc in same st and in each sc across to center sc of next corner 3-sc group, ★ 3 sc in center sc, sc in each sc across to center sc of next corner 3-sc group; repeat from ★ 2 times **more**, 2 sc in same st as first sc; join with slip st to **both** loops of first sc: 288 sc.

Rnd 3: Ch 1, turn; working in both loops, 3 sc in next sc, work Puff St, ★ (sc in next 3 sc, work Puff St) across to center sc of next corner 3-sc group, 3 sc in center sc, work Puff St in same st as last Puff St; repeat from ★ 2 times **more**, sc in next 3 sc, (work Puff St, sc in next 3 sc) across to last sc, work Puff St in same st as first Puff St; join with slip st to Back Loop Only of first sc: 74 Puff Sts and 222 sc.

Rnd 4: Ch 1, turn; working in Front Loops Only, sc in same st, ★ sc in each sc and in each Puff St across to center sc of next corner 3-sc group, 3 sc in center sc; repeat from ★ around; join with slip st to **both** loops of first sc, finish off.

ASSEMBLY

Place two Panels with **wrong** sides together and bottom edges at the same end. Working through inside loops only, whipstitch Panels together *(Fig. 27a, page 143)*, beginning in center sc of first corner 3-sc group and ending in center sc of next corner 3-sc group.

FALL FANCY

Ablaze with autumn color, this comfy creation sings with the excitement of cool-weather days! The quick and simple wrap is crocheted with a jumbo hook while holding four strands of black and variegated yarns.

Finished Size: 53" x 67"

MATERIALS
Worsted Weight Yarn:
Variegated - 63 ounces,
(1,790 grams, 3,655 yards)
Black - 38 ounces,
(1,080 grams, 2,145 yards)
Crochet hook, size Q (15.00 mm)

Each row is worked across length of Afghan holding four strands of yarn together.

GAUGE: 6 sc = 4½"; 8 rows = 5½"

Gauge Swatch: 4½"w x 5½"h
Ch 7 **loosely**.
Row 1: Sc in second ch from hook and in each ch across: 6 sc.
Rows 2-8: Ch 1, turn; sc in each sc across.
Finish off.

STITCH GUIDE

> **BEGINNING DECREASE**
> Pull up a loop in first 2 sc, YO and draw through all 3 loops on hook **(counts as one sc)**.
> **DECREASE**
> Pull up a loop in last 2 sc, YO and draw through all 3 loops on hook **(counts as one sc)**.

Holding 2 strands each of Variegated and Black together, ch 83 **loosely**.
Row 1 (Right side)**:** Sc in back ridge of second ch from hook *(Fig. 2b, page 139)* and each ch across: 82 sc.
Rows 2-4: Ch 1, turn; 2 sc in first sc, sc in each sc across to last sc, 2 sc in last sc: 88 sc.
Row 5: Ch 1, turn; 2 sc in first sc, sc in each sc across to last sc, 2 sc in last sc changing to 4 strands of Black in last sc *(Fig. 24, page 143)*: 90 sc.
Row 6: Ch 2, turn; skip first sc, (sc, dc) in next sc, ★ skip next sc, (sc, dc) in next sc; repeat from ★ across changing to 4 strands of Variegated in last dc: 45 dc and 45 sc.
Row 7: Ch 1, turn; sc in each dc and in each sc across: 90 sc.
Rows 8-10: Ch 1, turn; work beginning decrease, sc in each sc across to last 2 sc, decrease: 84 sc.
Row 11: Ch 1, turn; work beginning decrease, sc in each sc across to last 2 sc, decrease changing to 2 strands each of Variegated and Black: 82 sc.
Row 12: Ch 1, turn; sc in each sc across.
Rows 13-76: Repeat Rows 2-12, 5 times; then repeat Rows 2-10 once **more**.
Row 77: Ch 1, turn; work beginning decrease, sc in each sc across to last 2 sc, decrease; finish off.

BRILLIANT MUMS

Fall's favorite mums inspired these floral squares worked in seven shades. Rings of popcorn "petals" surround gold centers, and puffy popcorn stitches edge the floral throw.

Finished Size: 45" x 61"

MATERIALS

Note: For our Afghan, we used light, medium, and dark shades of Rose, Purple, Brown, Gold, Mauve, Peach, and Rust for the flowers.

Worsted Weight Yarn:
Black - 31 ounces, (880 grams, 2,125 yards)
Gold - 2 ounces, (60 grams, 135 yards)
Light shades - 3¹/₂ ounces
total,(100 grams, 240 yards)
Medium shades - 7 ounces
total,(200 grams, 480 yards)
Dark shades - 11 ounces
total,(310 grams, 755 yards)
Crochet hook, size H (5.00 mm) **or** size needed for gauge
Yarn needle

GAUGE: Each Square = 8"

Gauge Swatch: 3" in diameter
Work same as Square through Rnd 2.

STITCH GUIDE

BEGINNING POPCORN
Ch 3 **(counts as first dc, now and throughout)**, 3 dc in sp indicated, drop loop from hook, insert hook in first dc of 4-dc group, hook dropped loop and draw through *(Fig. 18, page 141)*.
POPCORN
4 Dc in sp indicated, drop loop from hook, insert hook in first dc of 4-dc group, hook dropped loop and draw through.

SQUARE (Make 35, 5 of each color family)

With Gold, ch 6; join with slip st to form a ring.
Rnd 1 (Right side)**:** Work Beginning Popcorn in ring, ch 3, (work Popcorn in ring, ch 3) 3 times; join with slip st to top of Beginning Popcorn, finish off: 4 ch-3 sps.
Rnd 2: With **right** side facing, join Light Shade with slip st in first ch-3 sp; work (Beginning Popcorn, ch 3, Popcorn) in same sp, ch 3, (work Popcorn, ch 3) twice in each ch-3 sp around; join with slip st to top of Beginning Popcorn, finish off: 8 ch-3 sps.
Rnd 3: With Medium Shade, repeat Rnd 2: 16 ch-3 sps.
Rnd 4: With Dark Shade, repeat Rnd 2: 32 ch-3 sps.
Rnd 5: With **right** side facing, join Black with slip st in first ch-3 sp; ch 3, (dc, ch 2, 2 dc) in same sp, ★ † 2 dc in next ch-3 sp, 2 hdc in next ch-3 sp, 2 sc in next ch-3 sp, 3 sc in next ch-3 sp, 2 sc in next ch-3 sp, 2 hdc in next ch-3 sp, 2 dc in next ch-3 sp †, (2 dc, ch 2, 2 dc) in next ch-3 sp; repeat from ★ 2 times **more**, then repeat from † to † once; join with slip st to first dc, do **not** finish off: 76 sts and 4 ch-2 sps.
Rnd 6: Ch 3, dc in next dc, ★ † (2 dc, ch 2, 2 dc) in next corner ch-2 sp, dc in next 2 dc, hdc in next 2 dc, sc in next 11 sts, hdc in next 2 dc †, dc in next 2 dc; repeat from ★ 2 times **more**, then repeat from † to † once; join with slip st to first dc: 92 sts and 4 ch-2 sps.
Rnd 7: Ch 3, dc in next dc and in each st around working (2 dc, ch 2, 2 dc) in each corner ch-2 sp; join with slip st to first dc, finish off: 108 dc and 4 ch-2 sps.

ASSEMBLY

With Black and working through inside loops only, whipstitch Squares together *(Fig. 27a, page 143)*, forming 5 vertical strips of 7 Squares each, beginning in second ch of first corner ch-2 and ending in first ch of next corner ch-2; whipstitch strips together in same manner.

EDGING

Rnd 1: With **right** side facing, join Black with slip st in any corner ch-2 sp; ch 5 **(counts as first dc plus ch 2)**, dc in same sp and in next dc, ★ † ch 1, (skip next dc, dc in next 2 dc, ch 1) 8 times, skip next dc, dc in next dc, [dc in next sp, ch 1, dc in next sp and in next dc, ch 1, (skip next dc, dc in next 2 dc, ch 1) 8 times, skip next dc, dc in next dc] across to next corner ch-2 sp †, (dc, ch 2, dc) in corner ch-2 sp, dc in next dc; repeat from ★ 2 times **more**, then repeat from † to † once; join with slip st to first dc: 240 sps.

Rnds 2-4: Slip st in first corner sp, work (Beginning Popcorn, ch 3, Popcorn) in same sp, ch 3, (work Popcorn in next sp, ch 3) across to next corner sp, ★ work (Popcorn, ch 3) twice in corner sp, (work Popcorn in next sp, ch 3) across to next corner sp; repeat from ★ 2 times **more**; join with slip st to top of Beginning Popcorn: 252 ch-3 sps.

Rnd 5: Ch 2, sc in next ch-3 sp, ch 2, ★ slip st in next Popcorn, ch 2, sc in next ch-3 sp, ch 2; repeat from ★ around; join with slip st to first slip st, finish off.

HARVEST MIST

As light and airy as mist in an autumn field, this soft cover-up brings to mind images of harvesttime frost. Quickly worked using double strands of brushed acrylic yarn, it has pretty crisscross stitch patterns and cable stitch edging.

Finished Size: 43" x 62"

MATERIALS
Worsted Weight Brushed Acrylic Yarn:
    39 ounces, (1,110 grams, 3,010 yards)
Crochet hook, size Q (15.00 mm)

Entire Afghan is worked holding two strands of yarn together.

GAUGE: In pattern, 15 sts = 7"; 10 rows = 7¹/₂"

Gauge Swatch: 8" square
Ch 18 **loosely**.
Work same as Afghan Body for 11 rows.
Finish off.

STITCH GUIDE

CABLE (uses next 3 sc)
Ch 3 **loosely**, skip next 2 sc, sc in next sc, **turn**; sc in next 3 chs *(Fig. 1a)*, slip st in next sc (sc made **before** ch-3) *(Fig. 1b)*.

Fig. 1a   **Fig. 1b**

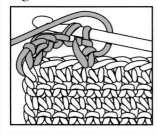 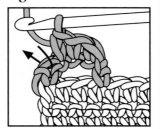

AFGHAN BODY
Ch 90 **loosely**.

Row 1: Sc in second ch from hook and in each ch across: 89 sc.

Row 2 (Right side)**:** Ch 3 **(counts as first dc, now and throughout)**, turn; ★ skip next 2 sc, dc in next sc, ch 1, working **around** last dc made, dc in first skipped sc; repeat from ★ across to last sc, dc in last sc: 29 ch-1 sps.

Row 3: Ch 1, turn; sc in each dc and in each ch-1 sp across: 89 sc.

Rows 4-81: Repeat Rows 2 and 3, 39 times; at end of Row 81, do **not** finish off.

EDGING

Rnd 1: Ch 1, turn; 3 sc in same st, skip next sc, sc in each sc across to last sc, 3 sc in last sc; working in end of rows, skip first row, 2 sc in next row, (sc in next row, 2 sc in next row) across to last row, skip last row; working in free loops of beginning ch *(Fig. 22b, page 142)*, 3 sc in ch at base of first sc, sc in each ch across to last ch, 3 sc in last ch; working in end of rows, skip first row, 2 sc in next row, (sc in next row, 2 sc in next row) across to last row, skip last row; join with slip st to first sc: 423 sc.

Rnd 2: Ch 1, do **not** turn; sc in same st, ★ work Cable, **turn**; working **behind** Cable, sc in 2 skipped sc *(Fig. 2)*; repeat from ★ around to last 2 sc, ch 3 **loosely**, skip last 2 sc, slip st in first sc, **turn**; sc in next 3 chs, slip st in next sc (sc made **before** ch-3), **turn**; working **behind** Cable, sc in 2 skipped sc; join with slip st to last slip st made.

Fig. 2

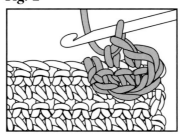

Rnd 3: Ch 1, turn; working in unworked sc in **front** of Cables, (2 sc in next sc, sc in next sc) around; join with slip st to first sc, finish off.

AUTUMN POPS

Sure to take the chill off moonlit evenings, this cozy fall warmer splashes variegated circles and squares against midnight black. Made with bright popcorn stitches, these geometric features add attractive texture.

Finished Size: 44" x 60"

MATERIALS
   Worsted Weight Yarn:
      Black - 25¼ ounces, (720 grams, 1,425 yards)
      Variegated - 18½ ounces, (530 grams, 1,075 yards)
   Crochet hook, size H (5.00 mm) **or** size needed
      for gauge
   Yarn needle

GAUGE: Each Square = 8¼"

Gauge Swatch: 3¼" diameter
Work same as Square through Rnd 3.

STITCH GUIDE

POPCORN
3 Dc in st or sp indicated, drop loop from hook, insert hook in first dc of 3-dc group, hook dropped loop and pull through *(Fig. 18, page 141)*, ch 1 to close Popcorn.

SQUARE (Make 35)
With Black, ch 4; join with slip st to form a ring.
Rnd 1 (Right side)**:** Ch 3 **(counts as first dc, now and throughout)**, 15 dc in ring; join with slip st to first dc, finish off: 16 dc.
Note: Loop a short piece of yarn around any stitch to mark Rnd 1 as **right** side.
Rnd 2: With **right** side facing, join Variegated with sc in any dc *(see Joining With Sc, page 142)*; sc in same st, work Popcorn in next dc, (2 sc in next dc, work Popcorn in next dc) around; join with slip st to first sc: 8 Popcorns and 16 sc.
Rnd 3: Ch 1, sc in same st, ch 3, sc in next sc, ch 3, skip next Popcorn, ★ (sc in next sc, ch 3) twice, skip next Popcorn; repeat from ★ around; join with slip st to first sc, finish off: 16 ch-3 sps.
Begin working in rows.
Row 1: With **right** side facing, join Black with slip st in any ch-3 sp; ch 7 **loosely**, hdc in fourth ch from hook **(3 skipped chs count as first dc)** and in next ch, sc in last 2 chs, slip st in same sp as joining.

Row 2: Ch 1, turn; working in Front Loops Only *(Fig. 21, page 142)*, sc in next 2 sc, hdc in next 2 hdc, dc in last dc.
Row 3: Ch 3, turn; working in Front Loops Only, hdc in next 2 hdc, sc in next 2 sc, slip st in next ch-3 sp on Rnd 3.
Row 4: Ch 1, turn; working in Front Loops Only, sc in next 2 sc, hdc in next 2 hdc, dc in last dc.
Rows 5-32: Repeat Rows 3 and 4, 14 times.
Finish off, leaving a long end for sewing.
Thread yarn needle with long end. With **right** side facing, sew free loops of beginning ch *(Fig. 22b, page 142)* to Front Loop Only of each st across Row 32.
Begin working in rnds.
Rnd 1: With **right** side facing and working in end of rows, join Variegated with sc in any row; 2 sc in same row, work Popcorn in next row, (3 sc in next row, work Popcorn in next row) around; join with slip st to first sc, finish off: 16 Popcorns and 48 sc.
Rnd 2: With **right** side facing, join Black with slip st in center sc of any 3-sc group; ch 7, (dtr, ch 3, tr) in same st, ★ † ch 2, (dc, ch 2) twice in center sc of next 3-sc group, (sc, ch 1, sc) in center sc of next 3-sc group, ch 2, (dc, ch 2) twice in center sc of next 3-sc group †, (tr, ch 3, dtr, ch 3, tr) in center sc of next 3-sc group; repeat from ★ 2 times **more**, then repeat from † to † once; join with slip st to fourth ch of beginning ch-7: 36 sts and 36 sps.
Rnd 3: Ch 1, sc in same st, ★ † 3 sc in next ch-3 sp, 3 sc in next dtr and in next ch-3 sp, sc in next tr, 2 sc in next ch-2 sp, sc in next dc, (sc in next sp and in next st) 5 times, 2 sc in next ch-2 sp †, sc in next tr; repeat from ★ 2 times **more**, then repeat from † to † once; join with slip st to first sc, finish off: 104 sc.
Rnd 4: With **right** side facing and working in Back Loops Only, join Variegated with sc in any sc; sc in each sc around working 3 sc in center sc of each corner 3-sc group; join with slip st to first sc, finish off: 112 sc.

ASSEMBLY
With Variegated and working through both loops, whipstitch Squares together *(Fig. 27b, page 143)*, forming 5 vertical strips of 7 Squares each, beginning in center sc of first corner 3-sc group and ending in center sc of next corner 3-sc group; whipstitch strips together in same manner.

EDGING

Rnd 1: With **right** side facing and working in both loops, join Variegated with sc in center sc of top right corner 3-sc group; sc in same st and in next 27 sc, † (sc in next joining and in next 27 sc) 4 times, 3 sc in center sc of next corner 3-sc group, skip next sc, sc in next 26 sc, (sc next joining and in next 27 sc) 6 times †, 3 sc in center sc of next corner 3-sc group, sc in next 27 sc, repeat from † to † once, sc in same st as first sc; join with slip st to first sc: 678 sc.

Rnd 2: Ch 1, 3 sc in same st, work Popcorn in next sc, ★ (sc in next sc, ch 4, skip next 2 sc, sc in next sc, work Popcorn in next sc) across to center sc of next corner 3-sc group, 3 sc in center sc, work Popcorn in next sc; repeat from ★ 2 times **more**, (sc in next sc, ch 4, skip next 2 sc, sc in next sc, work Popcorn in next sc) across; join with slip st to first sc, finish off: 138 Popcorns and 134 ch-4 sps.

Rnd 3: With **right** side facing, join Black with slip st in center sc of any corner 3-sc group; ★ † ch 2, (dc, ch 1, dc) in next Popcorn, ch 2, [slip st in next ch-4 sp, ch 2, (dc, ch 1, dc) in next Popcorn, ch 2] across to next corner 3-sc group, skip next sc †, slip st in next sc; repeat from ★ 2 times **more**, then repeat from † to † once; join with slip st to first slip st, finish off.

WOODLAND SHADOWS

A woodland walk on a brisk, sunny day reveals patterns of sunlight and shadow like those on this toasty throw. The ridges on the soothing ripple are created with front post stitches.

Finished Size: 48" x 60"

MATERIALS

Worsted Weight Yarn:
Grey - 38 ounces,
(1,080 grams, 2,390 yards)
Green - 19 ounces,
(540 grams, 1,195 yards)
Natural - 18 ounces,
(510 grams, 1,130 yards)
Crochet hook, size I (5.50 mm) **or** size
needed for gauge

GAUGE: Each repeat from point to point
and 10 rows = 4"

Gauge Swatch: 8"w x 4"h
Ch 37 **loosely**.
Work same as Afghan for 10 rows.
Finish off.

STITCH GUIDE

FRONT POST DOUBLE CROCHET (abbreviated FPdc)
YO, insert hook from **front** to **back** around post of st indicated, YO and pull up a loop **(Fig. 11, page 140)**, (YO and draw through 2 loops on hook) twice.

COLOR SEQUENCE
4 Rows **each**: Green **(Fig. 24, page 143)**, ★ Grey, Natural, Grey, Green; repeat from ★ throughout.

With Green, ch 217 **loosely**.
Row 1: Dc in fourth ch from hook and in next 7 chs, ch 3, dc in next 8 chs, ★ skip next 2 chs, dc in next 8 chs, ch 3, dc in next 8 chs; repeat from ★ across: 193 sts and 12 ch-3 sps.
Row 2 (Right side)**:** Ch 2, turn; work FPdc around each of next 7 dc, (dc, ch 1, dc) in next ch-3 sp, ★ work FPdc around each of next 7 dc, skip next 2 dc, work FPdc around each of next 7 dc, (dc, ch 1, dc) in next ch-3 sp; repeat from ★ 10 times **more**, work FPdc around each of next 6 dc, skip next dc, work FPdc around next dc, leave last st unworked: 193 sts and 12 ch-1 sps.
Row 3: Ch 2, turn; work FPdc around each of next 7 sts, (dc, ch 1, dc) in next ch-1 sp, ★ work FPdc around each of next 7 sts, skip next 2 FPdc, work FPdc around each of next 7 sts, (dc, ch 1, dc) in next ch-1 sp; repeat from ★ 10 times **more**, work FPdc around each of next 6 sts, skip next FPdc, work FPdc around next FPdc, leave last st unworked.
Repeat Row 3 until Afghan measures approximately 60" from beginning ch, ending by working 4 rows Green; finish off.

COUNTRY CASUAL

Wrap yourself in the country comfort of denim and calico! Worked holding double strands of yarn, the homey blanket features an appealing border and an interesting arrangement of rectangles set on the diagonal.

Finished Size: 52" x 68"

MATERIALS
Worsted Weight Yarn:
   Blue - 43 ounces, (1,220 grams, 2,330 yards)
   Variegated - 41 ounces, (1,160 grams, 2,380 yards)
Crochet hook, size P (10.00 mm) **or** size needed
   for gauge

Each row is worked across length of Afghan holding two strands of yarn together.

GAUGE: In pattern, 2 repeats = 4"; 2 rows = 1³/₄"

Gauge Swatch: 6³/₄"w x 3¹/₂"h
Row 1: ★ Ch 4, 3 dc in fourth ch from hook **(3 skipped chs count as first dc)**; repeat from ★ 2 times **more**: 12 dc.
Rows 2-4: Ch 4, turn; 3 dc in fourth ch from hook, skip first 3 dc, slip st in next dc, ★ ch 3 **(counts as first dc)**, 3 dc around post of same dc, skip next 3 dc, slip st in next dc; repeat from ★ once **more**.
Finish off.

AFGHAN BODY
Row 1 (Right side)**:** With Variegated, ★ ch 4, 3 dc in fourth ch from hook **(3 skipped chs count as first dc, now and throughout)**; repeat from ★ 31 times **more**: 128 dc.
Note: Loop a short piece of yarn around any stitch to mark Row 1 as **right** side.
Row 2: Ch 4, turn; 3 dc in fourth ch from hook, place marker in same ch for st placement, skip first 3 dc, slip st in next dc, ★ ch 3 **(counts as first dc, now and throughout)**, 3 dc around post of same dc, skip next 3 dc, slip st in next dc; repeat from ★ across; finish off.
Row 3: With **right** side facing, join Blue with slip st in first slip st; ch 4, 3 dc in fourth ch from hook, skip first 3 dc, slip st in next dc, ★ ch 3, 3 dc around post of same dc, skip next 3 dc, slip st in next dc; repeat from ★ across.
Row 4: Ch 4, turn; 3 dc in fourth ch from hook, skip first 3 dc, slip st in next dc, ★ ch 3, 3 dc around post of same dc, skip next 3 dc, slip st in next dc; repeat from ★ across; finish off.

Row 5: With **right** side facing, join Variegated with slip st in first slip st; ch 4, 3 dc in fourth ch from hook, skip first 3 dc, slip st in next dc, ★ ch 3, 3 dc around post of same dc, skip next 3 dc, slip st in next dc; repeat from ★ across.
Row 6: Ch 4, turn; 3 dc in fourth ch from hook, skip first 3 dc, slip st in next dc, ★ ch 3, 3 dc around post of same dc, skip next 3 dc, slip st in next dc; repeat from ★ across; finish off.
Rows 7-53: Repeat Rows 3-6, 11 times; then repeat Rows 3-5 once **more**.
Row 54: Ch 4, turn; 2 dc in fourth ch from hook, skip first 3 dc, slip st in next dc, ★ 3 dc in next slip st, skip next 3 dc, slip st in next dc; repeat from ★ across; do **not** finish off: 128 sts.

TRIM
FIRST SIDE
Ch 1, turn; slip st in first slip st, ch 3, ★ skip next 3 dc, slip st in next slip st, ch 3; repeat from ★ across to last 3 dc, skip next 2 dc, slip st in last dc; finish off.

SECOND SIDE
With **right** side facing and working in free loop of chs **(Fig. 22b, page 142)**, join Variegated with slip st in marked ch; ★ ch 3, slip st in ch at base of next 4-dc group; repeat from ★ across; finish off.

EDGING
Rnd 1: With **right** side facing, join Blue with slip st in last slip st made on Second Side of Trim; † ch 4, 3 dc in fourth ch from hook, working in end of rows, ★ skip next row, slip st in next row, ch 4, 3 dc in fourth ch from hook; repeat from ★ across to last 3 rows, skip last 3 rows †; working in slip sts on First Side of Trim, slip st in first slip st, (ch 4, 3 dc in fourth ch from hook, slip st in next slip st) across; repeat from † to † once, working in slip sts on Second Side of Trim, slip st in first slip st, ch 4, 3 dc in fourth ch from hook, (slip st in next slip st, ch 4, 3 dc in fourth ch from hook) across; join with slip st to first slip st.
Rnd 2: Ch 1, **turn**; slip st in first 4 dc, ch 3, 3 dc around post of same dc, skip next 3 dc, ★ slip st in next dc, ch 3, 3 dc around post of same dc, skip next 3 dc; repeat from ★ around; join with slip st to slip st at base of first dc, finish off.

SERAPE STRIPES

As warm and toasty as the shawl-like Mexican serape, this afghan features dramatic color combinations and interesting geometric patterns. In creating the blended stripes, you stitch over colors carried from one row to another.

Finished Size: 48" x 62"

MATERIALS
Worsted Weight Yarn:
    Black - 26 ounces, (740 grams, 1,470 yards)
    Green - 7½ ounces, (210 grams, 425 yards)
    Dk Green - 7½ ounces, (210 grams, 425 yards)
    Dk Peach - 6½ ounces, (180 grams, 365 yards)
    Peach - 6½ ounces, (180 grams, 365 yards)
    Crochet hook, size I (5.50 mm) **or** size needed
      for gauge

GAUGE: 13 dc and 7 rows = 4"

Gauge Swatch: 6"w x 4"h
With Black, ch 22 **loosely**.
Work same as Afghan for 7 rows.

CHANGING COLORS
When changing colors **(Fig. 24, page 143)**, carry unused color **loosely** across **wrong** side of work. When working **next** row, work over strand **not** used **(Fig. 1)**.

Fig. 1

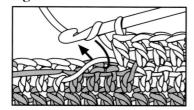

AFGHAN BODY
With Black, ch 158 **loosely**.
Row 1 (Right side)**:** Dc in fourth ch from hook **(3 skipped chs count as first dc)** and in each ch across: 156 dc.
Note: Loop a short piece of yarn around any stitch to mark Row 1 as **right** side.
Row 2: Ch 3 **(counts as first dc, now and throughout)**, turn; dc in next dc and in each dc across; finish off.
Row 3: With **right** side facing, join Green with slip st in first dc; ch 3, dc in next dc and in each dc across.

Row 4: Ch 3, turn; dc in next 3 dc changing to Dk Green in last dc, ★ dc in next 4 dc changing to Green in last dc, dc in next 4 dc changing to Dk Green in last dc; repeat from ★ across, cut Green. Continue to change colors in same manner throughout.
Row 5: Ch 3, turn; dc in next dc and in each dc across; finish off.
Row 6: With **wrong** side facing, join Black with slip st in first dc; ch 3, dc in next dc and in each dc across.
Row 7: Ch 3, turn; dc in next dc and in each dc across; finish off.
Row 8: With **wrong** side facing, join Dk Peach with slip st in first dc; ch 3, dc in next dc and in each dc across.
Row 9: Ch 3, turn; dc in next 3 dc, ★ with Peach dc in next 4 dc, with Dk Peach dc in next 4 dc; repeat from ★ across changing to Peach in last dc, cut Dk Peach.
Row 10: Ch 3, turn; dc in next dc and in each dc across; finish off.
Row 11: With **right** side facing, join Black with slip st in first dc; ch 3, dc in next dc and in each dc across.
Row 12: Ch 3, turn; dc in next dc and in each dc across; finish off.
Row 13: With **right** side facing, join Green with slip st in first dc; ch 3, dc in next dc and in each dc across.
Row 14: Ch 3, turn; dc in next 3 dc, ★ with Dk Green dc in next 4 dc, with Green dc in next 4 dc; repeat from ★ across changing to Dk Green in last dc, cut Green.
Rows 15-107: Repeat Rows 5-14, 9 times; then repeat Rows 5-7 once **more**; do **not** finish off.

EDGING
TOP
With **right** side facing and working across last row, join Black with sc in first dc **(see Joining With Sc, page 142)**; ch 3, ★ skip next 2 dc, sc in next 2 dc, ch 3; repeat from ★ across to last 3 dc, skip next 2 dc, sc in last dc; finish off.

BOTTOM
With **right** side facing and working in free loops of beginning ch **(Fig. 22b, page 142)**, join Black with sc in first ch; ch 3, ★ skip next 2 chs, sc in next 2 chs, ch 3; repeat from ★ 37 times **more**, skip next 2 chs, sc in next ch; finish off.

Holding 8 strands of Black together, add fringe in each ch-3 sp across short edges of Afghan **(Figs. 28a & c, page 143)**.

HANDSOME MEDLEY

Rich, deep shades invite you to enjoy an autumn wrap that's sure to bring comfort to your life. Finished with a lush, multicolor fringe, the handsome throw is crocheted in strips. The pattern is made by working contrasting stitches into previously worked rows.

Finished Size: 51" x 65"

MATERIALS
Worsted Weight Yarn:
    Brown - 26$\frac{1}{2}$ ounces, (750 grams, 1,815 yards)
    Purple - 8$\frac{3}{4}$ ounces, (250 grams, 600 yards)
    Gold - 8$\frac{1}{2}$ ounces, (240 grams, 585 yards)
    Green - 7$\frac{1}{2}$ ounces, (210 grams, 515 yards)
    Burgundy - 7 ounces, (200 grams, 480 yards)
Crochet hook, size H (5.00 mm) **or** size needed
    for gauge
Yarn needle

GAUGE: Each Strip = 7$\frac{1}{4}$" wide; 14 dc = 4"

Gauge Swatch: 4$\frac{1}{4}$"w x 3$\frac{1}{4}$"h
Ch 17 **loosely**.
Work same as Strip First Side for 8 rows.

Each row is worked across length of Afghan. When joining yarn and finishing off, always leave an 8" end to be worked into fringe.

STRIP (Make 7)
FIRST SIDE
With Brown, ch 229 **loosely**.
Row 1 (Right side): Dc in fourth ch from hook (**3 skipped chs count as first dc**) and in each ch across: 227 dc.
Note: Loop a short piece of yarn around any stitch to mark Row 1 as **right** side.
Row 2: Ch 3 **(counts as first dc)**, turn; dc in next dc and in each dc across.
Row 3: Ch 1, turn; sc in each dc across.
Row 4: Ch 3 **(counts as first hdc plus ch 1, now and throughout)**, turn; ★ skip next sc, hdc in next 3 sc, ch 1; repeat from ★ across to last 2 sc, skip next sc, hdc in last sc; finish off: 170 hdc and 57 ch-1 sps.

Row 5: With **right** side facing, join Burgundy with sc in first hdc *(see Joining With Sc, page 142)*; working in **front** of next ch-1, dc in skipped sc one row **below** ch-1, ch 1, skip next hdc, sc in next hdc, ★ working in **front** of next ch-1, dc in skipped sc one row **below** ch-1, sc in ch-1 sp, working in **front** of same ch-1, dc in same sc one row **below** ch-1, skip next hdc, sc in next hdc; repeat from ★ across to last ch-1 sp, ch 1, working in **front** of last ch-1, dc in skipped sc one row **below** ch-1, sc in last hdc; finish off: 227 sts.
Row 6: With **wrong** side facing, join Brown with slip st in first sc; ch 2 **(counts as first hdc, now and throughout)**, hdc in next dc, ch 2, ★ skip next 3 sts, 2 hdc in next sc, ch 2; repeat from ★ across to last 5 sts, skip next 3 sts, hdc in last 2 sts; finish off: 114 hdc and 56 ch-2 sps.
Row 7: With **right** side facing, join Gold with sc in first hdc; ★ sc in next hdc, working in **front** of next ch-2, dc in skipped sc one row **below** ch-2, sc in ch-2 sp, working in **front** of same ch-2, dc in same sc one row **below** ch-2; repeat from ★ across to last 2 hdc, sc in last 2 hdc; finish off: 227 sts.
Row 8: With **wrong** side facing, join Brown with slip st in first sc; ch 3, skip next 2 sts, 2 hdc in next sc, ★ ch 2, skip next 3 sts, 2 hdc in next sc; repeat from ★ across to last 3 sts, ch 1, skip next 2 sts, hdc in last sc; finish off: 114 hdc and 57 sps.
Row 9: With **right** side facing, join Green with sc in first hdc; working in **front** of next ch-1, dc in skipped sc one row **below** ch-1, ch 1, skip next hdc, sc in next hdc, ★ working in **front** of next ch-2, dc in skipped sc one row **below** ch-2, sc in ch-2 sp, working in **front** of same ch-2, dc in same sc one row **below** ch-2, skip next hdc, sc in next hdc; repeat from ★ across to last ch-1 sp, ch 1, working in **front** of last ch-1, dc in skipped sc one row **below** ch-1, sc in last hdc; finish off: 227 sts.
Row 10: With **wrong** side facing, join Brown with slip st in first sc; ch 2, hdc in next dc, ch 2, ★ skip next 3 sts, 2 hdc in next sc, ch 2; repeat from ★ across to last 5 sts, skip next 3 sts, hdc in last 2 sts; finish off: 114 hdc and 56 ch-2 sps.
Row 11: With **right** side facing, join Purple with sc in first hdc; ★ sc in next hdc, working in **front** of next ch-2, dc in skipped sc one row **below** ch-2, sc in ch-2 sp, working in **front** of same ch-2, dc in same sc one row **below** ch-2; repeat from ★ across to last 2 hdc, sc in last 2 hdc; finish off: 227 sts.

SECOND SIDE

Row 1: With **right** side facing and working in free loops of beginning ch *(Fig. 22b, page 142)*, join Brown with sc in first ch; sc in next 226 chs: 227 sc.

Rows 2-9: Repeat Rows 4-11 of First Side.

ASSEMBLY

Place two Strips with **wrong** sides together. With Purple and working through both loops, whipstitch Strips together *(Fig. 27b, page 143)*, beginning in first sc and ending in last sc.

Holding one strand of each color together, add additional fringe in end of every other row across short edges of Afghan *(Figs. 28b & d, page 143)*.

HOLLY AND IVY

Equally welcome on a sleigh ride or at the fireside, this holiday cuddler is merry and bright. The look of holly and ivy against a snowy background is produced by repeating one super-simple row in three festive colors.

COLOR SEQUENCE

2 Rows Maroon *(Fig. 24, page 143)*, one row Natural, one row Green, one row Natural, 2 rows Maroon, ★ 7 rows Natural, 2 rows Green, one row Natural, one row Maroon, one row Natural, 2 rows Green, 7 rows Natural, 2 rows Maroon, one row Natural, one row Green, one row Natural, 2 rows Maroon; repeat from ★ 2 times **more**.

With Maroon, ch 199 **loosely**.

Row 1 (Right side): 3 Dc in seventh ch from hook **(6 skipped chs count as first dc plus ch 3)**, ★ (skip next 2 chs, 3 dc in next ch) twice, skip next 3 chs, (3 dc in next ch, skip next 2 chs) twice, (3 dc, ch 3, 3 dc) in next ch; repeat from ★ across: 220 dc and 13 ch-3 sps.

Row 2: Ch 6 **(counts as first dc plus ch 3)**, turn; 3 dc in first ch-3 sp, ★ [skip next 3 dc, 3 dc in sp **before** next dc *(Fig. 25, page 143)*] twice, skip next 6 dc, (3 dc in sp **before** next dc, skip next 3 dc) twice, (3 dc, ch 3, 3 dc) in next ch-3 sp; repeat from ★ across to last dc, leave last dc unworked.

Rows 3-91: Repeat Row 2.
Finish off.

Finished Size: 48" x 57"

MATERIALS

Worsted Weight Yarn:
  Natural - 28 ounces,
    (800 grams, 1,760 yards)
  Maroon - 10 ounces,
    (280 grams, 630 yards)
  Green - 8 ounces,
    (230 grams, 505 yards)
Crochet hook, size H (5.00 mm) **or** size needed for gauge

GAUGE: Each repeat from point to point = 4";
    8 rows = 5"

Gauge Swatch: 8¹/₂"w x 5"h
Ch 39 **loosely**.
Work same as Afghan for 8 rows.
Finish off.

CELESTIAL SONG

*Inspired by angels, this elegant throw is as uplifting as a heavenly hymn
of praise. Angels with popcorn-stitch heads and rippled skirts trim the
ends of the lovely afghan, which is radiant with glorious shells.*

Finished Size: 46" x 58"

MATERIALS
Worsted Weight Brushed Acrylic Yarn:
   34 ounces, (970 grams, 1,720 yards)
Crochet hook, size G (4.00 mm) **or** size needed
   for gauge

GAUGE: 14 dc and 7 rows = 4";
        (5 dc, ch 1) twice = 3¼"; 6 rows = 4¼"

Gauge Swatch: 4" square
Ch 16 **loosely**.
Row 1: Dc in fourth ch from hook **(3 skipped chs count as first dc)** and in each ch across: 14 dc.
Rows 2-7: Ch 3 **(counts as first dc)**, turn; dc in next dc and in each dc across.
Finish off.

STITCH GUIDE

> **POPCORN**
> 5 Dc in ch indicated, drop loop from hook, insert hook in first dc of 5-dc group, hook dropped loop and draw through *(Fig. 18, page 141)*.

BOTTOM BORDER
Ch 160 **loosely**, place marker in last ch made for st placement on Afghan Body, ch 2 **loosely**, place second marker in last ch made for st placement on Row 2, ch 2 **loosely**: 164 chs.
Row 1: Dc in eighth ch from hook, ★ ch 2, skip next 2 chs, dc in next ch; repeat from ★ across: 53 sps.
Row 2 (Right side): Ch 3 **(counts as first dc, now and throughout)**, turn; (2 dc in next sp, dc in next dc) across to last sp, 2 dc in last sp, dc in marked ch, remove marker: 160 dc.
Note: Loop a short piece of yarn around any stitch to mark Row 2 as **right** side.

Row 3: Ch 5 **(counts as first dc plus ch 2, now and throughout)**, turn; skip next 2 dc, dc in next dc, ch 2, skip next 2 dc, dc in next dc, ch 5, skip next 2 dc, dc in next dc, ★ (ch 2, skip next 2 dc, dc in next dc) 3 times, ch 5, skip next 2 dc, dc in next dc; repeat from ★ across to last 6 dc, (ch 2, skip next 2 dc, dc in next dc) twice: 54 dc and 53 sps.
Row 4: Ch 5, turn; dc in next dc, ★ ch 5, skip next dc, work Popcorn in center ch of next ch-5, ch 5, skip next dc, dc in next dc, ch 2, dc in next dc; repeat from ★ across: 13 Popcorns, 28 dc, and 40 sps.
Row 5: Ch 5, turn; dc in next dc, ★ ch 2, (3 dc, ch 3, 3 dc) in next Popcorn, (ch 2, dc in next dc) twice; repeat from ★ across: 106 dc and 53 sps.
Row 6: Ch 5, turn; dc in next dc, ★ ch 2, skip next ch-2 sp, (3 dc, ch 3, 3 dc) in next ch-3 sp, ch 2, skip next 3 dc, dc in next dc, ch 2, dc in next dc; repeat from ★ across.
Row 7: Ch 5, turn; ★ dc in next 4 dc, (3 dc, ch 3, 3 dc) in next ch-3 sp, dc in next 4 dc, ch 2; repeat from ★ across to last dc, dc in last dc: 184 dc and 27 sps.
Row 8: Ch 3, turn; skip next dc, dc in next 6 dc, (3 dc, ch 3, 3 dc) in next ch-3 sp, dc in next 6 dc, ★ skip next 2 dc, dc in next 6 dc, (3 dc, ch 3, 3 dc) in next ch-3 sp, dc in next 6 dc; repeat from ★ across to last 2 dc, skip next dc, dc in last dc: 236 dc and 13 ch-3 sps.
Row 9: Ch 3, turn; skip next 3 dc, dc in next 6 dc, (3 dc, ch 3, 3 dc) in next ch-3 sp, dc in next 6 dc, ★ skip next 6 dc, dc in next 6 dc, (3 dc, ch 3, 3 dc) in next ch-3 sp, dc in next 6 dc; repeat from ★ across to last 4 dc, skip next 3 dc, dc in last dc.
Row 10: Ch 1, turn; skip first dc, sc in next 9 dc, 3 sc in next ch-3 sp, ★ sc in next 8 dc, skip next 2 dc, sc in next 8 dc, 3 sc in next ch-3 sp; repeat from ★ across to last 10 dc, sc in next 9 dc, leave remaining dc unworked; finish off.

AFGHAN BODY
Row 1: With **right** side facing and working in sps and in free loops across beginning ch *(Fig. 22b, page 142)*, join yarn with slip st in marked ch, remove marker; ch 3, (2 dc in next sp, dc in next ch) across: 160 dc.
Row 2: Ch 3, turn; dc in next dc and in each dc across.
Row 3: Ch 3, turn; dc in next dc, skip next 2 dc, 5 dc in next dc, ★ ch 1, skip next 5 dc, 5 dc in next dc; repeat from ★ across to last 5 dc, skip next 3 dc, dc in last 2 dc: 134 dc and 25 ch-1 sps.

Rows 4-58: Ch 3, turn; dc in next dc, skip next 2 dc, 5 dc in next dc, ★ ch 1, skip next 4 dc, 5 dc in next dc; repeat from ★ across to last 4 dc, skip next 2 dc, dc in last 2 dc.

Row 59: Ch 1, turn; sc in first 2 dc, ch 3, skip next 2 dc, sc in next dc, ★ ch 5, skip next 4 dc, sc in next dc; repeat from ★ across to last 4 dc, ch 3, skip next 2 dc, sc in last 2 dc: 27 sps.

Row 60: Ch 3, turn; dc in next sc, 3 dc in next ch-3 sp, dc in next sc, (5 dc in next ch-5 sp, dc in next sc) across to last ch-3 sp, 2 dc in last ch-3 sp, dc in last 2 sc: 160 dc.

Row 61: Ch 3, turn; dc in next dc and in each dc across; do **not** finish off.

Continued on page 136.

CHRISTMAS EVE

Pretty as a snow-covered landscape, this elaborate coverlet wraps you in the wonderment of the year's most joyful evening. Its various panels get their luscious textures from front and back post treble crochets, popcorns, and cable stitches.

Finished Size: 42" x 60"

MATERIALS
Worsted Weight Yarn:
50 ounces, (1,420 grams, 2,915 yards)
Crochet hook, size I (5.50 mm) **or** size needed for gauge
Yarn needle

GAUGES: Panel A - 10" wide
Panel B - 5¼" wide
Panel C - 2¾" wide

Gauge Swatches:
Panel A - 4" square
Ch 14 **loosely.**
Work same as Panel A for 12 rows.
Finish off.

Panel B - 5¼"w x 5"h
Work same as Panel B through Row 9, page 137.

Panel C - 2¾"w x 4¼"h
Work same as Panel C through Row 8, page 137.

STITCH GUIDE

BACK POST TREBLE CROCHET (*abbreviated BPtr*)
YO twice, insert hook from **back** to **front** around post of st indicated, YO and pull up a loop **(*Fig. 15, page 141*)**, (YO and draw through 2 loops on hook) 3 times. Skip st behind BPtr.

FRONT POST TREBLE CROCHET (*abbreviated FPtr*)
YO twice, insert hook from **front** to **back** around post of st indicated, YO and pull up a loop **(*Fig. 12, page 141*)**, (YO and draw through 2 loops on hook) 3 times. Skip st behind FPtr.

SHELL
(2 Dc, ch 2, 2 dc) in st or sp indicated.
POPCORN
4 Dc in next dc, drop loop from hook, insert hook in first dc of 4-dc group, hook dropped loop and draw through **(*Fig. 18, page 141*)**.
CABLE
Ch 5 **loosely**, slip st from **front** to **back** around post of dc 2 rows **below** last dc **(*Fig. 1a*)**, hdc in each ch across **(*Fig. 1b*)**.

Fig. 1a

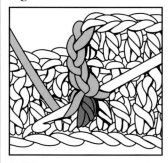

Fig. 1b

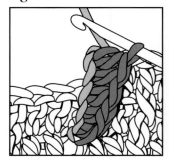

PANEL A (Make 2)

Ch 34 **loosely.**

Row 1 (Right side): Working in back ridges of beginning ch **(*Fig. 2b, page 139*)**, hdc in third ch from hook **(2 skipped chs count as first hdc)** and in each ch across: 33 hdc.
Note: Loop a short piece of yarn around any stitch to mark Row 1 as **right** side and bottom edge.
Row 2: Ch 2 **(counts as first hdc, now and throughout)**, turn; hdc in next hdc, sc in next hdc, (tr in next hdc, sc in next hdc) across to last 2 hdc, hdc in last 2 hdc.
Row 3: Ch 2, turn; work FPtr around hdc one row **below** next hdc, sc in next sc, (tr in next tr, sc in next sc) across to last 2 hdc, work FPtr around hdc one row **below** next hdc, hdc in last hdc; do **not** finish off.

Continued on page 136.

WINTER WARMTH

A festive warmer, this cozy throw underlines the spirit of the season. Worked on the diagonal, the afghan features front and back post double crochets and clusters that give depth to green and ecru stitches. Red puff stitches punctuate the stripes and border.

Finished Size: 45" x 65"

MATERIALS

Worsted Weight yarn:
  Green - 33 ounces, (940 grams, 2,075 yards)
  Red - 12½ ounces, (360 grams, 785 yards)
  Ecru - 11¼ ounces, (320 grams, 710 yards)
Crochet hook, size I (5.50 mm) **or** size needed
  for gauge

GAUGE: 12 sts = 3¾"

Gauge Swatch: 6" x 6" x 8¼" triangle
Work same as Afghan through Row 8.

STITCH GUIDE

FRONT POST SINGLE CROCHET (abbreviated FPsc)
Insert hook from **front** to **back** around post of st indicated, YO and pull up a loop *(Fig. 10, page 140)*, YO and draw through both loops on hook.

FRONT POST DOUBLE CROCHET (abbreviated FPdc)
YO, insert hook from **front** to **back** around post of st indicated, YO and pull up a loop *(Fig. 11, page 140)*, (YO and draw through 2 loops on hook) twice. Skip st behind FPdc unless otherwise indicated.

BACK POST DOUBLE CROCHET (abbreviated BPdc)
YO, insert hook from **back** to **front** around post of st indicated, YO and pull up a loop *(Fig. 14, page 141)*, (YO and draw through 2 loops on hook) twice. Skip st in front of BPdc unless otherwise indicated.

PUFF ST
★ YO, insert hook in st indicated, YO and pull up a loop; repeat from ★ 3 times **more**, YO and draw through all 9 loops on hook *(Fig. 19, page 142)*.

SINGLE CROCHET DECREASE
  (abbreviated sc decrease)
Pull up a loop in next 2 sts, YO and draw through all 3 loops on hook **(counts as one sc)**.

HALF DOUBLE CROCHET DECREASE
  (abbreviated hdc decrease) (uses next 2 sts)
(YO, insert hook in **next** st, YO and pull up a loop) twice, YO and draw through all 5 loops on hook **(counts as one hdc)**.

DOUBLE CROCHET DECREASE
  (abbreviated dc decrease) (uses last 2 sts)
★ YO, insert hook in **next** st, YO and pull up a loop, YO and draw through 2 loops on hook; repeat from ★ once **more**, YO and draw through all 3 loops on hook **(counts as one dc)**.

FRONT POST DOUBLE CROCHET DECREASE
  (abbreviated FPdc decrease) (uses next 2 sts)
YO, insert hook in next st, YO and pull up a loop, YO and draw through 2 loops on hook, YO, insert hook from **front** to **back** around post of next st *(Fig. 9, page 140)*, YO and pull up a loop, YO and draw through 2 loops on hook, YO and draw through all 3 loops on hook.

BACK POST DOUBLE CROCHET DECREASE
  (abbreviated BPdc decrease) (uses next 2 sts)
YO, insert hook in next dc, YO and pull up a loop, YO and draw through 2 loops on hook, YO, insert hook from **back** to **front** around post of next FPdc *(Fig. 9, page 140)*, YO and pull up a loop, YO and draw through 2 loops on hook, YO and draw through all 3 loops on hook.

FRONT POST DOUBLE CROCHET CLUSTER
  (abbreviated FPdc Cluster) (uses next 2 sts)
YO, insert hook from **front** to **back** around post of next st *(Fig. 9, page 140)*, YO and pull up a loop, YO and draw through 2 loops on hook, YO, insert hook in next st, YO and pull up a loop, YO and draw through 2 loops on hook, YO and draw through all 3 loops on hook *(Figs. 17a & b, page 141)*.

BACK POST DOUBLE CROCHET CLUSTER
  (abbreviated BPdc Cluster) (uses next 2 sts)
YO, insert hook from **back** to **front** around post of next FPdc *(Fig. 9, page 140)*, YO and pull up a loop, YO and draw through 2 loops on hook, YO, insert hook in next dc, YO and pull up a loop, YO and draw through 2 loops on hook, YO and draw through all 3 loops on hook *(Figs. 17a & b, page 141)*.

Continued on page 132.

AFGHAN BODY

Row 1 (Right side): With Green, ch 4, 4 dc in fourth ch from hook **(3 skipped chs count as first dc)**: 5 dc.

Note: Loop a short piece of yarn around any stitch to mark Row 1 as **right** side.

Row 2: Ch 3 **(counts as first dc, now and throughout)**, turn; work BPdc around first dc, working in **front** of BPdc just made, dc in same st, work BPdc around next dc, dc in next dc, work BPdc around next dc, 2 dc in last dc: 8 sts.

Row 3: Ch 3, turn; dc in same st, work FPdc around first dc, (dc in next dc, work FPdc around next BPdc) 3 times, 2 dc in last dc: 11 sts.

Row 4: Ch 3, turn; work BPdc around first dc, dc in next dc, (work BPdc around next FPdc, dc in next dc) across to last dc, work BPdc around last dc, working in **front** of BPdc just made, 2 dc in last dc: 14 sts.

Row 5: Ch 3, turn; work FPdc around first dc, dc in next dc, (work FPdc around next BPdc, dc in next dc) across to last 2 sts, ★ work FPdc around next st, working **behind** FPdc just made, dc in same st; repeat from ★ once **more**: 17 sts.

Row 6: Ch 3, turn; dc in same st, (work BPdc around next FPdc, dc in next dc) across, work BPdc around last dc, working in **front** of BPdc just made, dc in same st: 20 sts.

Row 7: Ch 3, turn; dc in same st, (work FPdc around next BPdc, dc in next dc) across to last dc, work FPdc around last dc, working **behind** FPdc just made, 2 dc in last dc: 23 sts.

Row 8: Ch 3, turn; work BPdc around first dc, dc in next dc, (work BPdc around next FPdc, dc in next dc) across to last dc, work BPdc around last dc, working in **front** of BPdc just made, 2 dc in last dc; finish off: 26 sts.

Row 9: With **right** side facing, join Red with slip st in first dc; ch 2 **(counts as first hdc)**, sc in same st and in each st across to last dc, (2 sc, hdc) in last dc; finish off: 29 sts.

Row 10: With **right** side facing, join Ecru with sc in first hdc **(see Joining With Sc, page 142)**; sc in same st and in next 2 sc, work FPdc around BPdc one row **below** next sc, (sc in next sc, work FPdc around BPdc one row **below** next sc) across to last 3 sts, sc in next 2 sc, 2 sc in last hdc; finish off: 31 sts.

Row 11: With **wrong** side facing, join Red with slip st in first sc; ch 3, hdc in same st and in next 2 sc, ch 1, ★ skip next st, work Puff St in next sc, ch 1; repeat from ★ across to last 3 sc, skip next sc, hdc in next sc, (hdc, dc) in last sc; finish off: 13 Puff Sts and 14 ch-1 sps.

Row 12: With **right** side facing, join Ecru with sc in first dc; sc in same st and in each st and each ch across to last dc, 2 sc in last dc; finish off: 35 sc.

Row 13: With **right** side facing, join Red with slip st in first sc; ch 2 **(counts as first hdc)**, sc in same st and in each sc across to last sc, (sc, hdc) in last sc; finish off: 37 sts.

Row 14: With **right** side facing, join Ecru with slip st in first hdc; ch 2 **(counts as first hdc)**, sc in same st and in next sc, (work FPdc around sc one row **below** next sc, sc in next sc) across to last hdc, (sc, hdc) in last hdc; finish off: 39 sts.

Row 15: With **wrong** side facing, join Green with slip st in first hdc; ch 3, dc in same st, work BPdc around next sc, dc in next sc, (work BPdc around next FPdc, dc in next sc) across to last 2 sts, work BPdc around next sc, 2 dc in last hdc; do **not** finish off: 41 sts.

Row 16: Ch 3, turn; dc in same st, work FPdc around first dc, dc in next dc, (work FPdc around next BPdc, dc in next dc) across to last dc, work FPdc around last dc, working **behind** FPdc just made, dc in last dc: 44 sts.

Row 17: Ch 3, turn; work BPdc around first dc, working in **front** of BPdc just made, dc in same st, (work BPdc around next FPdc, dc in next dc) across to last dc, work BPdc around last dc, working in **front** of BPdc just made, dc in last dc: 47 sts.

Row 18: Ch 3, turn; work FPdc around first dc, working **behind** FPdc just made, dc in same st, work FPdc around next BPdc, (dc in next dc, work FPdc around next BPdc) across to last dc, 2 dc in last dc: 50 sts.

Row 19: Ch 3, turn; dc in same st, work BPdc around first dc, (dc in next dc, work BPdc around next FPdc) across to last dc, 2 dc in last dc: 53 sts.

Rows 20-22: Repeat Rows 16-18: 62 sts. Finish off.

Row 23: Repeat Row 9: 65 sts.

Row 24: With **right** side facing, join Ecru with sc in first hdc; sc in same st and in next sc, (work FPdc around FPdc one row **below** next sc, sc in next sc) across to last 3 sts, work FPdc around dc one row **below** next sc, sc in next sc, 2 sc in last hdc; finish off: 67 sts.

Row 25: With **wrong** side facing, join Red with slip st in first sc; ch 3, hdc in same st, ch 1, ★ skip next st, work Puff St in next sc, ch 1; repeat from ★ across to last 2 sc, skip next sc, (hdc, dc) in last sc; finish off: 32 Puff Sts and 33 ch-1 sps.

Rows 26 and 27: Repeat Rows 12 and 13: 73 sts.

Row 28: With **right** side facing, join Ecru with slip st in first hdc; ch 2 **(counts as first hdc)**, sc in same st, work FPdc around sc one row **below** next sc, (sc in next sc, work FPdc around sc one row **below** next sc) across to last hdc, (sc, hdc) in last hdc; finish off: 75 sts.

Row 29: With **wrong** side facing, join Green with slip st in first hdc; ch 3, dc in same st, work BPdc around first hdc, dc in next sc, (work BPdc around next FPdc, dc in next sc) across to last hdc, work BPdc around last hdc, working in **front** of BPdc just made, dc in last hdc; do **not** finish off: 78 sts.

Row 30: Ch 3, turn; work FPdc around first dc, working **behind** FPdc just made, dc in same st, (work FPdc around next BPdc, dc in next dc) across to last dc, work FPdc around last dc, working **behind** FPdc just made, dc in last dc: 81 sts.

Row 31: Ch 3, turn; work BPdc around first dc, working in **front** of BPdc just made, dc in same st, work BPdc around next FPdc, (dc in next dc, work BPdc around next FPdc) across to last dc, 2 dc in last dc: 84 sts.

Row 32: Ch 3, turn; dc in same st, work FPdc around first dc, (dc in next dc, work FPdc around next BPdc) across to last dc, 2 dc in last dc: 87 sts.

Row 33: Ch 3, turn; dc in same st, work BPdc around first dc, dc in next dc, (work BPdc around next FPdc, dc in next dc) across to last dc, work BPdc around last dc, working in **front** of BPdc just made, dc in last dc: 90 sts.

Rows 34-36: Repeat Rows 30-32: 99 sts. Finish off.

Row 37: Repeat Row 9: 102 sts.

Row 38: With **right** side facing, join Ecru with sc in first hdc; sc in same st, work FPdc around dc one row **below** next sc, sc in next sc, (work FPdc around FPdc one row **below** next sc, sc in next sc) across to last 3 sts, work FPdc around dc one row **below** next sc, sc in next sc, 2 sc in last hdc; finish off: 104 sts.

Row 39: With **wrong** side facing, join Red with slip st in first sc; ch 3, hdc in same st, ch 1, ★ skip next st, work Puff St in next sc, ch 1; repeat from ★ across to last 3 sts, skip next FPdc, hdc in next sc, (hdc, dc) in last sc; finish off: 50 Puff Sts and 51 ch-1 sps.

Rows 40 and 41: Repeat Rows 12 and 13: 110 sts.

Row 42: With **right** side facing, join Ecru with slip st in first hdc; ch 2 (**counts as first hdc**), sc in same st, (sc in next sc, work FPdc around sc one row **below** next sc) across to last hdc, (sc, hdc) in last hdc; finish off: 112 sts.

Row 43: With **wrong** side facing, join Green with slip st in first hdc; ch 3, dc in same st, work BPdc around first hdc, dc in next sc, (work BPdc around next FPdc, dc in next sc) across to last 2 sts, work BPdc around next sc, 2 dc in last hdc; do **not** finish off: 115 sts.

Rows 44-50: Repeat Rows 16-19 once, then repeat Rows 16-18 once **more**: 136 sts.

Row 51: Repeat Row 9: 139 sts.

Rows 52 and 53: Repeat Rows 24 and 25: 69 Puff Sts and 70 ch-1 sps.

Rows 54 and 55: Repeat Rows 12 and 13: 147 sts.

Rows 56-61: Repeat Rows 28-33: 164 sts.

Rows 62-64: Repeat Rows 30-32: 173 sts. Finish off.

Row 65: Repeat Row 9: 176 sts.

Rows 66 and 67: Repeat Rows 38 and 39: 87 Puff Sts and 88 ch-1 sps.

Rows 68 and 69: Repeat Rows 12 and 13: 184 sts.

Row 70: Repeat Row 42: 186 sts.

Rows 71-106 will decrease on the right edge and increase on the left edge in order to maintain the same number of sts and shape the body of the Afghan. When working across, the beginning ch 2 (on previous row) is not counted as a st and remains unworked.

Row 71: With **right** side facing, join Green with slip st in first hdc; ch 2, work FPdc Cluster, (work FPdc around next FPdc, dc in next sc) across to last hdc, work FPdc around last hdc, working **behind** FPdc just made, 2 dc in last hdc; do **not** finish off.

Row 72: Ch 3, turn; work BPdc around first dc, dc in next dc, (work BPdc around next FPdc, dc in next dc) across to last 2 sts, work BPdc Cluster.

Row 73: Ch 2, turn; work FPdc decrease, (dc in next dc, work FPdc around next BPdc) across to last dc, dc in last dc, work FPdc around last dc, working **behind** FPdc just made, dc in same st.

Row 74: Ch 3, turn; dc in same st, work BPdc around next FPdc, (dc in next dc, work BPdc around next FPdc) across to last 2 sts, dc decrease.

Row 75: Ch 2, turn; work FPdc Cluster, (work FPdc around next BPdc, dc in next dc) across to last dc, work FPdc around last dc, working **behind** FPdc just made, 2 dc in last dc.

Rows 76-78: Repeat Rows 72-74. Finish off.

Row 79: With **right** side facing, join Red with slip st in first st; ch 1, sc in next st and in each st across to last dc, 2 sc in last dc; finish off.

Row 80: With **right** side facing, join Ecru with slip st in first sc; ch 1, sc in next sc, (work FPdc around BPdc one row **below** next sc, sc in next sc) across to last 2 sc, work FPdc around dc one row **below** next sc, 2 sc in last sc; finish off.

Row 81: With **wrong** side facing, join Red with slip st in first sc; ch 3, hdc in same st and in next sc, ch 1, ★ skip next FPdc, work Puff St in next sc, ch 1; repeat from ★ across to last 4 sts, skip next FPdc, hdc in next sc, hdc decrease; finish off: 90 Puff Sts and 91 ch-1 sps.

Continued on page 134.

Row 82: With **right** side facing, join Ecru with slip st in first hdc; ch 1, sc in next hdc and in each ch and each st across to last dc, 2 sc in last dc; finish off: 186 sc.

Row 83: With **right** side facing, join Red with slip st in first sc; ch 1, sc in next sc and in each sc across to last sc, 2 sc in last sc; finish off.

Row 84: With **right** side facing, join Ecru with slip st in first sc; ch 1, (work FPdc around sc one row **below** next sc, sc in next sc) across to last sc, 2 sc in last sc; finish off.

Row 85: With **right** side facing, join Green with slip st in first FPdc; ch 2, work FPdc decrease, dc in next sc, (work FPdc around next FPdc, dc in next sc) across to last 2 sc, work FPdc around next sc, dc in last sc, work FPdc around last sc, working **behind** FPdc just made, dc in same st; do **not** finish off.

Rows 86 and 87: Repeat Rows 74 and 75.

Rows 88-92: Repeat Rows 72-75 once, then repeat Row 72 once **more**. Finish off.

Row 93: Repeat Row 79.

Row 94: With **right** side facing, join Ecru with slip st in first sc; ch 1, (work FPdc around BPdc one row **below** next sc, sc in next sc) across to last sc, 2 sc in last sc; finish off.

Row 95: With **wrong** side facing, join Red with slip st in first sc; ch 3, hdc in same st, ch 1, ★ skip next st, work Puff St in next sc, ch 1; repeat from ★ across to last 5 sts, skip next FPdc, hdc in next 2 sts, hdc decrease; finish off: 90 Puff Sts and 91 ch-1 sps.

Rows 96 and 97: Repeat Rows 82 and 83.

Row 98: With **right** side facing, join Ecru with slip st in first sc; ch 1, (sc in next sc, work FPdc around sc one row **below** next sc) across to last sc, 2 sc in last sc; finish off.

Row 99: With **right** side facing, join Green with slip st in first sc; ch 2, work FPdc Cluster, (work FPdc around next FPdc, dc in next sc) across to last sc, work FPdc around last sc, working **behind** FPdc just made, 2 dc in last sc; do **not** finish off.

Row 100: Ch 3, turn; work BPdc around first dc, dc in next dc, (work BPdc around next FPdc, dc in next dc) across to last 2 sts, work BPdc Cluster.

Row 101: Ch 2, turn; work FPdc decrease, (dc in next dc, work FPdc around next BPdc) across to last dc, dc in last dc, work FPdc around last dc, working **behind** FPdc just made, dc in same st.

Row 102: Ch 3, turn; dc in same st, work BPdc around next FPdc, (dc in next dc, work BPdc around next FPdc) across to last 2 sts, dc decrease.

Row 103: Ch 2, turn; work FPdc Cluster, (work FPdc around next BPdc, dc in next dc) across to last dc, work FPdc around last dc, working **behind** FPdc just made, 2 dc in last dc.

Rows 104-106: Repeat Rows 100-102. Finish off.

Rows 107-176 decrease on both edges to complete shaping of Afghan. When working across, last ch 2 (on previous row) is not counted as a st and remains unworked.

Row 107: With **right** side facing, join Red with slip st in first st; ch 1, sc decrease, sc in next BPdc and in each st across to last 2 dc, sc decrease; finish off: 183 sc.

Row 108: With **right** side facing, join Ecru with slip st in first sc; ch 1, (work FPdc around BPdc one row **below** next sc, sc in next sc) across to last 2 sc, sc decrease; finish off: 181 sts.

Row 109: With **wrong** side facing, join Red with slip st in first sc; ch 1, hdc in next 3 sts, ch 1, ★ skip next FPdc, work Puff St in next sc, ch 1; repeat from ★ across to last 5 sts, skip next FPdc, hdc in next 2 sts, hdc decrease; finish off: 86 Puff Sts and 87 ch-1 sps.

Row 110: With **right** side facing, join Ecru with slip st in first hdc; ch 1, sc in next hdc and in each st and each ch across to last 2 hdc, sc decrease; finish off: 177 sc.

Row 111: With **right** side facing, join Red with slip st in first sc; ch 1, sc in next sc and in each sc across to last 2 sc, sc decrease; finish off: 175 sc.

Row 112: With **right** side facing, join Ecru with slip st in first sc; ch 1, sc decrease, (sc in next sc, work FPdc around sc one row **below** next sc) across to last 2 sc, sc decrease; finish off: 172 sts.

Row 113: With **right** side facing, join Green with slip st in first sc; ch 2, work FPdc decrease, dc in next sc, (work FPdc around next FPdc, dc in next sc) across to last 2 sts, work FPdc Cluster; do **not** finish off: 169 sts.

Row 114: Ch 2, turn; work BPdc decrease, (dc in next dc, work BPdc around next FPdc) across to last 2 sts, dc decrease: 166 sts.

Row 115: Ch 2, turn; work FPdc Cluster, work FPdc around next BPdc, (dc in next dc, work FPdc around next BPdc) across to last 2 sts, dc decrease: 163 sts.

Row 116: Ch 2, turn; work BPdc Cluster, (work BPdc around next FPdc, dc in next dc) across to last 2 sts, work BPdc Cluster: 160 sts.

Row 117: Ch 2, turn; work FPdc decrease, dc in next dc, (work FPdc around next BPdc, dc in next dc) across to last 2 sts, work FPdc Cluster: 157 sts.

Rows 118-120: Repeat Rows 114-116: 148 sts. Finish off.

Row 121: With **right** side facing, join Red with slip st in first st; ch 1, sc in next dc and in each st across to last 2 sts, sc decrease; finish off: 146 sc.

Row 122: With **right** side facing, join Ecru with slip st in first sc; ch 1, work FPdc around BPdc one row **below** next sc, (sc in next sc, work FPdc around BPdc one row **below** next sc) across to last 2 sc, sc decrease; finish off: 144 sts.

Row 123: With **wrong** side facing, join Red with slip st in first sc; ch 1, hdc in next 2 sts, ch 1, ★ skip next FPdc, work Puff St in next sc, ch 1; repeat from ★ across to last 3 sts, skip next FPdc, hdc decrease; finish off: 69 Puff Sts and 70 ch-1 sps.

Row 124: With **right** side facing, join Ecru with slip st in first hdc; ch 1, sc in next ch and in each st and each ch across to last 2 hdc, sc decrease; finish off: 140 sc.

Row 125: Repeat Row 111: 138 sc.

Row 126: With **right** side facing, join Ecru with slip st in first sc; ch 1, sc decrease, sc in next sc, (work FPdc around sc one row **below** next sc, sc in next sc) across to last 2 sc, sc decrease; finish off: 135 sts.

Row 127: With **right** side facing, join Green with slip st in first sc; ch 2, work FPdc decrease, (dc in next sc, work FPdc around next FPdc) across to last 2 sts, dc decrease; do **not** finish off: 132 sts.

Row 128: Ch 2, turn; work BPdc Cluster, work BPdc around next FPdc, (dc in next dc, work BPdc around next FPdc) across to last 2 sts, dc decrease: 129 sts.

Row 129: Ch 2, turn; work FPdc Cluster, (work FPdc around next BPdc, dc in next dc) across to last 2 sts, work FPdc Cluster: 126 sts.

Row 130: Ch 2, turn; work BPdc decrease, dc in next dc, (work BPdc around next FPdc, dc in next dc) across to last 2 sts, work BPdc Cluster: 123 sts.

Row 131: Ch 2, turn; work FPdc decrease, (dc in next dc, work FPdc around next FPdc) across to last 2 sts, dc decrease: 120 sts.

Rows 132-134: Repeat Rows 128-130: 111 sts. Finish off.

Row 135: Repeat Row 121: 109 sc.

Rows 136-145: Repeat Rows 108-117: 83 sts.

Rows 146-148: Repeat Rows 114-116: 74 sts. Finish off.

Rows 149-152: Repeat Rows 121-124: 66 sc.

Row 153: Repeat Row 111: 64 sc.

Rows 154-159: Repeat Rows 126-131: 46 sts.

Rows 160-162: Repeat Rows 128-130: 37 sts. Finish off.

Row 163: Repeat Row 121: 35 sc.

Rows 164-173: Repeat Rows 108-117: 9 sts.

Row 174: Repeat Row 114: 6 sts.

Row 175: Ch 2, turn; (work FPdc around next BPdc, dc in next dc) twice, dc in last st: 5 sts.

Row 176: Ch 2, turn; ★ YO, insert hook in **next** st, YO and pull up a loop, YO and draw through 2 loops on hook; repeat from ★ 3 times **more**, YO and draw through all 5 loops on hook; do **not** finish off.

EDGING

Rnd 1: Ch 1, turn; 5 sc in same st; † working in end of rows across short edge, 2 sc in each of next 8 rows, (sc in next 6 rows, 2 sc in each of next 8 rows) 4 times, sc in next 5 rows, 5 sc in last row; working in end of rows across long edge, (2 sc in each of next 8 rows, sc in next 6 rows) 7 times, 2 sc in each of next 7 rows, sc in last row †; 5 sc in ch at base of first 5-dc group; repeat from † to † once; join with slip st to first sc, finish off: 576 sc.

Rnd 2: With **right** side facing, join Red with sc in center sc of any corner 5-sc group; 2 sc in same st, sc in each sc around working 3 sc in center sc of each corner 5-sc group; join with slip st to first sc, finish off: 584 sc.

Rnd 3: With **right** side facing, join Ecru with sc in center sc of any corner 3-sc group; 2 sc in same st, sc in next sc, ★ (work FPdc around sc one rnd **below** next sc, sc in next sc) across to center sc of next corner 3-sc group, 3 sc in center sc, sc in next sc; repeat from ★ 2 times **more**, (work FPdc around sc one rnd **below** next sc, sc in next sc) across; join with slip st to first sc, finish off: 592 sts.

Rnd 4: With **right** side facing, join Red with slip st in center sc of any corner 3-sc group; ch 1, work (Puff St, ch 3, Puff St) in same st, ch 1, skip next sc, ★ (work Puff St in next sc, ch 1, skip next st) across to center sc of next corner 3-sc group, work (Puff St, ch 3, Puff St) in center sc, ch 1, skip next sc; repeat from ★ 2 times **more**, (work Puff St in next sc, ch 1, skip next st) across; join with slip st to top of first Puff St, finish off: 300 Puff Sts and 300 sps.

Rnd 5: With **right** side facing, join Ecru with sc in any corner ch-3 sp; ch 2, sc in same sp, ★ sc in each st and in each ch across to next corner ch-3 sp, (sc, ch 2, sc) in corner ch-3 sp; repeat from ★ 2 times **more**, sc in each st and in each ch across; join with slip st to first sc, finish off: 604 sc and 4 ch-2 sps.

Continued on page 136.

WINTER WARMTH Continued from page 135.

Rnd 6: With **right** side facing, join Red with sc in any corner ch-2 sp; 2 sc in same sp, ★ sc in each sc across to next corner ch-2 sp, 3 sc in corner ch-2 sp; repeat from ★ 2 times **more**, sc in each sc across; join with slip st to first sc, finish off: 616 sc.

Rnd 7: With **right** side facing, join Ecru with sc in center sc of any corner 3-sc group; 2 sc in same st, sc in next sc, ★ (work FPdc around sc one rnd **below** next sc, sc in next sc) across to center sc of next corner 3-sc group, 3 sc in center sc, sc in next sc; repeat from ★ 2 times **more**, (work FPdc around sc one rnd **below** next sc, sc in next sc) across; join with slip st to first sc, finish off: 624 sts.

Rnd 8: With **right** side facing, join Green with sc in first sc of any corner 3-sc group; ★ † ch 3, dc in third ch from hook, skip next sc, sc in next sc, ch 3, dc in third ch from hook, skip next sc, (work FPsc around next FPdc, ch 3, dc in third ch from hook, skip next sc) across to next corner 3-sc group †, sc in next sc; repeat from ★ 2 times **more**, then repeat from † to † once; join with slip st to first sc, finish off.

CELESTIAL SONG Continued from page 127.

TOP BORDER
Row 1: Ch 5, turn; skip next 2 dc, dc in next dc, ★ ch 2, skip next 2 dc, dc in next dc; repeat from ★ across: 53 ch-2 sps.
Row 2: Ch 3, turn; (2 dc in next ch-2 sp, dc in next dc) across: 160 dc.
Rows 3-10: Work same as Bottom Border Rows 3-10.

EDGING
FIRST SIDE
Row 1: With **right** side facing and working in end of rows, join yarn with slip st in first row; ch 2 **(counts as first hdc, now and throughout)**, hdc evenly across.
Rows 2 and 3: Ch 2, turn; hdc in next hdc and in each hdc across.
Finish off.

SECOND SIDE
Work same as First Side.

CHRISTMAS EVE Continued from page 128.

Row 4: Ch 2, turn; hdc in next FPtr, tr in next sc, (sc in next tr, tr in next sc) across to last 2 sts, hdc in last 2 sts.
Row 5: Ch 2, turn; work FPtr around FPtr one row **below** next hdc, tr in next tr, (sc in next sc, tr in next tr) across to last 2 hdc, work FPtr around FPtr one row **below** next hdc, hdc in last hdc.
Row 6: Ch 2, turn; hdc in next FPtr, tr in next tr, (sc in next sc, tr in next tr) across to last 2 sts, hdc in last 2 sts.
Row 7: Ch 2, turn; work FPtr around FPtr one row **below** next hdc, sc in next tr, (tr in next sc, sc in next tr) across to last 2 hdc, work FPtr around FPtr one row **below** next hdc, hdc in last hdc.

Row 8: Ch 2, turn; hdc in next FPtr, sc in next sc, (tr in next tr, sc in next sc) across to last 2 sts, hdc in last 2 sts.
Row 9: Ch 2, turn; work FPtr around FPtr one row **below** next hdc, sc in next sc, (tr in next tr, sc in next sc) across to last 2 hdc, work FPtr around FPtr one row **below** next hdc, hdc in last hdc.
Repeat Rows 4-9 until Panel measures approximately 59½" from beginning ch, ending by working a **wrong** side row.
Last Row: Ch 2, turn; work FPtr around FPtr one row **below** next hdc, hdc in each st across to last 2 hdc, work FPtr around FPtr one row **below** next hdc, hdc in last hdc; finish off.

PANEL B (Make 3)
Ch 23 **loosely**.

Row 1: Working in back ridges of beginning ch, dc in fourth ch from hook **(3 skipped chs count as first dc)**, skip next 2 chs, work Shell in next ch, skip next 2 chs, dc in next 7 chs, skip next 2 chs, work Shell in next ch, skip next 2 chs, dc in last 2 chs: 19 dc and 2 ch-2 sps.

Row 2 (Right side): Ch 3 **(counts as first dc, now and throughout)**, turn; work FPtr around next dc, ch 2, (sc, ch 3, sc) in next ch-2 sp, ch 2, skip next 2 dc, work FPtr around next dc, dc in next 2 dc, work Popcorn in next dc, dc in next 2 dc, work FPtr around next dc, ch 2, (sc, ch 3, sc) in next ch-2 sp, ch 2, skip next 2 dc, work FPtr around next dc, dc in last dc: 15 sts and 6 sps.

Note: Mark Row 2 as **right** side and bottom edge.

Row 3: Ch 3, turn; work BPtr around next FPtr, skip next ch-2 sp, work Shell in next ch-3 sp, work BPtr around next FPtr, dc in next 5 sts, work BPtr around next FPtr, skip next ch-2 sp, work Shell in next ch-3 sp, work BPtr around next FPtr, dc in last dc: 19 sts and 2 ch-2 sps.

Row 4: Ch 3, turn; work FPtr around next BPtr, ch 2, (sc, ch 3, sc) in next ch-2 sp, ch 2, work FPtr around next BPtr, dc in next 2 dc, work Popcorn in next dc, dc in next 2 dc, work FPtr around next BPtr, ch 2, (sc, ch 3, sc) in next ch-2 sp, ch 2, work FPtr around next BPtr, dc in last dc: 15 sts and 6 sps.
Repeat Rows 3 and 4 until Panel measures approximately 59½" from beginning ch, ending by working Row 4.

Last Row: Ch 2, turn; work BPtr around next FPtr, hdc in next sc, hdc in next ch-3 sp and in next sc, work BPtr around next FPtr, hdc in next 5 sts, work BPtr around next FPtr, hdc in next sc, hdc in next ch-3 sp and in next sc, work BPtr around next FPtr, hdc in last dc; finish off.

PANEL C (Make 2)
Ch 11 **loosely**.

Row 1 (Right side): Working in back ridges of beginning ch, dc in fourth ch from hook **(3 skipped chs count as first dc)** and in each ch across: 9 dc.

Note: Mark Row 1 as **right** side and bottom edge.

Row 2: Ch 3 **(counts as first dc, now and throughout)**, turn; work BPtr around next dc, dc in next 5 dc, work BPtr around next dc, dc in last dc.

Row 3: Ch 3, turn; work FPtr around next BPtr, dc in next 3 dc, work Cable, dc in next 2 dc, work FPtr around next BPtr, dc in last dc.

Row 4: Ch 3, turn; work BPtr around next FPtr, dc in next 5 dc, work BPtr around next FPtr, dc in last dc.
Repeat Rows 3 and 4 until Panel measures approximately 59¾" from beginning ch, ending by working Row 4; finish off.

ASSEMBLY
Using Placement Diagram as a guide, weave Panels together as follows:

With **right** side of two Panels facing you, bottom edges at same end and edges even, sew through both pieces once to secure the beginning of the seam, leaving an ample yarn end to weave in later. Insert the needle from **right** to **left** through one strand on each piece *(Fig. 2)*. Bring the needle around and insert it from **right** to **left** through the next strand on both pieces. Continue in this manner, drawing seam together as you work.

Fig. 2

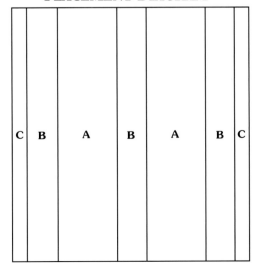

PLACEMENT DIAGRAM

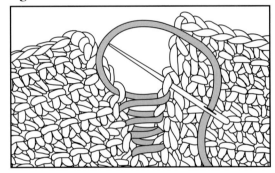

| C | B | A | B | A | B | C |

general instructions

BASIC INFORMATION

ABBREVIATIONS

BPdc	Back Post double crochet(s)
BPsc	Back Post single crochet(s)
BPtr	Back Post treble crochet(s)
ch(s)	chain(s)
dc	double crochet(s)
Dk	Dark
dtr	double treble crochet(s)
FP	Front Post
FPdc	Front Post double crochet(s)
FPsc	Front Post single crochet(s)
FPtr	Front Post treble crochet(s)
hdc	half double crochet(s)
Lt	Light
Med	Medium
mm	millimeters
Rnd(s)	Round(s)
sc	single crochet(s)
sp(s)	space(s)
st(s)	stitch(es)
tr	treble crochet(s)
YO	yarn over

SYMBOLS

★ — work instructions following ★ as many **more** times as indicated in addition to the first time.

† to † or ♥ to ♥ — work all instructions from first † to second † or from first ♥ to second ♥ **as many** times as specified.

( ) or [ ] — work enclosed instructions **as many** times as specified by the number immediately following **or** work all enclosed instructions in the stitch or space indicated **or** contains explanatory remarks.

colon (:) — the number(s) given after a colon at the end of a row or round denote(s) the number of stitches you should have on that row or round.

TERMS

chain loosely — work the chain **only** loose enough for the hook to pass through the chain easily when working the next row or round into the chain.

post — the vertical shaft of a stitch.

right side vs. wrong side — the right side of your work is the side that will show when the piece is finished.

work across or around — continue working in the established pattern.

GAUGE

Gauge is the number of stitches and rows or rounds per inch and is used to determine the finished size of a project. All crochet patterns specify the gauge that you must match to ensure proper size and to ensure that you will have enough yarn to complete the project.

Hook size given in instructions is merely a guide. Because everyone crochets differently — loosely, tightly, or somewhere in between — the finished size can vary, even when crocheters use the very same pattern, yarn, and hook.

Before beginning any crocheted item, it is absolutely necessary for you to crochet a gauge swatch in the pattern stitch indicated and with the weight of yarn and hook size suggested. Your swatch must be large enough to measure your gauge. Lay your swatch on a hard, smooth, flat surface. Then measure it, counting your stitches and rows or rounds carefully. If your swatch is smaller than specified or you have too many stitches per inch, try again with a larger size hook; if your swatch is larger than specified or you don't have enough stitches per inch, try again with a smaller size hook. Keep trying until you find the size that will give you the specified gauge. DO NOT HESITATE TO CHANGE HOOK SIZE TO OBTAIN CORRECT GAUGE. Once proper gauge is obtained, measure width of piece approximately every 3" to be sure gauge remains consistent.

BASIC STITCH GUIDE

CHAIN (abbreviated ch)

To work a chain stitch, begin with a slip knot on the hook. Bring the yarn **over** hook from **back** to **front**, catching the yarn with the hook and turning the hook slightly toward you to keep the yarn from slipping off. Draw the yarn through the slip knot **(Fig. 1)**.

Fig. 1

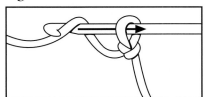

WORKING INTO THE CHAIN

When beginning a first row of crochet in a chain, always skip the first chain from the hook and work into the second chain from hook (for single crochet), third chain from hook (for half double crochet), or fourth chain from hook (for double crochet), etc. **(Fig. 2a)**.

Fig. 2a

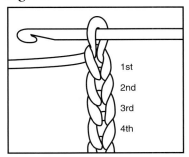

Method 1: Insert hook into back ridge of each chain indicated **(Fig. 2b)**.
Method 2: Insert hook under top loop **and** the back ridge of each chain indicated **(Fig. 2c)**.

Fig. 2b   **Fig. 2c**

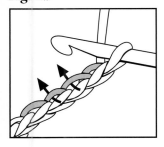   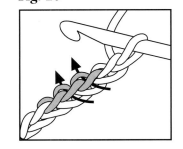

SLIP STITCH (abbreviated slip st)

This stitch is used to attach new yarn, to join work, or to move the yarn across a group of stitches without adding height. Insert hook in stitch or space indicated, YO and draw through stitch **and** loop on hook **(Fig. 3)**.

Fig. 3

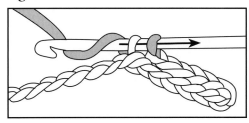

SINGLE CROCHET (abbreviated sc)

Insert hook in stitch or space indicated, YO and pull up a loop, YO and draw through both loops on hook **(Fig. 4)**.

Fig. 4

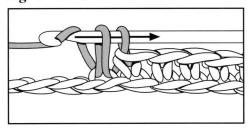

HALF DOUBLE CROCHET
(abbreviated hdc)

YO, insert hook in stitch or space indicated, YO and pull up a loop, YO and draw through all 3 loops on hook **(Fig. 5)**.

Fig. 5

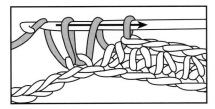

DOUBLE CROCHET (abbreviated dc)

YO, insert hook in stitch or space indicated, YO and pull up a loop (3 loops on hook), YO and draw through 2 loops on hook *(Fig. 6a)*, YO and draw through remaining 2 loops on hook *(Fig. 6b)*.

Fig. 6a

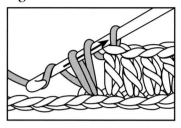

Fig. 6b

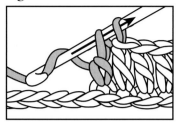

TREBLE CROCHET (abbreviated tr)

YO twice, insert hook in stitch or space indicated, YO and pull up a loop (4 loops on hook) *(Fig. 7a)*, (YO and draw through 2 loops on hook) 3 times *(Fig. 7b)*.

Fig. 7a

Fig. 7b

DOUBLE TREBLE CROCHET
(abbreviated dtr)

YO 3 times, insert hook in stitch or space indicated, YO and pull up a loop (5 loops on hook) *(Fig. 8a)*, (YO and draw through 2 loops on hook) 4 times *(Fig. 8b)*.

Fig. 8a

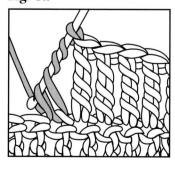

Fig. 8b

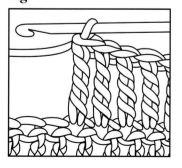

PATTERN STITCHES

POST STITCH

Work around post of stitch indicated, inserting hook in direction of arrow *(Fig. 9)*.

Fig. 9

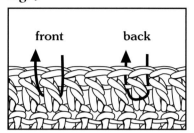

FRONT POST SINGLE CROCHET
(abbreviated FPsc)

Insert hook from **front** to **back** around post of stitch indicated *(Fig. 9)*, YO and pull up a loop *(Fig. 10)*, YO and draw through both loops on hook.

Fig. 10

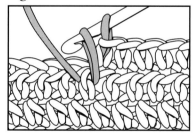

FRONT POST DOUBLE CROCHET
(abbreviated FPdc)

YO, insert hook from **front** to **back** around post of stitch indicated *(Fig. 9)*, YO and pull up a loop (3 loops on hook) *(Fig. 11)*, (YO and draw through 2 loops on hook) twice.

Fig. 11

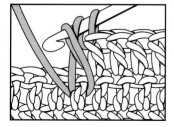

FRONT POST TREBLE CROCHET
(abbreviated FPtr)

YO twice, insert hook from **front** to **back** around post of stitch indicated *(Fig. 9)*, YO and pull up a loop (4 loops on hook) *(Fig. 12)*, (YO and draw through 2 loops on hook) 3 times.

Fig. 12

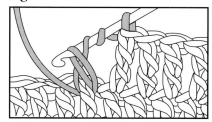

BACK POST SINGLE CROCHET
(abbreviated BPsc)

Insert hook from **back** to **front** around post of stitch indicated *(Fig. 9)*, YO and pull up a loop *(Fig. 13)*, YO and draw through both loops on hook.

Fig. 13

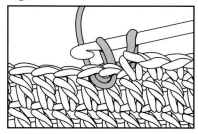

BACK POST DOUBLE CROCHET
(abbreviated BPdc)

YO, insert hook from **back** to **front** around post of stitch indicated *(Fig. 9)*, YO and pull up a loop (3 loops on hook) *(Fig. 14)*, (YO and draw through 2 loops on hook) twice.

Fig. 14

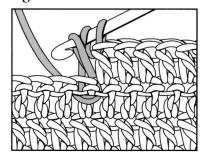

BACK POST TREBLE CROCHET
(abbreviated BPtr)

YO twice, insert hook from **back** to **front** around post of stitch indicated *(Fig. 9)*, YO and pull up a loop (4 loops on hook) *(Fig. 15)*, (YO and draw through 2 loops on hook) 3 times.

Fig. 15

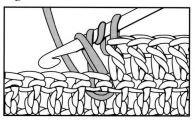

CLUSTER

A Cluster can be worked all in the same stitch or space *(Figs. 16a & b)*, **or** across several stitches *(Figs. 17a & b)*.

Fig. 16a

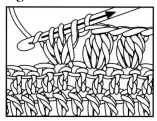

Fig. 16b

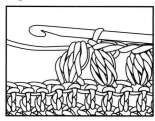

Fig. 17a

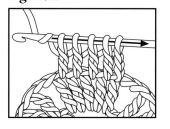

Fig. 17b

POPCORN

Work specified number of dc in stitch or space indicated, drop loop from hook, insert hook in first dc of dc group, hook dropped loop and draw through *(Fig. 18)*.

Fig. 18 **5-dc Popcorn**

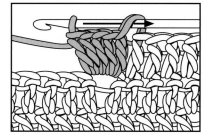

PUFF STITCH

★ YO, insert hook in stitch indicated, YO and pull up a loop even with loop on hook; repeat from ★ as many times as specified, YO and draw through all loops on hook *(Fig. 19)*.

Fig. 19

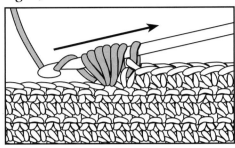

REVERSE SINGLE CROCHET
(abbreviated reverse sc)

Working from **left** to **right**, insert hook in st to right of hook *(Fig. 20a)*, YO and draw through, under, and to left of loop on hook (2 loops on hook) *(Fig. 20b)*, YO and draw through both loops on hook *(Fig. 20c)* **(reverse sc made, *Fig. 20d*)**.

Fig. 20a

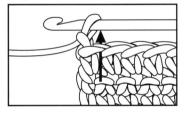

Fig. 20b

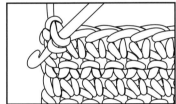

Fig. 20c

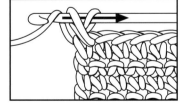

Fig. 20d

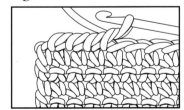

STITCHING TIPS

JOINING WITH SC

When instructed to join with sc, begin with a slip knot on hook. Insert hook in stitch or space indicated, YO and pull up a loop, YO and draw through both loops on hook.

BACK OR FRONT LOOP ONLY

Work only in loop(s) indicated by arrow *(Fig. 21)*.

Fig. 21

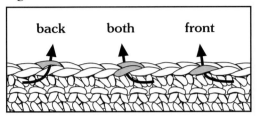

back   both   front

FREE LOOPS

After working in Back or Front Loops Only on a row or round, there will be a ridge of unused loops. These are called the free loops. Later, when instructed to work in the free loops of the same row or round, work in these loops *(Fig. 22a)*.
When instructed to work in a free loop of a beginning chain, work in loop indicated by arrow *(Fig. 22b)*.

Fig. 22a

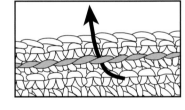

Fig. 22b

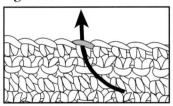

WORKING IN TOP OF STITCH

When instructed to work in top of stitch just worked, insert hook as indicated by arrow *(Fig. 23)*.

Fig. 23

CHANGING COLORS

Work the last stitch to within one step of completion, hook new yarn *(Fig. 24)* and draw through loops on hook. Cut old yarn and work over both ends unless otherwise specified.

Fig. 24

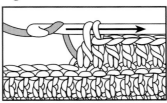

WORKING IN SPACE BEFORE STITCH

When instructed to work in space **before** a stitch or in spaces **between** stitches, insert hook in space indicated by arrow *(Fig. 25)*.

Fig. 25

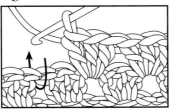

NO-SEW JOINING

Hold Squares, Motifs, or Strips with **wrong** sides together. Slip st or sc into space as indicated *(Fig. 26)*.

Fig. 26

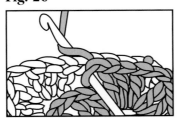

EDGING

SINGLE CROCHET EVENLY ACROSS OR AROUND

When instructed to single crochet evenly across or around, the single crochets should be spaced to keep the piece lying flat. Work a few single crochets at a time, checking periodically to be sure your edge is not distorted. If the edge is puckering, you need to add a few more single crochets; if the edge is ruffling, you need to remove some single crochets. Keep trying until the edge lies smooth and flat.

FINISHING

WHIPSTITCH

With **wrong** sides together and beginning in corner stitch, sew through both pieces once to secure the beginning of the seam, leaving an ample yarn end to weave in later. Insert needle from **front** to **back** through **inside** loops of **each** piece *(Fig. 27a)* **or** through **both** loops *(Fig. 27b)*. Bring needle around and insert it from **front** to **back** through the next loops of **both** pieces. Continue in this manner across to corner, keeping the sewing yarn fairly loose.

Fig. 27a

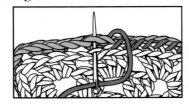

Fig. 27b

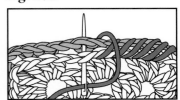

FRINGE

Cut a piece of cardboard 8" wide and ½" longer than desired fringe. Wind the yarn **loosely** and **evenly** around the length of the cardboard until the card is filled, then cut across one end; repeat as needed. Align the number of strands desired and fold in half.

With **wrong** side facing and using a crochet hook, draw the folded end up through a stitch, row, or loop, and pull the loose ends through the folded end *(Figs. 28a & b)*; draw the knot up **tightly** *(Figs. 28c & d)*. Repeat, spacing as specified. Lay flat on a hard surface and trim the ends.

Fig. 28a

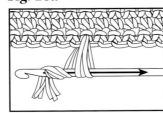

Fig. 28b

Fig. 28c

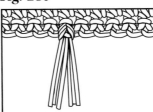

Fig. 28d

credits

To Magna IV Color Imaging of Little Rock, Arkansas, we say thank you for the superb color reproduction and excellent pre-press preparation.

We want to especially thank photographers Ken West, Larry Pennington, Mark Mathews, and Karen Shirey of Peerless Photography, Little Rock, Arkansas, and Jerry R. Davis of Jerry Davis Photography, Little Rock, Arkansas, for their time, patience, and excellent work.

We would like to extend a special word of thanks to the talented designers who created the lovely projects in this book:

Alexander-Stratton: *Homegrown Goodness,* page 80
Mary Lamb Becker: *Peaceful Promenade,* page 76
Nair Carswell: *Granny's Posy Patch,* page 28, and *Windowpane Posies,* page 52
Sue Galucki: *All-American Stars,* page 82
Anne Halliday: *Nostalgic Granny,* page 12; *Sentimental Swirls,* page 18; *Sweetheart Squares,* page 22; *Spring Ripple,* page 36; *Bunny Tales,* page 42; *Peaceful Garden,* page 66; *Daisy Delight,* page 70; *Buttercups and Bluebells,* page 84; *Paw Prints,* page 86; *Country Ripple,* page 96; and *School Days Silhouettes,* page 102
Jan Hatfield: *Carefree Pleasures,* page 64, and *Home on the Range,* page 94
Marion L. Kelley: *Fall Fancy,* page 108
Terry Kimbrough: *Victorian Elegance,* page 20; *Romantic Ribbons,* page 32; *Sweet Dreams,* page 68; *Blushing Seashells,* page 90; and *Delicate Diamonds,* page 92
Ann Kirtley: *Mother's Treasure,* page 54
Patty Kowaleski: *Ladylike Charm,* page 62
Tammy Kreimeyer: *Scrap-Basket Kaleidoscope,* page 6; *Royal Vineyard,* page 56; *Autumn Pops,* page 114; *Handsome Medley,* page 122; and *Winter Warmth,* page 130
Patricia Kristoffersen: *Pastel Garden,* page 50
Melissa Leapman: *American Heritage,* page 78; *Southwestern Stripes,* page 98; and *Serape Stripes,* page 120
Frances Moore-Kyle: *Emerald Trellis,* page 30
Carole Prior: *Rose Petal Ripple,* page 16; *Summer Ablaze,* page 88; *Woodland Shadows,* page 116; and *Holly and Ivy,* page 124
Katherine Satterfield: *Lilac Bouquet,* page 38
Mary Ann Sipes: *Snowy Day,* page 8; *Jeweled Diamonds,* page 100; *Harvest Mist,* page 112; and *Country Casual,* page 118
Martha Brooks Stein: *Country Pines,* page 10; *Irish Patchwork,* page 34; *Tulips in Bloom,* page 44; and *Brilliant Mums,* page 110
Gail Tanquary: *Celestial Song,* page 126
Carole Rutter Tippett: *Christmas Eve,* page 128
Maggie Weldon: *Vivacious Violets,* page 40